WRITING REVOLUTION

Studies in Critical Social Sciences Book Series

Haymarket Books is proud to be working with Brill Academic Publishers (www.brill.nl) to republish the *Studies in Critical Social Sciences* book series in paperback editions. This peer-reviewed book series offers insights into our current reality by exploring the content and consequences of power relationships under capitalism, and by considering the spaces of opposition and resistance to these changes that have been defining our new age. Our full catalog of *SCSS* volumes can be viewed at https://www.haymarketbooks.org/series_collections/4-studies-in-critical-social-sciences.

Series Editor
David Fasenfest (York University, Canada)

Editorial Board
Eduardo Bonilla-Silva (Duke University)
Chris Chase-Dunn (University of California–Riverside)
William Carroll (University of Victoria)
Raewyn Connell (University of Sydney)
Kimberlé W. Crenshaw (University of California–LA and Columbia University)
Heidi Gottfried (Wayne State University)
Alfredo Saad-Filho (King's College London)
Chizuko Ueno (University of Tokyo)
Sylvia Walby (Lancaster University)
Raju Das (York University)

WRITING REVOLUTION

Representation, Rhetoric,
and Revolutionary Politics

SHEILA DELANY

Haymarket Books
Chicago, IL

First published in 2023 by Brill Academic Publishers, The Netherlands
© 2023 Koninklijke Brill NV, Leiden, The Netherlands

Published in paperback in 2024 by
Haymarket Books
P.O. Box 180165
Chicago, IL 60618
773-583-7884
www.haymarketbooks.org

ISBN: 979-8-88890-323-0

Distributed to the trade in the US through Consortium Book Sales and Distribution (www.cbsd.com) and internationally through Ingram Publisher Services International (www.ingramcontent.com).

This book was published with the generous support of Lannan Foundation, Wallace Action Fund, and the Marguerite Casey Foundation.

Special discounts are available for bulk purchases by organizations and institutions. Please call 773-583-7884 or email info@haymarketbooks.org for more information.

Cover design by Jamie Kerry and Ragina Johnson.

Printed in the United States.

Library of Congress Cataloging-in-Publication data is available.

Contents

Acknowledgments VII

Introduction 1

1 Political Style/Political Stylistics 8

2 Marxist Medievalists
 A Tradition 25

3 Red Rosa
 Bread and Roses 37

4 Politics of the Signified in Bertolt Brecht's *The Measures Taken* 57

5 Women, Culture, Revolution
 Boris Lavrenov's "The Forty-first" 73

6 Anti-saints
 A Revolutionary's Legendary 96

7 St. Genevieve in the Revolution
 Sylvain Maréchal's Counter-History 119

8 The Woman Priest
 Obsession, Cross-Dressing, and Canada in an Eighteenth-Century French Novella 134

9 An Atheist Reads the Bible in Revolutionary France 154

10 Bible, Jews, Revolution 179

Index 195

Acknowledgments

Much appreciation to those "without whom" … My friend, co-thinker, and indefatigable colleague Raju Das of York University for his confidence in me and my work; Raju's collaborators at York, Robert Latham and Nitya Nagarajan, for posing important questions in their interview with me for York's Left Consortium; Darko Suvin, emeritus of McGill University and now resident in Lucca, Italy, for invaluable references and comradely commentary drawn from his vast treasury of literary, philosophical, and historical knowledge; David Fasenfest, chair of the Brill committee under whose welcoming auspices this collection appears and from whose advice it has benefited; Karyn Huenemann, my editorial assistant, whose IT savvy and meticulous attention to detail have made this an enjoyable project and a better book; Steve Mongrain, Associate Dean of Arts for Research at Simon Fraser University, for his office's tech help and financial support to this project.

Most of the chapters in this collection have appeared elsewhere, and have been updated to take account of subsequent scholarship or events and my own evolved style. Specifics can be found on the last page of each chapter. All translations from French and German in previous versions and in this collection are mine unless otherwise noted.

Introduction

This collection represents a lifelong interest in—a sense of partnership with, really—writers who supported the revolutions of their times. For some of those introduced here, scholarship or other writing was an important dimension to their support, often along with activism in organizations committed to social change; for a few of these writers, leadership in the workers movement or in a revolutionary party was also part of their achievement.

The revolutions these authors worked toward might have been of their own time or of a future they might not live to see—or both. For Sylvain Maréchal, it was the great, ambiguous, multi-faceted French Revolution that began in 1789 and ended, depending on one's criteria, anywhere from five to nine years later. It was not yet the egalitarian revolution he had hoped, written, and risked his freedom for. In his last book, Mike Davis refers to "the prescience of the original *sans-culotte* communists, Gracchus Babeuf and Sylvain Maréchal" (Davis 2018, 11). Although Davis was right about Babeuf and arguably wrong about Sylvain (see Chapter 6), it is good to see the presence of both in current anglophone work.

For Marx and his followers, it was the French Revolution with its continuations in the uprisings of 1830 and 1848, plus the Paris Commune, as well as possible revolutions in industrialized England or Germany, and, more remotely, in awakening Russia. That potential, adumbrated in 1905 and fulfilled in October 1917, became reality for Lenin, Trotsky, and Stalin: indeed, a reality they had themselves worked to create. Lavrenov's story chronicles a moment in the civil war that followed the October Revolution, though eventually he tacked his sail to the wind as the Bolshevik revolution, under Stalin after Lenin's death in 1924, deteriorated into bureaucratic dictatorship (see Chapter 5). For Brecht, it was all of the foregoing and the aborted Spartacist revolt of 1918 led by Rosa Luxemburg and Karl Liebknecht, both of whom would soon be assassinated by the Social Democratic government. This defeat, the German dramatist Heiner Müller called, "probably the most consequential mishap in recent history", inasmuch as it resulted in "the isolation of the socialist experiment inside the Soviet Union, a testing ground with undeveloped conditions" (Müller 1990, 124). Brecht and his co-thinkers also paid close attention to the revolution proceeding in China: a long, slow process starting in the 1920s, against which background Brecht set his play *The Measures Taken* (*Die Massnahme*: see Chapter 4).

These are some links in the "golden chain" (as Yiddish writers described their literary tradition) with its continuities and its breaks. Many more of the modern links—Mexico, Cuba, Spain, Hungary, and others—are verbally and photographically documented in Michael Lowy's *Revolutions* (2020) and, in a different register, Georges Didi-Huberman's compendious *Uprisings* (2016). Among these many insurrections, few have gone all the way to state power; it is a history of hope, of liberatory energy, and often of defeat. About this, Rosa Luxemburg, after the failed uprising she led, wrote in her last published article: "The question is, under what circumstances did each defeat occur? ... Tomorrow the revolution will rear its head once again, and ... will proclaim, I was, I am, I will be!" (Luxemburg 1919, 306)

My own coordinates, the ones most relevant to this collection, are as activist, writer, and teacher. The activism has been for Cuba, for Palestinian rights, for labor struggle, black rights, and revolutionary change. (I won't trouble the reader with a list of acronyms and initials here; some further detail is recounted in Chapter 2.) The writing has been in several genres. The teaching—in medieval and later English, medieval French, classical and biblical literatures—has attempted to incorporate the sensibility shaped by the activism and by the reading in Marxist theory underpinning all of it. My previous collections have been in medieval literature and in writing by and about women (see Delany 1983 and 1990). In a sense, this collection might be seen as obverse to the others, in that where they brought political theory and social history to texts meant first and foremost as literary, this one brings literary categories to political writing or to writing meant as primarily political, even propagandistic in the best sense.

Many of my interlocutors have been skeptical about the possibility of a harmonious integration of the two realms—literature—(especially old literature)—and radical politics—so that a question I was often asked early on in my professional life was "Why Chaucer?" The assumption was that in order to find suitable terrain to work, a scholar of left-wing convictions would want or need to take on modern, left-oriented, or labor-oriented literatures, not the products of a conservative, even reactionary, author, culture, or period. The unspoken premise was that only an ideologically similar object could yield conclusions or analyses consistent with a left point of view. Or perhaps those who posed this question thought that only a similar viewpoint could be interesting to a leftist. Of course, there were also those whose question was rather "Why Marx?", the assumption here being that medievalism could in no way benefit from the ministrations of modern theory of any type, especially not one so generally condemned, at least in North America, as communism. I encountered this perspective, often quite overtly or aggressively stated, from editors of prestigious academic journals and audiences at scholarly conferences, among others. Of course, in good dialectical fashion, in responding to "Why Chaucer?" as fully as possible, one necessarily responds at the same time to "Why Marx?"

But the former question is likely the more challenging to readers of this volume, so I would like to take a slight detour to respond to it, despite the fact that, unlike other collections of my work, this one does focus on modern rather than on medieval writing. Such a detour will, I think, provide a groundwork for what follows, despite the temporal difference.

First, despite the temporal difference, the Middle Ages—the very long Middle Ages!—remained relevant, even immediate, to some of these modern authors. Perhaps to Sylvain most of all, for feudalism survived during his lifetime in its most visible and palpable institutions of government and ideology in France: feudal laws governing land tenure, the Roman Catholic Church, and the monarchy. The Middle Ages lived for Marx as well, as it must for the elaboration of his economic theories and his grasp of European history. In Russia, serfdom—a post-medieval institution—was abolished in 1861, but feudal-style labor obligations remained; the Russian Orthodox Church, dating from the tenth century, was robustly powerful at all levels of society, and aristocrats of varying wealth, such as Lavrenov's White Guard officer, remained until the 1917 revolution abolished the class as a legal category along with its privileges.

Considering medieval or ancient literature in its social context, as a dialectical approach would require, one can hardly avoid noticing the frequency of rebellion, revolt, protest: class struggle in its many forms whether legal, vocal, written, or armed. Throughout Europe, peasants revolted against feudal lay or clerical landlords' oppressive laws; so did well-to-do bourgeois requiring more latitude for business and commerce; barons rose against kings (as in the Magna Carta); small businesspeople rose against the local oligarchs and guildmasters; serfs left the land and moved to cities to breathe the air that made them free (*Stadtluft macht frei*, the German saying went); slaves rose against their masters especially, though not only, in the famed Roman uprising led by the former slave Spartacus that came close to becoming a revolution. It would be foolishly sentimental to think that the twentieth-century German revival of the slave leader's name boded ill or that it was taken "quite by chance" as one recent biographer of Rosa claims (Brie and Schütrumpf 2021, vii). Rather, it suggests a sense of the recurrence of struggle down the ages.

This is part of the value of teaching and writing about the past from a class perspective: to let it be understood, perhaps to the surprise of younger generations, that class conflict is normal, it is usual, and can be accessed even, perhaps especially, through and despite the most reactionary texts—which are, after all, typically the ones that have survived or become best known down the centuries. As an instance, I might cite Lynn Arner's study of Geoffrey Chaucer and John Gower—conservative late-medieval poets of the middle class with courtly connections and privileges—showing how their work effaces the popular struggles of their day to replace them with conservative modes of thought, behavior, and political governance that became normative (Arner 2013). This is, to be sure, a variant and contemporary affirmation of what Friedrich Engels had already laid out in his fulsome appreciation of the royalist Balzac, whose novels so effectively expose the very class with which he sympathizes (Engels 1888). Similarly, Lenin and Trotsky wrote appreciatively about Tolstoy, with whose political vision they did not sympathize; indeed, both of them wrote about gifted reactionary or counter-revolutionary writers whose work, despite the author's opinion, can't help but reveal the social truth.[1]

Another through-line that is evident in this collection is rhetoric, from classical through medieval and renaissance to modern. Certainly, Sylvain Maréchal, educated in classics and law, practiced the rhetorical arts of his day in the many genres he wrote in, whether poetry, newspaper editorial, treatise, or novella. In doing so he contributed to the vast current and flow of eighteenth-century Parisian culture. Virtually all of the classic Marxist writers had a proper middle-class education as befitted their petty-bourgeois or bourgeois origins; this education would include Greek and Latin languages, mythologies, and literatures. They became class traitors in not only promoting the demands of workers and the oppressed, but in understanding—on the basis of Marx's work—the revolutionary potential of the international proletariat. Their education in rhetoric served them well in speech and writing needed to promote their vision, and I think this is not accidental inasmuch as rhetoric is what provides structure in language, form in communication. If we were to transpose this function into the political arena, it would have to do with party program and with the desired form for a future state, the state that would be a transition to a stateless, because classless, society. For the present and the foreseeable future, though, the anarchic perspective or hope remains counter-productive. While many critics—as we shall see in Chapter 1—have analyzed the function and theoretical meaning of various rhetorical techniques in the language of Marx and Lenin particularly—irony, metaphor, apostrophe, antithesis, etc.—it is rhetoric itself as form imposed on the infinite, as structuring the overwhelmingly unstructured, that is the starting point.

An interwoven theme that surfaces in several of the essays collected here is sexual politics. This was a constant concern for Sylvain Maréchal, who understood—in fact, saw for himself—that women were a powerful revolutionary force. They led the famous attack on the Bastille prison, led the crowd

---

1 For Lenin, see *Lenin on Literature and Art* (1967), 30–35, 52–68, 170–171; for Trotsky see *Art & Revolution* (1970), 127–147, 167–206.

INTRODUCTION   5

to Versailles to bring the king back to Paris, enlisted and fought in the revolutionary army (sometimes dressed or disguised as men), spoke in women's political clubs (until these were shut down by Robespierre in 1793) and at the National Assembly to demand more rights than their male compatriots were willing to grant. Not that Maréchal's views on women's role were endorsable by us, or by me, for they mirrored the ambivalence typical of most supporters of the revolution. Nonetheless, he understood the importance of addressing a female audience in order to win them away from the old ways; this he did in his parodic legendary, the *Nouvelle légende dorée* or *New Golden Legend* (see Chapter 6). Yet the ambivalence shows through in his novella, *La femme abbé* or *The Woman Priest,* whose heroine—or perhaps anti-heroine—Agatha, succumbs at last to the then-inevitable fate of the woman who dares to flout ancient tradition (see Chapter 8).

For Lavrenov's Maryutka, who challenges tradition in many different ways, the outcome is unknown though not hard to guess; it is likely to be the same as Agatha's, albeit after a very different trajectory (see Chapter 5). And in real life, not fiction, the lived experience of Rosa Luxemburg in the German Social Democratic Party replicated much of the ambivalence of a century and a half earlier, as she and her comrade Clara Zetkin were subjected to all-too-familiar sexist remarks and obstacles from their radical male comrades (see Chapter 3). Like the fictional Agatha and Maryutka, Rosa too suffers an unnatural death; as with Maryutka, it is at the hands of the class enemy; unlike Maryutka, Rosa was able, thanks to her class and education, not only to write but to leave us a powerful body of work that continues to inspire.

∙ ∙ ∙

Is writing or teaching from a left perspective a form of activism? Some have thought so; I don't. One who hoped and thought so was Brecht himself, author of a versified version of *The Communist Manifesto* (Brecht 1945). The story of this effort provides, in my view, a case in point about the fallacy of considering writing as activism. Written in 1945 as part of an intended longer opus modeled on Lucretius's *De rerum naturae,* the poem, a German verse epic imitating Greek hexameters, was meant as an intervention into the post-war German political environment, a way to "rediscover for German workers the obviously forgotten teachings of Marxism" (Suvin 2020, 65). Brecht believed that the practice of the Second and Third Internationals—social-democratic and communist had caused this text and its ideas to become so automatized and ossified that it could no longer inspire the reader but required a new form in order to recapture its authority and effectiveness (Suvin 2020, 82). In other words, Brecht's solution to the stultification of Stalinized Communist parties was not to change the practice—that is, in organizational action along the lines exemplified by Rosa Luxemburg or Leon Trotsky—but rather to change the founding document by presenting it in a new form. The text of Brecht's versification effort was never published in its day, so it's impossible to say with certainty what its reception would have been. Nonetheless, it seems to me that the relevant classical concept here is 'hubris', authorial hubris, in expecting that one person's literary effort could create a mass revolutionary consciousness in the face of social and historical conditions to the contrary. As Ernst Fischer observed, "Bertolt Brecht was not able to contribute to the strengthening of the G.D.R. [German Democratic Republic], although he certainly increased its prestige" (Fischer 1969, 175). I want to add that I write this as someone who loves, and has translated and taught, Brecht's poetry, and will see any play of his when I can.

What can leftist or Marxist scholarship accomplish? I haven't had the illusion that it is a weapon in real-world political struggle—this despite the ironic fact that one of my early essays (on Pope's *Rape of the Lock*) appeared in a volume with the hopeful title *Weapons of Criticism*. The editor quite rightly observed that the rarity of Marxist criticism in the U.S. to that point was the product of "the particular economic, political, cultural, and historical experience of American monopoly capitalism since World War II" (Rudich 1976, 16). "But times have changed", he notes, and indeed, a half century on, Marxist criticism has been more or less mainstreamed, along with other, newer approaches: queer, disability, ecological, feminist, black, Asian, intersectional. And yet the organized labor movement has shrunk disastrously; wealth inequality has expanded beyond belief, fascism by various means is a realistic possibility in the U.S. and elsewhere; poverty is rampant. As transnational capital seeks to survive, it will sacrifice innumerable people—as the conflict in Ukraine shows (I write this in January 2023)—along with the planetary environment (see, for example, Davis 2006; Desmond 2016). At best, I have hoped that my teaching and writing might help the reader or listener or interrogator to understand reality better. As William Robinson observes: "Theory needs to illuminate reality; it is useless as a tool for social action" (Robinson 2018, 108). Academics and other writers, no matter how innovative their work or how leftist their opinions, change the world as anyone else does: through active engagement in the political battles of their time, ideally in the company of like-minded comrades with a serious program for revolutionary change. I've written here about the "afterlife" or long survival of the Middle Ages, and in some of the chapters that follow, the long survival of an ancient genre, hagiography. This collection represents another type of afterlife, or—even better—a renewed life, for some of my previous work. If, as a consequence of their reading or studying, someone joins the issues engaged here (and I'm happy to say that some of my students have done so), all the better. *Avanti*!

References

Arner, Lynn. 2013. *Chaucer, Gower, and the Vernacular Rising: Poetry and the Problem of the Populace after 1381*. University Park: University of Pennsylvania Press.

Brecht, Bertolt. 1945. *The Manifesto*, translated by Darko Suvin. In Suvin 2020, 42–63.

Brie, Michael, and Jörn Schütrumpf. 2021. *Rosa Luxemburg: a Revolutionary Marxist at the Limits of Marxism*. Cham, Switzerland: Palgrave.

Davis, Mike. 2006. *Planet of Slums*. London: Verso.

Davis, Mike. 2018. *Old Gods, New Enigmas*. London: Verso.

Delany, Sheila. 1983. *Writing Woman: Women Writers and Women in Literature, Medieval to Modern*. New York: Schocken Books.

Delany, Sheila. 1990. *Medieval Literary Politics: Shapes of Ideology*. Manchester: Manchester University Press.

Desmond, Matthew. 2016. *Evicted: Poverty and Profit in the American City*. New York: Crown Publishers.

Didi-Huberman, Georges, ed. 2016. *Uprisings*. Paris: Éditions Gallimard/Jeu de Paume.

Engels, Friedrich. [1888] 1978. "Letter to Margaret Harkness". In *Marx and Engels on Literature and Art*, 89–92. Moscow: Progress Publishers.

Fischer, Ernst. 1969. *Art Against Ideology*, translated by Anna Bostock. London: Penguin.

Lenin, V.I. 1967. *Lenin on Literature and Art*. Moscow: Progress Publishers.

Lowy, Michael, ed. 2020. *Revolutions*. Chicago: Haymarket. First published 2000, Paris: Hazan.

Luxemburg, Rosa. [1919] 1972. "Order Reigns in Berlin". *Die Rote Fahne*, January 14, 1919. In *Rosa Luxemburg: Selected Political Writings*, edited by Robert Looker, translated by William D. Graf, 300–6. London: Jonathan Cape.

Müller, Heiner. 1990. "Brecht vs. Brecht". In *Germania*, translated by Bernard and Caroline Schütze. New York: Semiotext(e).

Robinson, William I. 2018. "Beyond the Theory of Imperialism". In *Into the Tempest*, 99–121. Chicago: Haymarket.

Rudich, Norman, ed. 1976. *Weapons of Criticism: Marxism in America and the Literary Tradition*. Palo Alto: Ramparts Press.

Suvin, Darko. 2020. *Brecht's Communist Manifesto Today: Poetry, Utopia, Doctrine*. Delhi: Aakar.

Trotsky, Leon. 1970. *Art & Revolution*, edited by Paul N. Siegel. New York: Pathfinder Press.

CHAPTER 1

Political Style/Political Stylistics

When I was asked to contribute to a special issue of *Style* an essay on the relation of style to politics, my response was: "There is none". Yet the request itself indicated that some qualification and elaboration of my initial response might not be as unnecessary as I had at first thought. Other experiences came to mind: the staff of a local left–labor and community newspaper take a stand against what they call "psychedelic" color, design, or layout in the paper; the young proprietor of a Vancouver used-bookstore denounces bourgeois culture as reactionary and worthless; a professor of English asks me what I, a Marxist, can possibly find of interest in Chaucer. This essay, then, takes up an assumption common to those three experiences and perhaps to the original request as well: that a political commitment means a stylistic commitment, and *vice versa*. Dialectical contradiction is the essay's conceptual center—a notion which, in fending off the obvious and the merely apparent, may function as a disorganizing as much as an organizing concept. My thesis is that a given politics *may* be deducible from a given style, and that a certain politics *may* generate a certain style; but that the relationship cannot be fixed for all time in a formula resembling that of a reversible chemical equation. This is why the first section makes a case for stylistic flexibility in art and in political writing, while the second section demonstrates possible connections between style and political vision. Only to the most mechanical view will this appear inconsistent; in my terms it is the only possible consistency. I hope that the variables will become clear in the essay itself.

• • •

"There is no such thing as bourgeois or proletarian, capitalist or socialist forms or means of expression in art. There is such a thing as a socialist way of thinking". Ernst Fischer's statement (1969, 60) may provoke some protest from readers already familiar with Marxist esthetics. Some of their objections might even be taken from Fischer's earlier book, *The Necessity of Art* (1963), a chapter of which analyzes the development of art under capitalism. Yet there, in discussing impressionism, nihilism, mysticism, and other tendencies, Fischer writes not about style but about attitudes toward society. Fischer's view remains consistent, for his chapter on "Art and Capitalism" concludes with the hope that the socialist artist will absorb the lessons of Egyptian and Aztec sculpture, Gothic art and Russian ikons, Homer and the Bible, Shakespeare and Strindberg, Rimbaud and Yeats: "All doctrinaire clinging to particular artistic methods, whatever they may be, is at variance with the task of making a synthesis of the result of many thousands of years of human development" (Fischer 1963, 114).

Agreed, Fischer's statement is simplified, even propagandistic, occurring as it does in a book whose original title is *Kunst und Koexistenz*—a book, moreover, which praises the efforts of Khrushchev, John F. Kennedy, and Pope John XXIII to achieve 'peaceful coexistence'. To paint Khrushchev as a real socialist, or to imagine that capital and religion can or want to coexist with genuine socialism, is worse than wishful thinking: it is deplorably bad politics.

Yet Fischer's position on art is, I believe, correct: a contradiction of a type familiar enough in the tradition of revolutionary writing. Lenin reminds us constantly of such contradictions, whether in history, contemporary politics, philosophy, or literature. Indeed, Lenin's balanced appreciation of progressive and reactionary elements in the work of Tolstoy, on the death of that great writer, is a model of the dialectical criticism whose principles Engels had already demonstrated in his brief and well-known critique of Balzac:

> Well, Balzac was politically a legitimist, his great work is a constant elegy on the irreparable decay of good society; his sympathies are with the class that is doomed to extinction. But for all that, his satire is never keener, his irony never more bitter, than when he sets in motion the very men and women with whom he sympathizes most deeply—the nobles … That Balzac was thus compelled to go against his own class sympathies and political prejudices, … that he saw the real men of the future where, for the time being, they alone were to be found—that I consider one of the greatest triumphs of realism, and one of the greatest features in old Balzac.
> ENGELS 1888, 91–92

History and the experience of history create the contradictions observed in the work of Tolstoy and Balzac; the list can be extended at length and includes critics as well as artists.

As I take it, Fischer suggests that style—the deliberate manipulation of language or plastic form—is a complex cultural phenomenon which in any given period may be used by a ruling class or by an oppressed class, or which may be accepted and rejected by the same class at different phases in its development. The point is flexibility, and I would suggest that rhetoric—nearly as versatile as religion in lending itself to opposite causes—does not confer meaning but receives it. No technique can be entirely value-free, for no technique exists outside of history, which produces and confers meaning. Style itself can't always or permanently certify intention or value, for the meaning of a style necessarily shifts with events. Roland Barthes uses the language of the French Revolution to make this point:

> The Revolution was in the highest degree, one of those great occasions when truth, through the bloodshed that it costs, becomes so weighty that its expression demands the very forms of theatrical amplification ... What today appears turgid was then no more than life-size.
> BARTHES 1967, 21–22

By the same token, "because the writer cannot modify in any way the objective data which govern the consumption of literature" (Barthes 1967, 15), many progressive writers have used available techniques to express the consciousness that will eventually be fleshed out in social form.

Equivocation is one problem besetting most discussions of politics and style: several questions are being asked at once, which need to be distinguished from one another. The question "Has style a politics?" can be broken down as follows:

1) Is style in general amenable to political or class analysis?
2) Is political discourse in general amenable to stylistic analysis?
3) Does a particular style necessarily reveal or serve a particular class or a particular politics?
4) Does a given political commitment require or imply commitment to a given style?

To the first pair the answer is, in my view, affirmative; to the second, negative.

These are not new questions in the revolutionary tradition. They were taken up, for instance, by Mao Tse-tung in a 1942 speech in Yenan. There, Mao notes that the old feudal literary dogmas and stereotypes have been replaced by new dogmatism and by a new stereotyped style of party writing which expresses "the fanaticism and one-sidedness of petty-bourgeois revolutionaries" (Mao 1942, questions 1 and 2). Mao proposes three sources of stylistic vitality in revolutionary writing: the vigorous, vivid, and effective language of the masses; fresh foreign expressions for ideas to which the old Chinese vocabulary was inadequate; and anything useful and lively in the classical Chinese tradition (questions 3 and 4). Mao's own style in this short talk clearly illustrates his principles. The structure of the piece imitates the ancient "eight-legged essay" with which candidates used to apply for the imperial civil service; the eight "legs" or sections are used for Mao's major indictments of the new dogmatism. As for vividness of language, a few examples will suffice:

> Some of our comrades love to write long articles with no substance, very much like the footbindings of a slattern, long and smelly.
>
> Like our stereotyped Party writing, the creatures known in Shanghai as "little *piehsan*" are wizened and ugly.
>
> Go and take a look at any Chinese pharmacy, and you will see cabinets with numerous drawers, each bearing the name of a drug—toncal, foxglove, rhubarb, saltpetre, indeed, everything that should be there. This method has been picked up by our comrades. In their articles and speeches, their books and reports, they use first the big Chinese numerals, second the small Chinese numerals, third the characters for the ten celestial stems, fourth the characters for the twelve earthly branches, and then capital A, B, C, D, then small a, b, c, d, followed by the Arabic numerals, and what not! ... The method borrowed from the Chinese pharmacy is really the most crude, infantile and philistine of all. It is a formalist method, classifying things according to their external features instead of their internal relations.
>
> MAO 1942, 97, 101, 103

In a more leisurely and theoretical vein, Lenin also addressed the problem of how revolutionaries ought to use the legacy of bourgeois culture, in a speech given to a congress of the Russian Young Communist League. The new culture, he said, "must be the logical development of the store of knowledge mankind has accumulated under the yoke of capitalist, landlord and bureaucratic society" (Lenin 1920, 152). No other approach is possible in the context of a dialectical and materialist view of history or epistemology:

> All these roads have been leading, and will continue to lead up to proletarian culture, in the same way as political economy, reshaped by Marx, has shown us what human society must arrive at, shown us the passage to the class struggle, to the beginning of the proletarian revolution ... It would be mistaken to think it sufficient to learn communist slogans and the conclusions of communist science, without acquiring that sum of knowledge of which communism itself is a result. Marxism is an example which shows how communism arose out of the sum of human knowledge.
>
> LENIN 1920, 152

Trotsky expanded the point in writing about proletarian culture and art, adding the reminder that "the proletariat cannot postpone Socialist reconstruction until the time when its new scientists [or critics or artists—S.D.], many of whom are still running about in short trousers, will test and clean all the instruments and channels of knowledge" (Trotsky 1924, 199).

Is there, then, a 'revolutionary style' in art? I think not; rather, many revolutionary styles are possible and desirable. To insist on a single revolutionary style is both undialectical and ultra-left. Yet even that insistence has its historical roots as the unfortunate consequence of the development of the Russian and Chinese revolutions, in which stylistic experimentation, along with intellectual and artistic freedom generally, threatened the authority of entrenched party bureaucracies. Trotsky remarked that "the art of the Stalinist period will remain as the frankest expression of the profound decline of the proletarian revolution", and his statement on architectural style is equally applicable to literature and the visual arts:

> The effort to reason out such a style by the method of deduction from the nature of the proletariat, from its collectivism, activism, atheism, and so forth, is the purest idealism, and will give nothing but an ingenious expression of one's ego, an arbitrary allegorism, and the same old provincial dilettantism.
>
> TROTSKY 1924, 136

A second difficulty in discussing politics and style comes from a certain functional similarity between the two. By creating the impression of isomorphism, this functional similarity obscures the fluctuating relation between politics and style. Politics and style are two things that no one is without; they are concomitants of the human condition, inasmuch as work and language are concomitants of the human condition. Short of suicide, there is no abstention from politics or from style. One may of course refuse to commit oneself to a definite political philosophy, analysis, party, or action, but there is no effective difference between such refusal and explicit acquiescence to the status quo. So that 'abstention' from politics in a pre-revolutionary situation doesn't produce *no* politics, it produces in effect a counter-revolutionary politics. Similarly, the refusal or failure to develop a particular style of communication results not in the absence of style, but rather in whichever style dominates culturally or prevails in one's immediate environment. In either case, if you don't choose, the choice is made for you. It appears by extension, then, that choice in the area of politics implies analogous choice in the area of style: that there is a right and wrong in either case. That analogy, though, is only apparent: it is mechanistic, neither theoretically justifiable nor historically true.

History shows many permutations of politics and style. Writers in the same historical period, but with opposed ideologies, may display stylistic similarities. In the writing of Thomas Paine and of Samuel Johnson one notes identical cadences, alliterations and antitheses and balances, rhythms of long and short sentences, of abstract statement and concrete image. Or one can compare Carlyle's 1843 "Gospel of Mammonism" with Marx's 1844 "The Power of Money in Bourgeois Society".[1] A second case in point: socialist writers have often borrowed the art forms and stylistic techniques of earlier periods and cultures—Mao and classical Chinese poetry, Brecht and oriental theater and poetry, Mayakovsky and the medieval morality play. Indeed, Brecht's theory of alienation effect was strongly influenced by his study of traditional Chinese theater (see Brecht 1936). Nor is this remarkable, for new social content has often been expressed in old forms (although here we move out of style as such into form generally). Christian art in the late Roman period used the pagan style; the sonnet had a continuous existence from the thirteenth through the nineteenth centuries; the epic surfaces (with changes that ensure its survival) over two and a half millennia with Homer, Virgil, and Milton. Further, the purist or mechanical position on the relation of style to politics conceals a potential *reductio ad absurdum,* which becomes blatant as soon as we apply the position to an individual artist in the process of change. Will anyone seriously argue that William Morris's conversion to revolutionary socialism should have altered the style of his painting? Or, conversely, that Russian revolutionary posters should have avoided the art-nouveau style?

It comes down to the old idea of fruit and chaff, or kernel and husk, or in contemporary terms, content and form:

> But ye that holden this tale a folye,
> As of a fox, or of a cok and hen,
> Taketh the moralite, goode men.

---

1 Marx and Engels knew Carlyle's work: Marx uses Carlyle's "cash-nexus" image in the *Communist Manifesto* (sec. 1), and Engels translated parts of *Past and Present* for publication in Germany. Yet Carlyle's denunciation of the bourgeoisie was profoundly unhistorical in its assumptions, and the remarks of Marx and Engels, in the third section of the *Communist Manifesto*, on "feudal socialism", can also be applied to Carlyle: "half lamentation, half lampoon; half echo of the past, half menace of the future; at times, by its bitter, witty and incisive criticism striking the bourgeoisie to the very heart's core; but always ludicrous in its effect, through total incapacity to comprehend the march of modern history".

> For seint Paul seith that al that writen is,
> To oure doctrine it is ywrite, ywis;
> Taketh the fruyt, and lat the chaf be stille.
>
> CHAUCER, *Nun's Priest's Tale* 3438–43

In this Augustinian formulation, literary form, style, or craft is the expendable chaff, while the useful fruit is orthodox Christian doctrine, which may infuse any form. That I borrow an image from the patristic tradition is no coincidence, inasmuch as that image addressed a situation similar in some respects to that of socialists in the twentieth century: a relatively new popular movement with rapidly growing international strength, confronted an immense but decadent and obsolescent imperial power.[2] It had to find a stance from which to challenge the old dominant culture which it would eventually replace, and it especially required an attitude toward the corpus of Greco-Roman secular literature. In a letter (dated 797) to the Bishop of Lindisfarne, the monk Alcuin presents the traditional sectarian approach to this problem. "What has Ingeld [a popular legendary hero] to do with Christ?" asks Alcuin; as Jerome before him had asked (in 384), "What has Horace to do with the Psalter? Or Vergil with the Gospels? Or Cicero with the Apostle?"; and before Jerome, St. Paul: "What part hath the faithful with the unbeliever? And what agreement hath the temple of God with idols?" (II Cor. 6:16).

In contrast to this rigid 'Proletkult' view, the dominant tendency was represented by Augustine:

> If those who are called philosophers ... have said things which are indeed true and are well accommodated to our faith, they should not be feared; rather, what they have said should be taken from them as from unjust possessors and converted to our use. Just as the Egyptians had not only idols, ... which the people of Israel avoided, so also they had vases and ornaments of gold and silver and clothing which the Israelites took with them secretly when they fled, as if to put them to a better use.
>
> AUGUSTINE 1958, 75

---

2 See Engels: "One good thing, however, Ernest Renan has said: 'When you want to get a distinct idea of what the first Christian communities were, do not compare them to the parish congregations of our day; they were rather like local sections of the International Working Men's Association'. ... Christianity got hold of the masses, exactly as modern socialism does, under the shape of a variety of sects ... all opposed to the ruling system, to 'the powers that be'" (1883, 205–6). See also Engels's comparison of early Christianity with "the modern working-class movement" (1894, 316).

Those who feel uncomfortable with the comparison to early Christianity haven't understood, as Augustine and Lenin in their radically different ways understood, the uses of the past: in both cases an understanding based on confidence in the long-term future. Again, it's Trotsky who illustrates my point, with a modern version of the fruit–chaff image:

> The methods of formal analysis are necessary, but insufficient. You may count up the alliterations in popular proverbs, classify metaphors, count up the number of vowels and consonants in a wedding song. It will undoubtedly enrich our knowledge of folk art, in one way or another; but if you don't know the peasant system of sowing, and the life that is based on it, if you don't know the part the scythe plays, and if you have not mastered the meaning of the church calendar to the peasant, of the time when the peasant marries, or when the peasant women give birth, you will have only understood the outer shell of folk art, but the kernel will not have been reached.
> TROTSKY 1924, 180

In letting the image grow organically (as it were) from his discussion of the art of an agricultural population; in requiring both formal and social analysis (fruit and chaff together); in using the old image for a new social purpose, Trotsky preserves, destroys, and creates at once. It is an emblem of revolutionary artistic process.

• • •

If the relation between politics and style isn't necessarily predictable, then what can legitimately be said of the style of political writers? Can one subject the writing of political theorists to stylistic analysis, and derive from such analysis any genuine political insights? A good deal depends here on the breadth of the word 'political' for it's at the level of style that politics takes on the nebulous outlines of temperament. In making this connection, we are no longer dealing with politics alone. Rather, we are considering that substratum of personality which provides more or less consistent patterns in different areas of behavior and expression. If style can be broadly defined to include both personal and cultural factors—i.e., style as the way a personality operates in a cultural context—then the inclusion of both factors is not simply psychologistic.

The analysis of style in communist writing starts with consideration of the work of Marx and Engels. With them, as with Lenin, Trotsky, Rosa Luxemburg, and Mao, rhetoric and figurative language are a striking aspect of the work.

This is a tradition defined by the coruscating polemics of Marx, by Engels's biting wit, by the lucid precision and vitality of Lenin, the passion and rhetorical Polish of Trotsky and of Luxemburg, and by Mao's pointed homely parables. Constantly in their works we meet hyperbole, antithesis, climax and anticlimax, metonymy, personification and apostrophe, dialogue, rhetorical question, irony and sarcasm, simile and metaphor, pun, classical and biblical reference, parody, etc., as well as deep sensitivity to rhythm and clausal structure—all evident even when translated out of the original language. The following examples, from Marx's *Wage-Labor and Capital,* will give some sense of the norm:

> What [the laborer] produces for himself is not the silk that he weaves, not the gold that he draws up from the mining shaft, not the palace that he builds. What he produces for himself is wages ... Is this twelve hours' weaving, spinning, boring, turning, building, shoveling, stone-breaking, regarded by him as a manifestation of life? Quite the contrary. Life for him begins where this activity ceases ... If the silk-worm's object in spinning were to prolong its existence as a caterpillar, it would be a perfect example of a wage-worker.
> MARX 1847, 19

> The working class is also recruited from the higher strata of society; a mass of small businessmen and of people living on the interest of their capitals is precipitated into the ranks of the working class, and they will have nothing else to do than to stretch out their arms alongside of the arms of the workers. Thus the forest of outstretched arms, begging for work, grows ever thicker, while the arms themselves grow ever thinner.
> MARX 1847, 47

Not surprisingly, modern critics have found plenty in Marx on which to exercise their skills, regardless of their political inclinations. Stanley Edgar Hyman treated all of Marx's writing, including *Capital,* as "imaginative literature" (Hyman 1962, 133): the *Communist Manifesto* is "Marx's great masterpiece of rhetoric" (98). Hyman's treatment of the Marx oeuvre includes "comic devices" and "wild parody" (88, 90) in *The Holy Family;* a "riot of metaphor ... fireworks ... comprehensive imaginative visions" (92–93) in *The German Ideology;* organic and sexual imagery (111–12) in *The Eighteenth Brumaire,* and much more. These qualities were not lost on contemporary reviewers across Europe, England, and Russia or on followers in the next generation (see Toscano 2023). In his biographical memoir of Marx, Rosa Luxemburg's comrade Karl Liebknecht wrote of Marx's style through an etymological image:

> The style here is what it—the stylus—originally was in the hands of the Romans—a sharp-pointed steel pencil for writing as well as stabbing. The style is the dagger used for a well-aimed thrust at the heart.
> HYMAN 1962, 111

In a more philosophical vein, Bertell Ollman acknowledges Marx's "'peculiar' use of words", ambiguity and even apparent inconsistency: "Thinkers ... have noticed how hard it is to pin Marx down to particular meanings" (Ollman 1976, 3); the issue is resolved by way of Marx's complicated understanding of social reality. Ludovico Silva's project, originally published in 1971 and translated into English only in 2023, had taken a similar approach, emphasizing several key metaphors throughout the Marxian œuvre. Jacques Derrida used Marx's relation to Shakespeare, especially the image of the ghost or specter, as the scaffolding for his brilliant investigation of issues confronting Marx and ourselves (see Derrida 1994). For philosopher Robert Wolff, Marx was "the greatest ironist since Swift" (Wolff 1988, 11), asserting

> the inner connection between the linear equations of Marxian value theory and the satiric thrust of Marx's literary invocations ... in the aid of explicating the objectively contradictory character of capitalist social reality in its ironic relation to those of us who strive to understand capitalism from within.
> WOLFF 1988, 5

Lenin's language burst upon the Russian scene with even more impact than Marx's had done in Europe, as the language of action and an achieved revolution. It would be as well the language of other revolutions: "Just as the word was Lenin's primary weapon until the October revolution, so does the word also serve as the primary weapon of the international revolutions taking place in Europe, Asia, American and Australia" (Kruchenykh 1928, 287). Literary people who welcomed the new government and the new forms it brought to every area of life—personal relations, marriage and parenthood, architecture, sculpture, painting, poetry—saw Lenin's spoken and written style as a model for revitalizing and cleansing what Lenin himself called "the mighty Russian language" (see Shklovsky 1924, 152).

Shortly after Lenin's death in 1924, a group of Russia's avant-garde cultural luminaries published a collection of essays on Lenin's language, in the journal of their group, the *Left Front of the Arts* (*LEF*); this has now been translated into English for the first time (see Boynik 2018). Lenin's precision and directness are agreed on by all, an absence of grandiloquence. Another point of general agreement is Lenin's use of the colloquial language of workers and peasants, typically absent from—indeed, unacceptable in—the speech and writing of the intelligentsia and polite society. This might include slang, localisms, completely new words or expressions, proverbs, sarcasm, mockery. As Boynik observes, "Bolshevik vituperation was a style unto itself" with its "list of rich, succulent, dirty words" (Boynik 2018, 62). At the same time—as might be expected from a well-educated son of the provincial civil service—there is plenty of traditional rhetoric: anaphora, syntactic parallelism, antithesis, apostrophe, chiasmus, etc., noticed by most contributors even if not given their classical names. Eikhenbaum summarizes:

> Generally, Lenin's style is a unique combination of three stylistic layers: the bookish discourse of the Russian intelligentsia …; the Russian colloquial everyday speech …; and Latin oratorical style.
> EIKHENBAUM 1924, 170

Both Rosa Luxemburg and Leon Trotsky were also accomplished and effective rhetoricians in speaking and in writing. Here is Rosa Luxemburg's scathing denunciation of the Social Democratic Party's opportunism in supporting the German war effort:

> Where and when has the suspension of all constitutional rights been accepted so submissively as a matter of course? Where has such a hymn of praise to the most severe press censorship been sung from the ranks of the opposition as it has in the individual newspapers of German Social Democracy? Never before has a war found such Pindars; never has a military dictatorship found such obedience; never has a political party so fervently sacrificed all that it stood for and possessed on the altar of a cause which it had sworn a thousand times before the world to fight to the last drop of blood.
> LUXEMBURG 1915, 200

Trotsky's work offers many examples. Here I'll cite the effective use of sexual and biological imagery in his discussion of the abortive Chinese revolution of 1925–27 in *The Third International After Lenin*. The imagery invites the reader to perceive in history a dialectic similar to what can be observed in nature: there is health and disease; there is deformity; there are laws of development and interaction which can be perverted if they are not correctly understood. The imagery also bespeaks a profound integration of, and simultaneous commitment to, the sensual, intellectual, and active modes of life. Sexual pleasure, reproduction, detailed analysis, intellectual comprehension, and socialist revolution are healthy; rape, impotence, adventurism, and lack of correct class analysis are not.

> The fact that these attempts to rape the historical process [i.e., the Estonian and Bulgarian risings of 1924] by means of a putsch were left without a critical investigation, led to a relapse in Canton towards the end of 1927.
> Seeking to insure themselves against their past sins, the leadership [of the Comintern] monstrously forced the course of events at the end of last year and brought about the Canton miscarriage. However, even a miscarriage can teach us a good deal concerning the organism of the mother and the process of gestation.
> As to the agrarian overturn, the revolution gave birth to a perfectly healthy and strong baby, but it was the proletarian dictatorship that functioned as the midwife.
> The resolution ... condemns itself to utter impotence by the fact alone that ... it entirely ignores the class content of the Canton insurrection.
> TROTSKY 1928, 118, 181, 191, 200

As to Stalin: Those who consider Stalin's crudely mechanical interpretations of Marxism, or his opportunism and brutality, to have seriously handicapped the world communist movement and several revolutions internationally, will not be surprised to observe how rigidly dull, how repetitive and predictable, how devoid of wit, metaphor, irony, rhythm or indeed any awareness of the possibilities of language, is the prose style of Stalin. The plodding monotony of his style sets it apart in the mainstream of communist writing. Most conspicuous in Stalin's style is the virtually complete absence of figurative language, a feature the more striking because of the frequence, vigor, and variety of figurative language with which the other writers mentioned convey many of their most important and deeply felt principles.

That the classic communist writers rely so heavily on figurative language is not simply the effect of their class background, although their academic training and wide reading in world literature are important influences. Nor should their style be understood only as the consequence of a hortatory or propagandistic intention: to move rather than to instruct. On the contrary, that distinction can scarcely apply to communist literature, for it assumes the fragmentation of consciousness into intellect (to which instruction appeals) and passion (the target of rhetoric)—a fragmentation corresponding to that which divides theory from practice. The works and passages I have cited are simultaneously analytic and hortatory: their analysis implies action; their exhortation is based on analysis. No other condition is possible for a prose whose writers are committed to the view that psychological fragmentation is a form of our alienation from ourselves, and that such alienation can be overcome through revolutionary activity—the fusion of understanding and action—and the new society to be created through that activity.

Beyond training and purpose, though, the predilection of communist writers for figurative language expresses a principle basic to both figurative language and historical process: the principle of contradiction, or tension, between or among opposed forces. In requiring our attention to vibrate between literal and symbolic levels of meaning, between concrete and abstract, real and hyperbolic, stated and implied, or among multiple literal meanings, figurative language reflects the perceived complexities of natural and social existence. It preserves an otherwise tenuous equilibrium, bringing contradiction within our range of understanding and within our verbal control in a primary act of white magic, the power of naming. It mitigates the harshness of irreconcilable oppositions in nature and in social life, while—indeed by—expressing that harshness as illogicality. Hence André Breton:

> Everything leads us to believe that there exists a mental position from which life and death, real and imaginary, past and future, communicable and incommunicable, high and low cease to be perceived as contradictions … [T]he position in question is … one where construction and destruction can no longer be brandished against one another.[3]

Nor is the sense of contradiction only the product of class antagonism. It is, I suggest, as basic to humanity as language itself, or as work: adult human consciousness is conscious of its difference from the rest of nature, and of its opposition to nature. The song of a Canadian indigenous (Gitksan) shaman, Isaac Tens, apologizes to nature for disturbing it, for its life is sacrificed to his own:

> Death of the salmon,
> my death

---

3 The passage appears in various versions. I was unable to document the one I have used here, but a close version appears in Rosemont 1978, 129.

> but the city
> finds life in it.
>> ROTHENBERG 1969, 52

The ceremony of sacrifice, common to most early societies, expresses this sense of the necessity to restore to nature some part of what we take from it. The ceremony, like art itself, helps to overcome that alienation, that contradiction which is literally as fundamental as opening one's eyes and becoming aware of self and other:

> Repose for man's thought consists in the firmness and certainty with which he eternally creates this contradiction between thought and object and eternally overcomes it. ... Cognition is the eternal endless approximation of thought to the object. The reflection of nature in man's thought must be understood not lifelessly, not abstractly, not devoid of movement, not without contradictions, but in the eternal process of movement, the arising of contradictions and their solution.
>> LENIN 1916, 195

Besides being partner to contradiction, nature is also paradoxical within itself: it nurtures and destroys, it is beneficent and dangerous at once, as in a Dahomey chant:

> Softly softly Lisa-o
> Softly o sun-god
> Do not ravish the world
> Ram pawing the earth with hooves of flame
> Ram pounding the earth with horns of fire
> Do not ravish the world
> Do not destroy us.
>> HERSKOVITZ 1934, 75–76

Society is as paradoxical as nature, with this difference: it is not an Other. Because humanity doesn't simply inhabit nature but deliberately uses and controls it, society (like history) is nothing distinct from human action but is itself that process of use and control (that is, appropriation of nature and wealth through wars, migrations, monarchies, priestly castes, religion, technology, and the rest). The effort, then, is to understand the rationale of experiential paradox.

> Religious distress is at the same time the expression of real distress and the protest against real distress.
>
> MARX 1844, 42

> And bourgeoisdom ... crucifies liberty upon a cross of gold, and if you ask in whose name it does this, it replies, "In the name of personal freedom".
>
> CAUDWELL 1938, 228

> Production becomes social but appropriation remains private.
>
> LENIN 1916, 25

To understand this language is to understand reality. That is perhaps the distinctive contribution of socialist style in the service of truth, not of mystification: to suggest that ultimate reality is, after all, comprehensible, and as capable of bending to different needs as style in art or the language we use.[4]

References

Augustine. [427] 1958. *On Christian Doctrine*, translated by D.W. Robertson. New York: Liberal Arts Press.

Barthes, Roland. 1967. *Writing Degree Zero*. New York: Hill and Wang. First published 1953, Paris: Editions du Seuil.

Boynik, Sezgin. 2018. *Coiled Verbal Spring: Devices of Lenin's Language*. Helsinki: Rab-Rab Press.

Brecht, Bertolt. [1936] 1964. "Alienation Effects in Chinese Acting". In *Brecht on Theatre*, translated and edited by John Willett, 91–99. New York: Hill and Wang.

Caudwell, Christopher. [1938] 1971. *Studies in a Dying Culture*. In *Studies and Further Studies in a Dying Culture*, v–228. New York: Monthly Review Press.

Derrida, Jacques. 1994. *Specters of Marx: the State of the Debt; The Work of Mourning; and The New International*, translated by Peggy Kamuf. New York: Routledge.

Eikhenbaum, Boris. 1924. "Lenin's Basic Stylistic Tendencies". In Boynik 2018, 155–73.

Engels, Friedrich. [1883] 1974. "The Book of Revelation". In *Marx and Engels on Religion*, 205–12. New York: Schocken Books.

---

4 This chapter is a revised version of "Political Style/Political Stylistics", *Style* 8, no. 3 (1974): 437–51.

Engels, Friedrich. [1888] 1976. "Letter to Margaret Harkness". In *Marx and Engels on Literature and Art*, 89–92. Moscow: Progress Publishers.

Engels, Friedrich. [1894] 1974. "On the History of Early Christianity". In *Marx and Engels on Religion*, 316–47. New York: Schocken Books.

Fischer, Ernst. 1963. *The Necessity of Art: a Marxist Approach*, translated by Anna Bostock. Harmondsworth: Penguin.

Fischer, Ernst. 1969. *Art Against Ideology*, translated by Anna Bostock. London: Penguin.

Herskovitz, Frances. 1934. "Dahomean songs". *Poetry: A Magazine of Verse* 45 (2): 75–76.

Hyman, Stanley Edgar. 1962. *The Tangled Bank: Darwin, Marx, Frazer and Freud as Imaginative Writers*. New York: Atheneum.

Kruchenykh, Alexei. 1928. "Devices of Lenin's Speech". In Boynik 2018, 283–334.

Lenin, V.I. [1916] 1965. *Imperialism, the Highest Stage of Capitalism*. Peking: Foreign Languages Press.

Lenin, V.I. [1920] 1978. "The Tasks of the Youth Leagues". In *Lenin on Literature and Art*, 148–66. Moscow: Progress Publishers.

Lenin, V.I. 1910, 1911. "Tolstoy". In *Lenin on Literature and Art*, 52–68. 1978. Moscow: Progress Publishers.

Lenin, V.I. 1916 1[1972]. *Conspectus of Hegel's Science of Logic*. Bk. 3, "Subjective Logic", sec. 3, "The Idea". In *Collected Works*, vol. 38. Moscow: Progress Publishers.

Luxemburg, Rosa. [1915] 1972. "Rebuilding the International". In *Rosa Luxemburg. Selected Political Writings*, edited by Robert Looker, translated by William D. Graf, 197–210. London: Jonathan Cape.

Mao Tse-tung. [1942] 1967. "Oppose Stereotyped Party Writing". In *Mao Tse-tung on Literature and Art*, 91–114. Peking: Foreign Languages Press.

Marx, Karl. [1844] 1974. "Introduction to a Contribution to the Critique of Hegel's Philosophy of Right". In *Marx and Engels on Religion*, 41–58. New York: Schocken Books.

Marx, Karl. [1847] 1999. "Wage-Labour and Capital". In *Wage-Labour and Capital; and Value, Price and Profit*, 15–48. New York: International Publishers.

Ollman, Bertell. 1976. *Alienation: Marx's Conception of Man in Capitalist Society*. Cambridge: Cambridge University Press.

Rosemont, Franklin, ed. 1978. *André Breton: What Is Surrealism? Selected Writings*. New York: Monad Press.

Rothenberg, Jerome, ed. 1969. *Technicians of the Sacred*. Garden City, NJ: Anchor Books.

Shklovsky, Viktor. 1924. "Lenin as Decanonizer". In Boynik 2018, 149–53.

Toscano, Alberto. 2023. "Foreword. Echoes of Marx". In Ludovico Silva. [1973] 2023. *Marx's Literary Style*, translated by Paco Brito Núñez. London: Verso. Ebook.

Trotsky, Leon. [1924] 1971. *Literature and Revolution*, translated by Rose Strunsky. Ann Arbor: University of Michigan Press.

Trotsky, Leon. [1928] 1970. *The Third International After Lenin*, translated by John G. Wright. New York: Pathfinder Press.

Wolff, Robert Paul. 1988. *Moneybags Must Be So Lucky: On the Literary Structure of Capital.* Amherst: University of Massachusetts Press.

CHAPTER 2

Marxist Medievalists
A Tradition

I begin with two disclaimers. The first is that this is not a formal chapter but rather a series of impressions and anecdotes about several people in this and the last two centuries who were committed to medieval studies and to revolutionary social change. It originated as a talk in a panel on women medievalists at the International Medieval Congress at Kalamazoo, Michigan. I was asked to speak about my career and chose instead to do a prosopographic piece, inserting myself into what could loosely be called a tradition, one to which Margaret Schlauch also belonged. Since the point of being a Marxist is precisely in community, context, and history, this seems appropriate, and I'm sure that Schlauch (with the modesty I've learned was characteristic of her) would have approved.[1]

My second disclaimer is about the looseness of what I am calling a tradition, because I don't claim to have been directly influenced by any of the people I will mention, except for the first one, who was not a medievalist. I will bring out some points of contact among these individuals and between them and myself as a Marxist medievalist.

Karl Marx wrote about medieval economics, as he had to in order to document the development of mercantile capitalism during the high Middle Ages. These scattered items, collected by Eric Hobsbawm in *Precapitalist Economic Formations*, have been used by many cultural historians—Ernst Fischer, Arnold Hauser, Norbert Elias, Marc Bloch, Fernand Braudel, Jacques LeGoff, Perry Anderson, among others—and remain useful to materialist-minded medievalists. Marx well understood the radical intellectual and social innovations of the high medieval period (such as the Italian city-state) and admired high medieval culture. He paid special tribute to Dante, ending his preface to

---

1   This talk developed into a keynote address given at the Schlauch Symposium in Poznan, Poland, in May 2002. The conference was organized by me and Dr. Jacek Fisiak of Adam Mickiewicz University in Poznan, who was Schlauch's graduate student and colleague. The conference brought together a small, compatible group of medievalists from Canada, the United States, Germany, Australia, and Poland working in literary-cultural history and in linguistics, the areas of Schlauch's specialization. A number of the contributions have been published in *Studia Anglica Posnaniensa* (see Fisiak 2002).

the first edition of *Capital* with a line from "the great Florentine" that might well have served as his own life motto: *"Segui il tuo corso e lascia dir le genti"* (Follow your own road and let people talk).

The beautiful and erudite Eleanor Marx, Karl's oldest daughter, had close friendships with two important figures in nineteenth-century medievalism who themselves were social activists. One was the artist and printer William Morris, with whom Eleanor, along with Friedrich Engels and others, founded the Socialist League in 1884. Morris's medievalism was a lifelong commitment, starting with his childhood reading of the novels of Sir Walter Scott, then reinforced at Oxford by John Ruskin's work, especially "The Nature of Gothic", and by fashionable anglo-Catholicism. His early (1858) poem "Defense of Guinevere" picks up the art-nouveau medievalism of the period (also exhibited in Tennyson's Arthurian cycles, in some of Browning's dramatic monologues, and in the work of several painters) as well as its nascent feminism. His epic *The Earthly Paradise* is set against the backdrop of the Black Plague; his "Dream of John Ball" commemorates a leader of the great and nearly successful 1381 rebellion; and his socialist utopia, *News from Nowhere*, combines certain aspects of medieval life with Marxian notions of revolutionary struggle, full genuine socialism and the development of human personality. As a craftsman, Morris produced what has been called one of the most beautiful books ever made, the *Kelmscott Chaucer* (1894). Morris had little use for what he called "the maundering side" of medievalism (Morris 1883, 31): he meant the merely aesthetic attraction to medieval art, and the sentimental romanticization of the period evident in the work of various poets and painters. Instead, Morris constructed a 'realistic' medievalism. For him, what tied Marxism and medievalism together was, in his own words, "hatred of modern civilization"— a hatred generated in turn by "the desire to produce beautiful things ... the love and practice of art" (Morris 1894, 36–37). In this sense, both his art and his politics were strategies of protest and of reconstruction.

Eleanor Marx was never as close to William Morris as she was to F.J. Furnivall, the famous editor of medieval texts, founder of the Chaucer, Ballad, Wyclif, and Early English Text Societies, and organizer of what eventually became the *Oxford English Dictionary*. Furnivall was a militant activist for the rights and education of working men and women: he organized; he marched; he demonstrated; he led protests in the streets. Furnivall's socialism, unlike Morris's, was not of the Marxian revolutionary type, but rather the semi-utopian, good-works Christian Socialism fashionable among English intellectuals at mid-century. His Middle Ages was far different from the one envisioned by his contemporary Thomas Carlyle, whose *Past and Present* evoked a peaceful, static feudalism in which everyone knew his or her place. Part of Furnivall's attraction to medieval literature lay in what he saw as its populist thrust; thus in 1858 he lectured on *Piers Plowman* "because of its sketch of working men in the fourteenth century", as he put it (Munro 1906, XXXVI). He must have felt deeply gratified when the introduction to the Early English Text Society volume for 1870—a collection of English guild records—became an important document in the development of English trade union law (see Haas 1989).

As an employee and friend of Furnivall, Eleanor Marx gave papers in several of his societies, especially the Browning Society and the Shelley Society, for Shelley's work in particular was a touchstone of social radicalism for many, including for Eleanor's famous father.[2] She took her dear papa to literary meetings, for he was a lover of romantic poetry and of Shakespeare's work.[3] A private Shakespeare club grew out of Furnivall's larger Shakespeare society. It often convened at the Marxes' house, and the two men evidently met there or elsewhere, for Marx described Furnivall as resembling "a pilgrim on the way to the Holy Land to seek St. Anthony's beard"[4] (Kapp 1976, 1:172 n). At least one can say that the two men were well matched in the matter of beardsmanship, as well as in literary taste and unconventional social views. Eleanor worked at the British Museum for Furnivall's massive dictionary project and for his Philological, Chaucer, and Shakespeare Societies. Among other items, she transcribed the manuscript of the so-called Macro plays in 1881–82: the three fifteenth-century morality plays in the collection of the Reverend Cox Macro (*Wisdom, Mankind*, and *The Castle of Perseverance*).

I started reading the revolutionary classics as a graduate student at Columbia University, in the period 1964–67. In 1969, I was fired from my first job, at Queens College, CUNY, for what now seems like fairly minor departmental political activity: agitating, with a group of my young new-hire colleagues and friends, for a range of departmental reforms that are now completely normal everywhere (e.g., maternity leave, an extra-departmental appeal procedure,

---

2   Eleanor and her companion, Edward Aveling, wrote a pamphlet called *Shelley's Socialism*; she recalls "the Byron and Shelley-worship of the Chartists" whom she knew in childhood, and Engels's comment, "We all knew Shelley by heart then" (quoted in Kapp 1976, 2:250).
3   Marx was also a writer of romantic poetry: see the City Lights edition, edited by Lawrence Ferlinghetti, of juvenilia addressed to, or about, his then-fiancée, Jenny (Marx 1977). As for Shakespeare, the quotes are everywhere, most notably in "The Power of Money in Bourgeois Society" from the *Economic and Philosophical Manuscripts*. For an exploration of this complex relationship, see Derrida 1994.
4   Another member of the Shakespeare Club described Marx senior this way: "As an audience he was delightful, never criticizing, always entering into the spirit of any fun that was going on, laughing when anything struck him as particularly comic, until the tears ran down his cheeks—the oldest in years, but in spirit as young as any of us" (Kapp 1976, 1:193).

untenured faculty's right to voice and vote in departmental meetings, etc.). I was then hired into a new remedial program (SEEK: Search for Education, Elevation and Knowledge) at City College during the period of open admissions, then fired from that before I could start, along with the two people who had hired me (one of them the illustrious and now recently deceased Aijaz Ahmad): in short, I was blacklisted. So, I had an enforced year off, which I used to become more political. I compiled my first book, *Counter-Tradition: The Literature of Dissent and Alternatives* (1970) and joined the New University Conference (NUC), a new-left organization in which I met the Progressive Labor Party (PL), a left, pro-China split from the Communist Party.

PL provided an attractively militant pro-labor alternative to the rather flaky new leftists of NUC. But flakiness has never prevented anti-communism, and when NUC expelled PL in its own little witch-hunt, I went with PL as a sympathizer. I sold their paper, *Challenge*, in the garment district downtown and cut my hair the better to do so: long hair whipped in the wind too much and provoked flirtation from garment workers to whom I wanted to sell the paper and with whom I wanted to discuss labor issues. One non-activist friend, Marshall Berman, was horrified: "You sacrificed your femininity for the party!" he gasped. I thought I had a better grasp on my femininity than that, so I was amused at his analysis. I should add that years later, when I sent for my FBI file under the Freedom of Information Act, I found all the most interesting parts blacked out: the parts that would have enabled me to identify the agency's informants at Queens, at Columbia, in NUC, or perhaps even in Progressive Labor.

With the help of my main PL contact, an astrophysicist, I began to read Marx, Lenin, and other classics. I wanted to integrate this into my scholarship, and I looked to Margaret Schlauch as a model, having heard that in 1951, some 15 years earlier, Schlauch, a Communist, had left her job as an English professor at New York University (NYU) and defected to Poland, which was then off-limits to Americans. Much later I learned that she had a number of reasons for going. Her sister was there, married to a Polish physicist, Dr. Inman, who had been expelled from Canada as a Soviet spy.[5] In the USA of 1951, the cold-war anti-communist witch-hunt was gathering strength under President Truman; the Korean War was in progress; Senator Joseph McCarthy was firmly in the saddle; and the famous televised Army–McCarthy hearings of 1954 would soon transfix the nation. I watched them daily after school. Margaret's close friend

---

5 Although not named in the infamous Gouzenko affair (1946–47), Inman's expulsion probably was a consequence of the Cold War hysteria that swept Canada in its wake. Gouzenko, a defector from the Soviet Union, accused various people of conveying classified information to the Russians, including atomic weapon secrets.

Edwin Berry Burgum, a critic of the modern novel, had just been fired from his position at NYU for refusing to sign the loyalty oath required of all public employees. Schlauch was about to be called before an NYU committee for interrogation; she too would have refused to sign and would have been fired, so her leaving was a pre-emptive gesture. Schlauch thus re-enacted the scenario of her best-known book, *Chaucer's Constance and Accused Queens*, the Columbia University doctoral thesis she published in 1927. It is a study of the romance topos of a falsely accused noblewoman forced to flee her homeland. A difference, of course, is that the romance heroine returns, but except for a few short visits, Margaret Schlauch did not. Nor, in Schlauch's case, was the accusation false.

In my search for a scholarly model, I read Schlauch's 1956a, 1956b book, *English Medieval Literature and Its Social Foundations*, and was disappointed. It juxtaposed social and literary data without demonstrating the interpenetration of the two on the level of consciousness and style, that is, apart from explicit social content or message. For example, when Schlauch discussed the literary influence of urban growth and commerce in the high Middle Ages, she did so in terms of the exotic stories brought back to Europe from distant lands, rather than in terms of what a bourgeois consciousness might mean to poetry, art, or ethical values. Or again, she explained troubador poetry with a rather heavy-handed and unilluminating quotation about adultery from Engels's *Origins of the Family, Private Property and the State* (1884). Through other reading, I eventually learned that this well-intentioned but schematic type of work was fairly typical of scholars sympathetic with Stalinist parties, and I realized that one had to return to Marx, Engels, Lenin, and Trotsky for models of how to work with subtlety as well as rigor.

A few years later—the early 70s, in Vancouver—I looked for a Marxist journal in which to publish, for at that time openly partisan work was not accepted in mainstream journals. (I recall being told face to face by the then-editor of *PMLA* (*Publications of the Modern Language Association*), the flagship academic journal in literary studies, that my scholarship was wonderful but I ought to "drop the Marxism".) I found *Science & Society*, a Marxist journal in New York, one of whose editors was Henry Mins, a non-academic polymath. Over the next few years, *S&S* took several of my long pieces, the first in 1974, and eventually invited me to serve as an advisory editor and later as a member of the Manuscript Collective, which decided on the fate of manuscripts submitted, as well as various issues and events confronting the journal. Founded in 1936 by Margaret Schlauch and several of her colleagues, *Science & Society* has the longest continuous publication history of any Marxist journal in the world. Among the responses I received from international readers was a congratulatory letter from Margaret Schlauch in Warsaw. In December 1974 she wrote: "I can only say that I wish [your article] had been available to me when I was writing my book (many years ago) on *English Medieval Literature and Its Social Foundations*. I could have profited from your exposition in many ways" (personal letter, December 11, 1974). This was wonderfully generous encouragement to a young scholar, especially one encountering bitter resistance to Marxian method from the anglophone medieval establishment. In a second letter a couple of months later, Schlauch wrote that her book on Constance "stemmed partly from my commitment to women's rights and votes for women in the period before World War I. I was an adolescent then, but I bicycled around in the suburb where I lived, getting signatures supporting an amendment to the Constitution of the U.S. that would give women the vote" (personal letter, February 28, 1975). It turned out that Schlauch had not only been a founding editor of *S&S*, but also that the journal had been an important outlet for her political writing. There, through the 30s and 40s, she published on topics both current and medieval, obviously understanding, like many before her and since, the contemporaneity of the medieval.

It is tempting to suggest that Schlauch's solution to the question of how to be a Marxist medievalist was to split the two functions, publishing relatively conventional medieval material in mainstream books and journals, and tough-minded political pieces in *S&S*. This would not be entirely fair, because she did, at several points, introduce a class or other political perspective into several of her books.[6] Nonetheless, Schlauch's scholarship overall seemed to me to implement the typical Communist Party strategy of the day: never reveal your whole agenda, keep a low profile, only rarely invoke the big trouble-making names, and influence people gradually. This has not been my approach, for a number of reasons I haven't space to specify here.

But then, besides scholarship, there is political activism. One of my colleagues on the *S&S* editorial board was the indefatigable Annette Rubinstein, who died in 2007 at the age of ninety-seven. Annette left the Communist Party in protest against the Party's self-liquidation into the Democratic Party. Schlauch was Annette's faculty advisor at NYU in 1925; later they became close friends and political co-workers. In a short unpublished memoir that

---

6 *The Gift of Tongues* (1942) has a chapter entitled "Social Aspects: Class, Taboos, Politics". *Modern English and American Poetry* (1956) is a no-nonsense manual meant to cut through what Schlauch calls the "tricks and devices" of formalism in order to get to "the heart of what poets are saying"; her models are Whitman, Neruda, Mayakovsky and Aragon—the last three communists or pro-revolutionary. Dalton Trumbo, a brilliant screenwriter and member of the blacklisted Hollywood Ten, is studied as a gifted experimental poet.

she graciously sent me,[7] Annette tells this story, set in 1949, about Margaret Schlauch's practical medievalism:

> Vito Marcantonio, the veteran radical congressman, had decided to run in the mayoralty election, and I was campaign manager. We planned an early morning sound truck appearance at the lower west side docks, which were almost entirely worked by Italian-Americans. Since the "shape-up" for the day's job took place at 5 A.M., our meeting began at 4. ... Marc and I rode down on top of the truck, and as we approached the designated corner, we saw Margaret chatting with a group of longshoremen. She had climbed the ladder and was with us before we could greet her. "Maggie" took over, said a few words of English then smoothly slid into Italian. When she ended her introduction of Marc with a quotation from Dante there was a roar of approval.
>
> RUBINSTEIN, n.d.

For me, what's significant about this anecdote is not only Schlauch's use of Dante (himself a consummately political writer) in her organizational work, and her knowledge of colloquial Italian, but the dockworkers' obvious familiarity with Dante—a tradition going back to the poet's own time.

Annette continues with a poignant sketch of how Margaret Schlauch left America. She had invited Margaret to speak on "Homer and the Iliad" at a left-wing adult evening school, the Jefferson School, on a Saturday evening.

> Wednesday I received a note from her: "My dear Annette, I've never done this to a chairman before, and I'm desperately sorry to do it to you, but when you see the papers tomorrow you'll understand why I have to stand you up and why I couldn't let you know earlier". Headlines the next day told me that Professor Schlauch ... had surreptitiously sailed the night before.

How was Schlauch received in Poland? She became chair of her department at Poland's top university in Warsaw, and had a small apartment of the type reserved for the privileged few, with a view of the river. Her letters say virtually nothing about politics or Polish social life generally; they were certainly subjected to the scrutiny of censors. So, it is again to Annette Rubinstein's memoir

---

7 Annette Rubinstein's papers are held in the Tamiment Library in New York.

that I am grateful for an account of Schlauch's "painful experiences during the first years" of her residence in exile:

> Her colleagues ... thought her appointment had been made entirely on political grounds, perhaps even through Soviet pressure, and many felt that she was usurping a position which should have gone to an antifascist Polish professor. ... Her first years were very lonely ones; while formal relations were always correct it was a very long time before she was invited for an informal meal at a colleague's home or included in any small social gatherings.

So, I found out that *S&S* had had a major medievalist as one of its editors during the 30s and 40s. I didn't know that Henry Mins, the editor I corresponded with, would provide yet another medieval connection. Mins was a linguist from NYU and, according to Annette, "a rigid and orthodox" CP member. He had several brothers and sisters, all of them CP members or sympathizers. One of his sisters, Helen Ann Mins, was married to Rossell Hope Robbins, the well-known editor of medieval lyrics. Helen's bridesmaid had been Margaret Schlauch, and Carleton Browne, another famous editor of medieval songs, married them. Henry Mins told his brother-in-law Ross about the Marxist medievalist in Vancouver, and I was invited to Robbins's gala retirement conference, "Chaucer at Albany II", in 1982. A few interesting things happened at the banquet. One is that Ross had asked for a medieval Latin grace before the meal, and everyone was asked to stand during this grace. Evidently, he did not realize how many well-known American Chaucerians—including myself—were Jewish, and therefore did not stand. Another sign of changing times was Helen Ann's after-dinner address, directed to the many women present, urging them to do as she had done in service of some great scholar and reminding us that (in John Milton's words) "they also serve who stand and wait". It was a welcome surprise to me when I recently learned from a nephew of Helen's that she was the radical of the pair—though I don't doubt for a moment that Ross saw his editorship of popular medieval songs much as F.J. Furnivall saw his: as an aid to historical, radical, and populist consciousness.

Those of you who knew Ross will remember how proudly he displayed the large medal he had been awarded by the French Legion of Honor; he always wore it over a black turtleneck sweater. It was given for writing, not fighting. As an army officer, Ross wrote propaganda for American troops in Europe, particularly on the subject of how they should interact with French culture. Helen Ann's politics were more pointedly left. During the Spanish Civil War, she worked in Paris for the Spanish Republican government in exile. Back home, she organized New York City public school teachers into the predecessor to the American Federation of Teachers, at a time when it was illegal for public servants to unionize. Even much later, when I was at Queens College from 1967 to 1969 and the American Federation of Teachers existed, the City University system was not yet organized. We untenured faculty had no voice or vote at department meetings; we had no means of appealing a tenure or termination decision, no maternity leave, no right to see our files, and so on. My involvement with a group of other new-hires attempting to change all this led to my being fired in 1969, despite my publications and educational pedigree. This coincided with a major student uprising led by the Students for a Democratic Society (SDS), and my rehiring became a student demand. There followed an exhilarating and much-publicized several weeks of sit-ins and occupations on the Queens College campus—which is, as they say, a "whole nother story".[8]

In Canada, in the 1970s, I sought out the organization closest to Progressive Labor: the Canadian Party of Labour (CPL). I sold their paper in a suburb called New Westminster, in front of the Army-Navy surplus store, where people often told us to "go back where we came from" (I think they usually meant Russia) and on a couple of occasions tried to set fire to our armful of papers with their cigarette lighters. On the other hand, 'socialist' was not a dirty word to many Canadians as it usually was in the United States—though by 'socialist', Canadians usually meant social democratic, for Canada has a conservative social-democratic party, the New Democratic Party—now, in 2023, even more conservative than ever. My reading continued, and the more I read of revolutionary history, the more I and CPL realized that I was not about to join any Stalinist organization, so we parted ways. Eventually I joined the Spartacist League (SL), an international group of a few hundred in the Bolshevik Trotskyist tradition. I sold their paper, *Workers Vanguard*, to students, longshoremen, and the general public. During my first five years at Simon Fraser University, I was active on campus and in town, leading Marxist reading groups first for CPL, then for the SL, organizing and participating in various demonstrations: on Chile, on campus cutbacks, etc. It is perhaps not surprising that I was denied tenure—that is, fired—despite even more publications, including two books. One offense was precisely having published in *S&S*, which one Tenure Committee member characterized as a "fly-by-night journal" that would publish any leftist who asked. With the help of many a student petition and sit-in,

---

8 Ample documentation of the 1969 events is available through the Queens College library archives. In 2019, a fiftieth anniversary celebration at the Queens College library was a wonderful opportunity for a reunion with some of the participants and a new generation of students seeking models for their own struggles.

my job was eventually saved by the same university president, Dr. Kenneth Strand, whose policies I had so often denounced in campus demonstrations. Later, I did thank him in person.

I was in the SL for about five years, and neither resigned nor was expelled: an unusual ending. Instead, the organization left town because of priorities elsewhere, and I chose not to follow, since I had a job, a writing career, and two children. When they left—about 1985—I had no money, no friends, no social life, and not a single dress. Demonstrations, marches, and meetings do not require a dress; people were comrades, contacts or opponents; and as for salary, party dues took a large chunk of it every month. I had also not published much during those five years, and had turned down various requests to speak as a rising young historicist medievalist (though I did speak at Spartacist events in various North American cities). Still, I always appreciated one of the party leaders, a former physicist, for offering me what he saw as a very generous leave of six months to write a book on Chaucer. I didn't take the leave nor write the book, nor inform him that it might take six years not six months.

What attracts a Marxist to medieval studies? I was often asked this question decades ago, before Marxist-inflected historicism became as accepted in scholarship as it is today. The question was usually posed with incredulity: what could an atheist, revolutionary Marxist possibly find interesting in such a reactionary, static, monarchic, religion-dominated, monolithic culture as that of the European Middle Ages? Of course, the first answer is that no culture is monolithic, and much of my work has been committed to demonstrating that proposition. My work in Jewish studies does the same from a different angle (see Delany 2002, 2007). However, for me it was the other way around: I was a medievalist first (though one with healthy anti-authoritarian instincts). My first Middle English graduate class at Berkeley, with Dorothée Finkelstein Metlitzki (another pioneering woman scholar; she died in 2001) made me a medievalist; classes with Alain Renoir and Charles Muscatine confirmed that choice, and all three professors became friends as well as colleagues. Later, at Columbia (where I transferred to accompany my husband), I became a Marxist.

What I found the two disciplines shared was, first, that they were challenging and difficult, and I tend to prefer something not too easy. Second, both Marxism and Catholicism were comprehensive, systematic, and inclusive theories; they could incorporate and make sense of anything: humor, love, death, nature, art. Third, they both offered conceptual and historical structure and elegant writing in a high intellectual tradition.

To wrap up: this sketch shows, I hope, that medievalism need not be an ivory-tower pursuit—that in the hands of some of its practitioners it has not only been compatible with militant social activism but has sometimes even been co-opted to that end. I hope it also suggests, most of all to an audience that has experienced life under Stalinism, that Marxism in its original formulations and genuine continuity is far from being that puritanical, anti-sensual dogma to which it was so disastrously reduced in the Stalin era. I can't say that I have brought medievalism into my activism, except insofar as revolutionary commitment may resemble *caritas*, but perhaps it suffices to have done it the other way around and attempted an activist medievalism.[9]

References

Delany, Sheila, ed. 1970. *Counter-Tradition: the Literature of Dissent and Alternatives*. New York: Basic Books.

Delany, Sheila, ed. 2002. *Chaucer and the Jews. Sources, Contexts, Meanings*. New York: Routledge.

Delany, Sheila, ed. 2007. *Turn It Again: Jewish Medieval Studies and Literary Theory*. Eugene, OR: Wipf and Stock. First published 2004, Asheville: Pegasus Press.

Derrida, Jacques. 1994. *Specters of Marx*. New York: Routledge.

Fisiak, Jacek, ed. 2002. *Studia Anglica Posnaniensia*. Poznan: UAM.

Haas, Renate. 1989. "The Social Functions of F.J. Furnivall's Medievalism". In *The Living Middle Ages: a Festschrift for Karl Heinz Goller*, edited by Uwe Boker, 319–32. Stuttgart: Belser.

Kapp, Yvonne. 1976. *Eleanor Marx*. 2 vols. London: Lawrence and Wishart.

Marx, Karl. 1977. *Love-poems of Karl Marx*, edited by Lawrence Ferlinghetti. San Francisco: City Lights.

Morris, William. [1883] 1962. "A Rather Long-winded Sketch of My Very Uneventful Life". In *Selected Writings and Designs*, edited by Asa Briggs, 29–33. Harmondsworth: Penguin Books.

Morris, William. [1894] 1962. "How I Became a Socialist". In *Selected Writings and Designs*, edited by Asa Briggs, 33–37. Harmondsworth: Penguin Books.

Munro, John. 1906. *Frederick James Furnivall: a Volume of Personal Record*. London: Oxford University Press.

Rubinstein, Annette. n.d. Unpublished memoir, typescript.

Schlauch, Margaret. 1927. *Chaucer's Constance and Accused Queens*. New York: New York University Press.

Schlauch, Margaret. 1942. *The Gift of Tongues*. New York: Modern Age Books.

---

9 This chapter is a revised version of "Marxist Medievalism: A Tradition", *Science & Society* 68, no. 2 (2004): 206–215.

Schlauch, Margaret. 1956a. *English Medieval Literature and Its Social Foundations.* Warsaw, Poland: Polish Scientific Publishers.

Schlauch, Margaret. 1956b. *Modern American Poetry: Techniques and Ideologies.* London: Watts.

CHAPTER 3

Red Rosa
Bread and Roses

> Now Red Rosa is also gone,
> Where she lies is quite unknown.
> Because she told the poor the truth,
> The rich have hunted her down.
> BERTOLT BRECHT, *"Grabschrift* 1919"

A woman, a Jew, and a Pole—it sounds like the beginning of a bad joke. Rosa Luxemburg was all three, but as a revolutionary Communist she transcends definition by sex, religion, or nationality.

Franz Mehring, the colleague and first biographer of Marx, called Luxemburg "the most brilliant intellect of all the scientific heirs of Marx and Engels" (Frölich 1972, 140). When Lenin paid homage to Luxemburg three years after her death at the hands of German police, he told "a good old Russian fable":

> "Eagles may at times fly lower than hens, but hens can never rise to the height of eagles". ... In spite of her mistakes, Rosa Luxemburg was and remains for us an eagle. Not only will Communists all over the world cherish her memory, but her biography and her *complete* works ... will serve as useful manuals in training many generations of Communists all over the world.
> LENIN 1922, 210; italics in the original

Despite Lenin's defense of "the great Communist" (Lenin 1922, 211), nonetheless six years later, Communist Party stalwarts were denouncing Rosa Luxemburg's work as "opportunist deviation" and even as a "syphilis bacillus" infecting the German proletariat. During Stalin's regime she was linked with Leon Trotsky as a heretic and deviant from 'official' Bolshevik doctrine. In East Germany, Luxemburg's reputation would revive in a limited way during the 1970s, although her antibureaucratic stance and uncompromising rejection of all opportunism continued to make party bureaucracies uncomfortable. Brecht's "Ballad of Red Rosa" was lost, but she remained an absent muse throughout his creative life, figuring in many of his songs and poems, by name or indirectly, down the years, including other epitaphs than the one given above.

In the West during the same period, a slow but steady revival of interest in Rosa Luxemburg developed. Several anthologies of her writing and speeches appeared; many of her pamphlets were made available in new editions; the important early biography by her comrade Paul Frölich was reissued in a new translation (1972), along with new editions of her letters; her doctoral dissertation became available in its first English translation.

Even this output is far from complete, for Luxemburg was an enormously prolific writer of pamphlets, newspaper articles, theoretical works, speeches, and letters. Much of this material remains unpublished or untranslated, and some was destroyed when Luxemburg's Berlin apartment was ransacked after her arrest and murder. Her major work has been taken up by a mixed audience of anarchists, surrealists, spontaneists, feminists, vanguard party theoreticians, revolutionary groupuscules, and disillusioned ex-leftists (I intend no equations here, nor any blanket evaluation). Obviously, their motives differ, as consequently does their understanding of Luxemburg's contribution to Marxist theory. Some see her as neither a theorist nor leader but rather as a gifted journalist and orator (Brie and Schütrumpf 2021, x). Luxemburg's work and her life are full of apparent paradox—like history itself, or like Marxist theory—and it's in part the inadequate understanding of such paradox that permits such a wide range of interpretation of her ideas. It isn't my purpose here to analyze Luxemburg's contribution to Marxist economics, and I am not convinced it is primarily as an economist that she is most usefully seen. As Luxemburg herself noted in a 1917 letter to Hans Diefenbach, the reader of her economic work must "thoroughly master political economy in general and Marxian economics in particular. And how many such mortals are there today? Not a half-dozen. From this standpoint my works really are luxury items and could be printed on handmade paper" (quoted in Bronner 1978, 185). Nonetheless I want to explore some of the meaning of this immensely powerful figure from our revolutionary past and to suggest some of her importance for our revolutionary future.

•••

She was born in 1871, the same year as Lenin and the year of the Paris Commune whose short life did so much to show the world revolutionary movement what proletarian democracy could and ought to be. Her family—like the families of Marx, Engels, Lenin, and Trotsky—was cultured and of comfortable means, although far from wealthy. A star pupil in high school, Rosa was denied the traditional gold medal for excellence "because of her oppositional attitude toward authority" (Frölich 1972, 6). In 1889, when Rosa was nineteen, her involvement in Warsaw with the Proletariat Party and with the new Polish Workers' League was discovered by the czarist police. It was an offense that carried the punishment of imprisonment or exile to Siberia; so, hidden under straw in a peasant's cart, Rosa Luxemburg left Poland. She escaped to Zurich, a major center of intellectual life and of international socialist activity.

In Zurich, Luxemburg made enduring friends and enemies. Among her enemies was Georgii Plekhanov, leader of the Russian exile group and 'grand old man' of the revolutionary movement abroad; for personal and political reasons Plekhanov was antagonistic to Luxemburg and her friends. And, most important, Luxemburg met Leo Jogiches, the young Polish revolutionary who was her lover for many years and her lifelong comrade in the Polish socialist movement.

The dissertation with which Rosa Luxemburg earned her doctorate was a study of the industrial development of Poland during the nineteenth century (see Luxemburg 1898). It was a pioneering effort, still used by modern historians in the field, which became an important part of Luxemburg's argument against the claims of the Polish nationalist movement for independence from Russia. The dissertation demonstrated that Poland's economic growth depended on the Russian market, so that separation would lead to economic chaos. Further, the ideological emphasis on patriotic nationalism would divert the Polish proletariat from class struggle and the struggle for socialism, thus benefiting the bourgeoisie. Luxemburg's position, then, was that Polish Communists should lend no support to the movement for national independence in Poland.

This stance was one of the mistakes that Lenin mentioned in his balanced eulogy of Luxemburg, for the Bolsheviks consistently supported the right of oppressed nations to self-determination, while at the same time recognizing the reactionary nature of nationalism—"national egoism", in Lenin's phrase—and the equally retrograde influence of such mystical trends as pan-Islamism. Luxemburg's mistakes here were several. She confused support for national liberation with capitulation to nationalism. And, in her zeal to avoid the reformist mistake of limitation to democratic demands, she recoiled to the opposite (ultra-left) extreme of rejecting the democratic demand—rather than, as Lenin urged in his writings on the question, taking up the democratic demand for national liberation, supporting it, and combining it with the struggle for socialism. Stalin's analogy to the religion question is helpful here: the Bolsheviks will defend freedom of religion, while simultaneously agitating against religion as an ideology hostile to the interests of the proletariat. Similarly, the revolutionary party will support the right of nations to self-determination while agitating for its own program. The Bolshevik position implied neither (as Trotsky put it) "an evangel of separation" (Trotsky 1930, 40) nor political support to the bourgeoisie of a colonial country, even if that bourgeoisie were waging a struggle for national independence. Here the key principle is the organizational and propagandistic independence of Communists within the movement: to support militarily the struggle for national liberation, while simultaneously exposing and opposing the colonial bourgeoisie and pushing the struggle toward socialist revolution.

It was partly through her polemics against Polish independence and her leadership of the Polish group that the young Rosa Luxemburg established her reputation as an important member of the international socialist movement. On completing her degree in 1898, she decided, against the advice of Jogiches, to continue her revolutionary career in Germany. The specific reasons for her decision are not known, but it must have been clear that Germany, with its rapidly growing (though already internally divided) socialist party, its developed capitalist economy, and its well-organized working class, offered the serious prospect of socialist revolution in the near future. It was in Germany that Luxemburg developed into one of the most formidable and creative leaders of world socialism, both a brilliant theoretician and a militant strategist. She sustained that position until she was arrested and killed by army officers during the abortive German revolution of 1918–19, when working-class militancy made her leadership (and that of her comrade Karl Liebknecht, who died with her) a serious and immediate threat to the government. She and Liebknecht were arrested in Berlin on January 15, 1919, beaten, and shot; Jogiches met the same fate two months later. Luxemburg's body was dumped into a canal, not to be recovered for another four months. O'Kane opens her study with a gruesomely vivid account of the arrest and assassination (O'Kane 2015, 1), and Frölich provides a fully detailed account of the episode, including names of the assassins (Frölich 1972, 299–300). In Goebbels's book-burning of 1933, her works were thrown into the fire along with those of Marx and Engels, Wilhelm Reich, and the rest of Europe's greatest artists, scientists, and revolutionaries. From exile, Bertolt Brecht complained that his works were not added to the pyre with hose of his friends and comrades:

> When the Regime ordered that books with dangerous teachings
> Should be publicly burnt and everywhere
> Oxen were forced to draw carts full of books
> To the funeral pyre, an exiled poet,
> One of the best, discovered with fury, when he studied the list
> Of the burned, that his books
> Had been forgotten. He rushed to his writing table
> On wings of anger and wrote a letter to those in power.
> Burn me, he wrote with hurrying pen, burn me!

> Do not treat me in this fashion. Don't leave me out. Have I not
> Always spoken the truth in my books? And now
> You treat me like a liar! I order you:
> Burn me!
>
> BRECHT 1947, 125

•••

The central struggle in Rosa Luxemburg's political life in Germany was the struggle against reformist revisionism: that is, against the abandonment of socialist revolution and class struggle in favor of legal and parliamentary reforms. Until World War I, 'social democracy' had been the general name for scientific or Marxian socialism as distinct from other currents such as Fourierist or Owenite utopian socialism. Lenin's party was the Russian Social Democratic Labor Party. What set scientific socialism apart from other programs for social change was, first, the dialectical and materialist understanding of history and of capitalist social relations (relations of production, together with the class structure and political institutions that followed from these relations of production); second, the understanding of the revolutionary tendency of the working class because of its position in capitalist society as the productive but exploited class; and third, understanding the necessity of revolution in order to expropriate the capitalist ruling class, smash—Marx's word (Tucker 1978, 607; Marx 1871, 86)—the bourgeois state, and establish new, genuinely democratic forms of social life.

Reformist revisionism began its major theoretical development in the European socialist movement in the work of the German social democrat and pacifist Eduard Bernstein who, even while revising the most basic economic and political premises of Marxist theory, continued to pose as a sincere socialist. Briefly, Bernstein's argument, supported by the economist and philosopher Konrad Schmidt, runs as follows. By means of various adaptive mechanisms such as the credit system, improved communications, and employers' organizations (cartels, trusts), capitalism can avoid the recurrent crises that Marxist economics sees as inevitable. In this way, capitalism becomes flexible enough to satisfy everyone, including the proletariat. Moreover, the trade union activity of the organized working class, along with assorted social reforms, will gradually improve its lot to the point where "the trade union struggle ... will lead to a progressively more extensive control over the conditions of production", while through legislation the capitalist, according to Schmidt, is eventually "reduced to the role of a simple administrator" (Luxemburg 1899, 19). Class struggle can thus be eliminated by parliamentary reforms, and capitalism can survive indefinitely. The net effect of enough reforms would be socialism: No revolution required.

The best short exposure of this sleight-of-hand is still Rosa Luxemburg's polemic against Bernstein and Schmidt, *Reform or Revolution*, first published in 1899. The pamphlet examines the economic assumptions and the practical political consequences of revisionism, counterposing the Marxist analysis of the question. It shows, for example, how credit and cartels, far from suppressing the anarchy of capitalism, intensify and precipitate its crises. In particular they "aggravate the antagonism existing between the mode of production and exchange by sharpening the struggle between the producer and the consumer"—a principle whose concrete operation affects us now in the artificially inflated prices of housing, food, and other consumer commodities, and in such carefully engineered "shortages" as the mid-1970s oil crisis. Nor will the trade union movement lead steadily to a proletarian paradise, for as capitalism proceeds through its decadent phase, the demand for labor power will increase more slowly than the supply. Moreover, losses suffered on the world market will be compensated by reduction of wages. For these reasons, unemployment and falling wages (real wages, if not nominal wages) can be expected, and the trade union movement will find its effort to protect the proletariat doubly difficult. Some of these problems are taken up in more detail by Lenin in *Imperialism, the Highest Stage of Capitalism* (1916).

This is not to say that revolutionary communism minimizes the importance of reform struggles, of safeguarding the gains made by the organized working class, or of defending democratic rights. In fact, as Luxemburg notes in her introduction to *Reform or Revolution*, it is only in Bernstein's work that one finds for the first time any opposition between the two indissolubly linked aspects of socialism. She writes,

> the daily struggle for reforms ... and for democratic institutions, offers to the Social-Democracy the only means of engaging in the proletarian class war and working in the direction of the final goal—the conquest of political power and the suppression of wage-labor. [For Social Democracy] the struggle for reforms is its means; the social revolution, its aim.
>
> LUXEMBURG 1899, 8

The difference from revisionism, then, is that revisionism declares the stated aim of socialism to be impossible, unknowable, or unimportant: "The final goal, no matter what it is, is nothing; the movement is everything". Yet since, as Luxemburg notes, "there can be no socialist movement without a socialist aim, [Bernstein] ends by renouncing the movement" (Luxemburg 1899, 56) as well. It remains painfully familiar; one thinks of Herbert Marcuse's advice in *Counter-Revolution and Revolt* to young revolutionaries: to abandon mass action and "labor fetishism" and retreat to the universities (Marcuse 1972, 55–57, 132).

Perhaps the worst practical consequence of the growing influence of revisionism in the German Social Democratic Party (SPD) was its inability to deal correctly with the outbreak of World War I. In 1914 the SPD, along with socialist parties of other countries, went patriotically in support of the national war effort, instead of refusing to participate in a war among imperialist nations. When the SPD voted war credits to the government, its theoretical and practical bankruptcy became as obvious to many as they had been for some time already to Rosa Luxemburg. 'Social democrat' has since remained the term for those who want to reform capitalism rather than destroy it. Such reformists allied with the bourgeoisie to protect interests now their own. Indeed, it was with the complicity of an SPD government (to which power had been handed over in November 1918) that Luxemburg and Liebknecht were arrested and killed.

Obviously, the collapse of German social democracy cannot be laid entirely at the feet of Bernstein. In the introduction to his edition of Luxemburg's political writings, Robert Looker points out that "a stress on the insidious influence of revisionism ... mistakes symptoms for causes" (Looker 1972, 35). Looker is surely correct in citing as important contributing factors the history of the German labor movement and the history of the SPD from the nineteenth century on. Still, the 1899 controversy with Bernstein and the 1914 abdication of a proletarian class line were symptoms of the same disease: opportunism. As Luxemburg wrote in "Either/Or", a Spartacus League pamphlet of 1916: "The proud old cry, 'Proletarians of all countries, unite!' has been transformed on the battlefield into the command, 'Proletarians of all countries, cut each other's throats!'" (Luxemburg 1916, 212). And the Marxist principle that all written history is the history of the class struggle, now had "except in time of war" added to it (Luxemburg 1915). This was the demise of the Second International, as Lenin, Luxemburg, and other revolutionary socialists recognized. At the Zimmerwald Conference in September 1915, the foundations of the Third International were laid, although not until 1919 was it officially established.

In spite of their shock and outrage at the SPD's defection, Luxemburg and other comrades were not paralyzed. Those who were committed to Marxian economics, to dialectical materialism, and to revolution formed an opposition faction within the Party, the *Spartakusbund* (Spartacus League), named after the famous leader of a Roman slave revolt. Some four years later, the group would become the Communist Party of Germany (KPD) and, in 1919, would affiliate with the Third International. In the intervening years before they split from the SPD, their tasks were to oppose the revisionist Party leadership especially around the war issue, to propagandize among the masses for a correct line, and to organize actions against the war—as best they could without too blatantly breaching party discipline. The opposition conference of March 1916 showed impressive support in key industrial areas and in the SPD youth: a solidarity squandered by the faction leadership's firm decision to remain inside the Party as long as possible. Their reason was to not abandon the social-democratic masses to the reformist leadership. The eventual effect—visible in the tragic defeat of the so-called Spartacus uprising of 1918–19—was to do exactly that, in failing to build the unambiguous and distinct revolutionary organization that in the critical moment could have provide the leadership abdicated by social democracy.

...

What was Rosa Luxemburg's experience as a woman leader of the SPD? In an ideal world, an ideal party, the question would be irrelevant. But since neither the world nor the party was perfect, gender was a factor both in inner-party life and in the SPD's external work around 'the woman question'.

For twenty-five years, this pioneering work was led by Rosa's good friend Clara Zetkin, who did more than anyone to produce a synthesis of Marxian theory, political principle, and organizational practice on the woman question, a synthesis imitated by the Bolsheviks before and after they came to power. Until 1908, women in most parts of the Habsburg empire were forbidden by law to join a political party. Since the SPD could not recruit women directly, at a time when millions of women were joining the industrial work-force, it devised special techniques to reach them. In order to organize working women, the SPD sponsored hundreds of educational societies for women, reading and discussion groups, or 'mutual-help societies' that were more or less organizationally autonomous, although in political agreement with the Party. Virtually all members were workers or the wives of SPD workers. They had their own conferences; they sent delegates to SPD congresses; they canvassed for SPD electoral candidates and raised money for the SPD; they published articles in the party press. The journal of this socialist women's movement, *Gleichheit* (*Equality*), was edited by Zetkin, first independently, then under Party sponsorship. However, since the SPD was far from rigorously centralist, *Gleichheit* became, as we shall see, a hotbed of opposition.

Luxemburg did not participate in the women's movement, nor need she have done. As a first-rate economist and political mind, her place was at the center of power and policy. Doubtless the revisionist SPD graybeards would have liked nothing better than to see their fiery young opponent safely relegated to the more marginal work among women, rather than raising left-wing resolutions at international congresses, editing Party press, and embarrassing them with her uncompromising radicalism. And, as Luxemburg noted in a letter to Jogiches, it was not only her enemies in the SPD who feared her as a rival, but even her allies who saw her as "someone who gives them the feeling that it might be best to put her off for as long as possible, because she might quickly surpass them" (quoted in Bronner 1978, 76). Although an older leader quickly retracted his snide "joke" about "petticoat politics" on Luxemburg's being offered an important position on the Press Commission, nonetheless it was not the last manifestation of sexual politics she would encounter in the SPD. Her short tenure (in 1899) as editor of an important Party newspaper ended in her indignant resignation in protest against lack of cooperation by her colleagues. For some revisionist leaders—a few of whom actually opposed equal rights for women—Luxemburg and Zetkin were "the two weird sisters" or "the two hysterical females" (Honeycutt 1975, 249).

Immensely ambitious, immensely conscious of her superior abilities, Rosa Luxemburg was not one to placate her rivals with feminine wiles. There can be no doubt of the sexuality of her private life: the tender ardent letters to Jogiches and Diefenbach make that clear. A rather fetching blend of sensuality and modesty is conveyed in her remark about a book of erotic poems. Wittily adapting a notorious line from the SPD debate on revisionism, Luxemburg commented on the poems, "one doesn't say things like that, one does them" (quoted in Bronner 1978, 165). Political work, though, should know no gender, except for the work among women, as Rosa sardonically remarked in a letter to Luise Kautsky in 1911: "Are you going to attend the women's conference? Can you imagine: I have become a female! I received a credential for the conference". (quoted in Bronner 1978, 145).

Luxemburg's oft-cited description of the work among women as "old ladies' business" should, I think, be put in context. The comment need not be blown out of proportion, as I believe some feminists have done, to imply that Luxemburg was not committed to the liberation of women. She was committed, and stood squarely in the normative Marxian tradition of full liberation for women and men through socialist revolution: She did not believe that full liberation was possible without socialism. Moreover, the great Russian revolutions of 1905 and 1917 must have made the municipal welfare projects and social work orientation of the German women's organizations seem tame, indeed diversionary, by comparison. Rosa was a constant and incisive supporter of the Russian events. In 1906 she traveled (illegally) on a speaking tour, also illegal, to Russian-controlled Poland, where she was imprisoned for months; then, in dangerously poor health, to Russia and to Finland, where she wrote one of her most important pamphlets, *The Mass Strike* (Frölich 1972, 117).

On the other hand, I believe that Luxemburg's early attitude toward the work among women was incorrect, although it was consistent with other of her positions. A woman, a Jew, and a Pole: triply oppressed—and as a Communist, Luxemburg saw all the oppressed as her constituency:

> What do you want with this particular suffering of the Jews? The poor victims on the rubber plantations of Putumayo, the Negroes in Africa with whose bodies the Europeans play a game of catch, are just as near to me. ... Oh, this "sublime silence of eternity" in which so many screams have faded away unheard. It rings within me so strongly that I have no special corner of my heart reserved for the ghetto.
> quoted in BRONNER 1978, 179–80

Doubtless Rosa Luxemburg considered her (ultra-left) position on national independence to be of a piece with this view, and the Bolsheviks' insistence on the democratic right of nations to self-determination a diversionary concession to backward popular sentiment, a concession to the immediate needs of a portion of the oppressed. And similarly, I would suggest, with the oppression of women.

In 1908, a new law granted women the right of association. Female membership in the SPD rose dramatically as the party both recruited directly and integrated the already existing sympathetic women's groups. Between 1908 and 1914 about 150,000 women joined. Although it would be simplistic to claim that all the new female recruits were more radical than the leadership, it is certain that *Gleichheit, und*er Zetkin's leadership, was a powerful instrument of opposition propaganda, especially after the war broke out in 1914. Zetkin was with the Spartacists, the most radical of the opposition factions, whose antiwar propaganda (contradicting the official national-patriotic party line) won an enthusiastic hearing among proletarian women. But the revisionist leadership did not for long tolerate this state of affairs: Zetkin was forced out of her position in 1916, and the new majority-loyal *Gleichheit* editorialized:

> Women are more influenced than men by their emotions. In this lies their strength and also their weakness. In this case, the strength is a passionate opposition to war. ... Their weakness is that, due to emotionalism,

they are more susceptible to the erroneous view that majority socialists favored war.

quoted in QUATAERT 1979, 215

• • •

Perhaps the most startling revelation in Luxemburg's letters is the stubbornness with which she created and clung to a private world, a sense of herself apart from political life. Her painting, her carefully classified collection of dried plants, her intense sympathy for the pain of animals and insects, her love for music and literature, her close friendships with women comrades, the poignant vignettes of ordinary life observed from prison—these testify to a many-sided personality that is most evident in Rosa's letters to Hans Diefenbach: "I still don't know what will become of me for, as you know, I too am a land of boundless possibilities" (quoted in Bronner 1978, 174). It was a sense of self that did not contradict her political commitment but complemented and confirmed it, as she could write with utter candor to a friend and comrade, Sonja Liebknecht:

> Inwardly, I feel so much more at home in a plot of garden like the one here ... than at one of our party congresses. Surely I can tell you this, since you will not immediately suspect me of betraying socialism! You know that, in spite of it all, I really hope to die at my post, in a street fight or in prison.
>
> But my innermost self belongs more to my titmice than to the "comrades". And not because I find a restful refuge in nature like so many morally bankrupt politicians. On the contrary, in nature, too ... I find so much that is cruel that I suffer very much.
>
> quoted in BRONNER 1978, 203

Precisely this strong, unerring sense of self gave Luxemburg her fierce tenacity in struggle; certainly it is what she drew on for her unique power as a writer and speaker:

> When people write, they forget ... to dig deeply into themselves and to feel the whole import and truth of what they are writing. I believe that every time, every day, in every article you must feel your way through it, and then fresh words—coming from the heart and going to the heart— would occur to express the old familiar thing. But you get so used to a truth that you rattle off the deepest and greatest things as if they were the

> "Our Father". I firmly intend, when I write, never to forget to be enthusiastic about what I write and to commune with myself.
>
> quoted in FRÖLICH 1972, 39

And it was surely this sense of self that enabled Luxemburg to survive so wonderfully intact the long sojourn in prison that left her sick and gray-haired but never touched her revolutionary will or her lifelong conviction that, as she wrote to Mathilde Wurm, "being a *Mensch* [person] is the main thing! And that means to be firm, lucid and cheerful" (quoted in Bronner 1978, 173). It is in a letter from prison, to Hans Diefenbach, that she reconstructs a domestic scene overheard from a neighboring tenement, a scene whose imagery repeats the roses in my title and seems to evoke the beauty she never lost sight of as the ultimate goal. It is night; a little girl is stubbornly singing a nursery song despite orders to go to bed:

> In this jumping rhythm of the nursery song, in the bubbling laughter, there was so much carefree and victorious lust for life that the whole dark, mouldy building of the police presidium seemed enveloped in a coat of silvery mist; it was as if, all of a sudden, my malodorous cell smelled of falling dark-red roses. Thus, wherever we are we can gather up a little happiness from the street, and we are reminded again that life is beautiful and rich.
>
> quoted in BRONNER 1978, 217

In 1916 Rosa Luxemburg was again arrested (taken into 'protective custody'), and it was in prison that she heard the news of the Bolshevik revolution in Russia. "For three years Europe has been like a musty room", she wrote in May 1917, "almost suffocating those living in it. Now all at once a window has been flung open, a fresh, invigorating gust of air is blowing in, and everyone in the room is breathing deeply of it" (Luxemburg 1917, 227). This was her enthusiastic welcome to long-awaited revolution, in the famous essay "The Old Mole".[1] It seemed that the old mole, revolutionary history, having gone underground for the time in Germany, had now surfaced in Russia. Its reappearance there

---

1 The title is taken from a phrase of Marx in *The Eighteenth Brumaire of Louis Bonaparte* (1852). Predicting an eventual uprising against the authoritarian regime, Marx writes: "And when it [the revolution] has done this ... work, Europe will leap from her seat and exultantly exclaim: Well grubbed, old mole!" Tucker explains that this refers to Shakespeare's *Hamlet* (Tucker 1978, 606) but without providing the locus: Act 1, scene 5, line 162, Hamlet addressing his father's ghost.

would and must herald similar events in Germany, not only by force of example, but because, as the Bolshevik leaders knew all too well, the success and even survival of their revolution depended on the rapid development of revolutions in other countries. They confronted the dangers of military invasion, economic strangulation, political compromises: these meant either more European revolutions in a fairly short time, or a worldwide setback for the international socialist movement as well as for the Russian Revolution itself. Naturally, the notion of 'socialism in one country', Stalin's invention, was never considered a realistic solution; since it is not dialectically—that is, politically or realistically—possible, it has no basis in the Marxist–Leninist tradition. Rather it represents both an absolute failure to understand the dialectic of revolutionary process, and a most opportunistic attempt to transform the concessions and defeats of the Russian Revolution into iron principle and virtue. Without denying that some of these concessions may have been necessary for the survival of the new state, one has nonetheless to call a spade a spade. As Luxemburg acknowledged in September 1918, even while (again incorrectly) denouncing the Treaty of Brest-Litovsk, "admittedly Lenin and his friends deluded neither themselves nor others about the facts. They admitted their capitulation. Unfortunately, they did deceive themselves in hoping to purchase a genuine respite at the price of capitulation" (Luxemburg 1918, 235). Such a deceptive slogan as "socialism in one country" could not have been and was not seriously entertained by the victorious Bolsheviks in 1917, although the idea (if not the explicit wording) was put forth by some Mensheviks and revisionists. "Imperialism or socialism! War or revolution! There is no third way!"—that was Luxemburg's battle cry (Luxemburg 1917, 234).

The proletarian rising of November 1918 to January 1919 seemed to fulfill these hopes. As a participant in what he calls "the German Revolution", Paul Frölich writes with vividness and pace of mass risings in Berlin and other major cities, of workers' councils, of the revolutionary alliance of sailors and factory workers, of the kaiser's abdication, and the proclamation by Karl Liebknecht of the Socialist Republic of Germany (see Frölich 1972, chaps. 13 and 14).

But, having shown its head all too briefly, the old mole disappeared in Germany with the defeat of the November rising. As Luxemburg foresaw it might, it soon went underground in Russia, too, after Lenin's death, and it is a favorite speculation among Luxemburg's biographers what her position might have been had she lived through the periods of the Third (Stalinist) and Fourth (Trotskyist) Internationals.

Luxemburg's criticism of the Bolshevik Party has been a thorny question on the left. Her position, and Lenin's too, has often been caricatured and oversimplified, as in Bertram D. Wolfe's introduction to his edition of two Luxemburg tracts (see Wolfe 1961, 1–24). Wolfe went so far as to publish Luxemburg's 1904 piece "Organizational Questions of the Russian Social Democracy" under the theatrical and misleading title given it by a later publisher: "Leninism or Marxism?"—as if a revolutionary of Luxemburg's caliber could formulate the problem so mechanically. It seems to me that Luxemburg never understood as profoundly as Lenin did two things: first, the necessity for "iron discipline" within a vanguard party so that it can be a unified fighting force and avoid the tragic capitulation of the Second International; and second, the unpleasant necessity to make certain compromises, such as the Brest-Litovsk peace treaty or the New Economic Policy, to ensure the immediate survival of the Russian Revolution so that genuine socialism could be built. Lenin was always painfully aware of the differences between dictatorship of the proletariat as it existed under his leadership and full socialism: it is a constantly recurrent theme in his writings of the 1920s.

It is important to bear in mind, and as far as possible to duplicate, the very finely balanced dialectical sensibility that permits support and criticism to exist simultaneously, in all their complexity, without taking the easy way out by a crudely mechanical solution (whether fanatical enthusiasm or outraged rejection). The Bolsheviks existed, for the moment, "under the conditions of bitter compulsion and necessity in the midst of the roaring whirlpool of events" (Luxemburg 1918, 29). In such circumstances, Luxemburg reiterates time and again, one does not expect perfection. Yet Rosa Luxemburg is also thinking of the long run, always pressing ahead to the long-range implications, the possibilities. As Georg Lukacs remarks, "she constantly opposes to the exigencies of the moment the principles of future stages of the revolution" (Lukacs 1971, 276–77). Some may view the idea of perfection as a luxury that few revolutionaries can afford. I suggest that Rosa Luxemburg saw it as a costly necessity and tool of the trade, without which there is no long-range criterion for specific situations. Worse, without a clear and constant vision of the ideal there can be no principled guide to practical action, no ability to predict or control events, therefore passivity and virtually certain defeat. Is this utopian? Only if we extend the 'no place' of utopia into 'never': it depends on your sense of possibility. At the same time, the vision of perfection can lead, and it sometimes led Luxemburg, into ultra-left and incorrect positions.

Operating, then, from the sense of maximum possibility, Luxemburg wrote "The Russian Revolution" (1918). Fourteen years earlier, in 1904, she had published in *Iskra*, the Bolshevik theoretical journal, a review of *One Step Forward, Two Steps Back*, "written by Lenin, an outstanding member of the *Iskra* group". There she had argued that the militant centralism of the Bolshevik tendency would paralyze the Party, rendering it "incapable of accomplishing its historic tasks". In 1918 the success of the Russian Revolution forced Luxemburg to revise at least part of her earlier judgment. In "The Russian Revolution", she addressed herself to the Bolsheviks in power. On one hand she eulogized their clear-sightedness and discipline:

> The Bolshevik tendency performs the historic service of having proclaimed from the very beginning, and having followed with iron consistency, those tactics which alone could save democracy and drive the revolution ahead. All power exclusively in the hands of the worker and peasant masses, in the hands of the Soviets—this was indeed the only way out of the difficulty which the revolution had got into; it was the sword which cut the Gordian knot and let the Revolution out of the impasse into the free and open fields where it could continue to develop ... The party of Lenin was thus the only one in Russia which grasped the true interest of the Revolution in that first period; it was the element that drove the Revolution forward, and thus ... the only party which pursued a really socialist policy.
>
> quoted in FRÖLICH 1972, 243

After the Paris Commune and, more recently, the Chilean coup of September 1973 as well as the failure of the African National Congress in South Africa, our generation can add to this that those who hesitate to take full power, hesitate to change the system at its basis, are driven brutally off the stage, along with thousands of revolutionary workers who sacrifice their lives in the process. Or they take the place of those whom they expelled in continuing the old system and its oppressions.

Besides praising, Luxemburg criticized Bolshevik land reform as inadequate and tending to create a conservative stratum of land-owning peasants. She also protested the suspension of certain democratic rights, especially for the opponents of Soviet rule. Such interference with free public life and political debate would certainly, she said, cut the Party off from its vital roots in the masses and turn it into an authoritarian bureaucracy. In both cases she was right theoretically but wrong practically—defeated, I would suggest, by that characteristic vision of perfection that enabled her to ignore the exigencies of the particular moment. Indeed, one could argue that her criticism was inconsistent, inasmuch as the compromise land reform did constitute one of Lenin's efforts to halt bureaucratic degeneration by satisfying, through temporary measures, a relatively backward part of the population who would otherwise have to be confronted with force and bureaucracy.

The bureaucratic degeneration of the Russian Revolution after Lenin's death in 1924 does not necessarily prove, as Frölich claims, that Luxemburg was prophetically correct in all her criticism of the Bolsheviks. Such a claim omits the necessary scrupulous analysis of world events, of the Russian situation at any given moment, and of the individuals involved. Certainly, to use her work in support of an anti-vanguard or 'spontaneist' position, as some groups and individuals have done, is partial and crude in ignoring her evolution. Moreover, it ignores the importance of correct leadership, which Luxemburg stressed throughout her life and which, after all, provided the impetus for her struggle against revisionism in the SPD. What was required was a leadership both disciplined enough and flexible enough to work with the spontaneous energies of the masses, to prepare the masses for the assumption of state power, and to direct its spontaneous energies toward that goal. This, like so many other Marxist positions, appears paradoxical; as a dialectical appreciation of reality, it is, I believe, correct.

Frölich's book has had many incarnations since its first edition in 1940 and up to the present: according to WorldCat, 104 editions in five languages. It is an extremely thorough political biography by a close associate of Luxemburg, for, with her, Frölich led the revolutionary Spartacus League, participated in the 1918 rising, and helped found the KPD. With clarity and detail, he sets out the historical and political context in which Luxemburg lived and worked.

As a biography, though, Frölich's book presents an almost one-dimensional view of its subject, and that dimension is the political. One gets little sense from his pages of the passion and inner conflict that emerge from Luxemburg's correspondence. All of the personal material is collected in a single chapter, in which Frölich briefly documents Luxemburg's love for music, poetry, and botany; her talent for painting; her romantic streak; and the intensity of her personal relations. Yet by confining this material to one chapter, Frölich sets it apart from her political life and diminishes it.

Frölich never alludes to sexual relations, not even the tempestuous long-term (and often long-distance) union with her comrade Leo Jogiches, whom Rosa met in Zurich and with whom she founded the Social Democracy of the Kingdom of Poland. To Jogiches Rosa wrote nearly a thousand letters over a period of twenty years, intense letters full of ardent self-revelation as well as history in the making. There is a great deal that Frölich does not mention: Jogiches' extreme possessive jealousy, which had both a sexual and a professionally rivalrous component; the breakup of their relationship over Jogiches' friendship with another woman; Rosa's romantic rebound affair with Konstantin, the twenty-two-year-old son of her close friend and comrade Clara Zetkin; nor even the last love of her life, Hans Diefenbach. Her expensive tastes and love of luxury and stylish shoes, her sarcasm often at the expense of friends, her craving for privacy and order, her desire to have a baby, her stubborn determination to "haggle for a daily portion" of personal happiness: all these traits are omitted.

For these reasons, it is not Frölich but J.P. Nettl's splendid two-volume biography (*Rosa Luxemburg*, 1966) that presents the recognizable human being, the political woman rather than the political machine. The lacunae in Frölich's biography can be partly explained, as the author himself points out in his preface, by the loss or inaccessibility of a good deal of material, particularly correspondence and manuscripts: there is simply a lot that he did not know. Beyond this, though, one senses that Frölich wanted us to concentrate on the important historical and political issues without being distracted by mere curiosity. Although such an approach is not always wrong, it does imply a certain elitism in this case. It suggests, wrongly, that great revolutionaries have easily escaped or transcended the personal difficulties that bourgeois society imposes on all its members. Frölich's presentation suggests further, and equally erroneously, that the personal dimension is not really worth the attention of serious political persons.

The tone of Frölich's biography is sustained eulogy. As Nettl observes, it is "an exercise in formal hagiography" (Nettl 1966, 1:14), and everywhere Luxemburg is described in glowing superlatives. Clearly, she was an extraordinary person in many respects. Everyone who knew or met her agrees on that, from Lenin to Luxemburg's housekeeper, and Frölich himself must often have felt the force of her intellect and personality. But the method tends to undercut the aim, for the exemplary figure instructs not by distance but by closeness to us: not by being without faults, but by overcoming them. Frölich's Rosa Luxemburg is an unattainable ideal, so that in my view it isn't in his biography that one finds a clear evaluation of Luxemburg's personal and political limitations, even though he does concede certain errors in her criticism of the Bolsheviks. For such an evaluation Frölich must be supplemented with other sources. Her letters show both the domineering and the sentimental aspects of her nature. Georg Lukacs's "Critical Observations on Rosa Luxemburg's 'Critique of the Russian Revolution'" shows that Luxemburg's view of certain aspects of the early phase of Bolshevik power was far too schematic (Lukacs 1922, 276–77). The writings of Lenin and Trotsky are an indispensable guide and an important corrective to her errors, and Nettl sheds light everywhere.

If, as Lukacs declares in the opening sentence of "The Marxism of Rosa Luxemburg", "it is not the primacy of economic motives in historical explanation that constitutes the decisive difference between Marxism and bourgeois thought, but the point of view of totality" (Lukacs 1921, 27), then certainly Rosa

Luxemburg's work remains permanently relevant in demonstrating the dialectical method. Lukacs concludes the essay: "The unity of theory and practice was preserved in her actions with exactly the same consistency and with exactly the same logic as that which earned her the enmity of her murderers: the opportunists of Social Democracy" (Lukacs 1921, 44). The essay itself progresses from focus on theory to focus on practice. Yet in his preface to the 1967 edition of *History and Class Consciousness*, Lukacs performs a self-criticism in which he notes "a—Hegelian—distortion, in which I put the totality in the center of the system, overriding the priority of economics" (Lukacs 1967, xx). The paradox that Lukacs notes here is as relevant today as Luxemburg herself, for his distortion will be repeated by many. Its source, as Lukacs says, is the ongoing conflict in his life between "Marxism and political activism on the one hand, and the constant intensification of my purely idealistic ethical preoccupations on the other" (Lukacs 1967, x). That or similar conflict still describes the condition of many intellectuals today. It is never a waste of time to read Luxemburg; but to read her without the desire to become what she was—a revolutionary Communist in theory and in practice—is to approach her as a curiosity, to distance the power of her work and her example. The day before Luxemburg died, an article of hers appeared in *Die Rote Fahne*. Its last words were:

> Order reigns in Berlin! You stupid lackeys! Your "order" is built on sand. Tomorrow the revolution will rear its head once again, and, to your horror, will proclaim, with trumpets blazing: I was, I am, I will be!
> LUXEMBURG 1919, 306

To understand Luxemburg is to understand that those sentences are no mere eschatology but a statement about history that wants to lay a claim on anyone who reads it.[2]

References

Brecht, Bertolt. 1947. *Selected Poems*, translated by H.R. Hays. New York: Grove Press.

Brie, Michael, and Jörn Schütrumpf. 2021. *Rosa Luxemburg: a Revolutionary Marxist at the Limits of Marxism*. Cham, Switzerland: Cham.

---

2 This chapter is a revised version of "Red Rosa: Bread and Roses", *The Massachusetts Review* 16, no. 2 (1975): 373–386.

Bronner, Stephen E., ed. and trans. 1978. *The Letters of Rosa Luxemburg*. Boulder: Westview Press.
Frölich, Paul. [1939] 1972. *Rosa Luxemburg: Her Life and Work*, translated by Johanna Hoornweg. New York: Monthly Review Press.
Honeycutt, Karen. 1975. *Clara Zetkin: A Left-wing Socialist and Feminist in Wilhelmian Germany*. PhD diss., Columbia University. Ann Arbor: University Microfilms.
Lenin, V.I. [1916] 1974. *Imperialism, the Highest Stage of Capitalism*. In *Collected Works*, vol. 22, 185–304. Moscow: Progress Publishers.
Lenin, V.I. [1922] 1973. "Notes of a Publicist". In *Collected Works*, vol. 33, 204–11. Moscow: Progress Publishers.
Looker, Robert, ed. 1972. *Rosa Luxemburg: Selected Political Writings*. London: Jonathan Cape.
Lukacs, Georg. 1967. "Preface to the New Edition". In *History and Class Consciousness: Studies in Marxist Dialectics*, translated by Rodney Livingstone, ix–xxxix.
Lukacs, Georg. [1921] 1971. "The Marxism of Rosa Luxemburg". In *History and Class Consciousness: Studies in Marxist Dialectics*, translated by Rodney Livingstone, 27–45. Cambridge: MIT Press.
Lukacs, Georg. [1922] 1971. "Critical Observations on Rosa Luxemburg's 'Critique of the Russian Revolution'". In *History and Class Consciousness: Studies in Marxist Dialectics*, translated by Rodney Livingstone, 272–94. Cambridge: MIT Press.
Luxemburg, Rosa. [1898] 1977. *The Industrial Development of Poland*, translated by Tessa DeCarlo. New York: Campaigner Publications.
Luxemburg, Rosa. [1899] 1970. *Reform or Revolution*. New York: Pathfinder Press.
Luxemburg, Rosa. [1916] 1972. "Either/Or". In Looker 1972, 211–26.
Luxemburg, Rosa. 1915. "Rebuilding the International". *Die Internationale*, no.1. In Looker, 197–210.
Luxemburg, Rosa. [1918] 1961. "The Russian Revolution". In *The Russian Revolution and Leninism or Marxism*, edited by Bertram D. Wolfe, 25–80. Ann Arbor: University of Michigan Press.
Luxemburg, Rosa. 1917. "The Old Mole". *Spartacus*, no.5. In Looker 1972, 227–34.
Luxemburg, Rosa. 1919. "Order Reigns in Berlin". *Die Rote Fahne*, January 14, 1919. In Looker 1972, 300–6.
Marcuse, Herbert. 1972. *Counter-Revolution and Revolt*. Boston: Beacon Press.
Marx, Karl. [1871] 1968. "Letter to Kugelmann". In *The Civil War in France: The Paris Commune*, 86–87. 1968. New York: International Publishers.
Nettl, J.P. 1966. *Rosa Luxemburg*. 2 vols. London: Oxford University Press.
O'Kane, Rosemary H.T. 2015. *Rosa Luxemburg in Action: For Revolution and Democracy*. New York: Routledge.
Quataert, Jean H. 1979. *Reluctant Feminists in German Social Democracy, 1885–1917*. Princeton: Princeton University Press.

Trotsky, Leon. [1930] 1967. *The History of the Russian Revolution*, translated by Max Eastman, 3 vols. London: Sphere Books.

Tucker, Robert C., ed. 1978. *The Marx–Engels Reader*. New York: W. W. Norton.

CHAPTER 4

Politics of the Signified in Bertolt Brecht's *The Measures Taken*

In the year of Brecht's death, Roland Barthes wrote of him that "Brecht's morality consists of a correct reading of history, and the plasticity of the morality ... derives from the very plasticity of history" (Barthes 1956, 76). The "plasticity of morality" is posed nowhere in Brecht's theater more sharply than in his 1930 *Lehrstück* (didactic piece) *The Measures Taken* (*Die Massnahme*). The piece is a play within a play, its frame scenario a meeting of the Party Control Commission convened to hear and evaluate the report of four Russian and German agitator–comrades just returned from duty in the Chinese city of Mukden. The inner play, the comrades' dramatization of their report before the Control Commission, enacts their murder of another young comrade, with his consent, in order to safeguard the revolution that his behavior has jeopardized. The verdict of the Control Chorus is for the liquidation: "You are assured of our sympathy / It was not easy to do what was right / ... We agree to what you have done".

In vindicating the killing, Brecht's play challenges two moralities: that of the audience, who presumably believe that murder is wrong; and that of the Young Comrade, whose sympathy for the suffering masses drives him to break party discipline in a series of impetuous but finally sentimental, premature, and dangerous actions. It would appear, then, that *The Measures Taken* conveys an orthodox revolutionary lesson about the inadequacy of bourgeois morality to the specialized requirements of revolution.

Barthes's statement is attractive not only for its rhetorical balance and wit, but also for its comfortable reassurance that Brecht did, indeed, read history correctly. In taking so much for granted, the statement resembles many discussions of so-called 'socialist realism', which often founder upon fundamentals. What notion of 'reality' is operative in the phrase 'socialist realism'—or indeed, what notion of socialism? And what definition of 'correct' is operative in Barthes's evaluation of Brecht? I want to propose that *The Measures Taken* can be seen as either 'correct' or 'incorrect' within a revolutionary context, depending on what signified we assign to its signifiers. The specification of a signified, however—that is, the production of meaning—will, in turn, depend on several prior decisions. Should the signifier be considered historically referential? If so, how do we interpret the events referred to? Finally, how do we assess Brecht's representation of history in the play?

Brecht's intention, I don't doubt, was pro-revolutionary. Whether his understanding equaled his intention is another question. To be sure, the play validates collective against individual, Communist Party against undisciplined member, long-range historical objectivity against immediate personal subjectivity. But if we are to avoid fetishizing or reifying these phenomena, we will have to know more before deciding whether *The Measures Taken* offers a correct reading of history. We will have to know, or at least hypothesize, what kind of party judges the comrades' actions in the play. We will have to know who or what the Young Comrade is likely to represent historically, in order to evaluate his behavior. The question here is not whether his assassination was justified (for this is a fake problem, a red herring appropriate only to parable, not to history) but rather whether his positions were historically—i.e., concretely and politically—right or wrong, useful or not, furthering or subverting the revolutionary movement. If we refuse this effort, then the effect of *The Measures Taken* will not be to illuminate reality but to mystify it. We will have retreated from history to myth: surely the opposite of what Brecht or Barthes would want an audience to do. If this effort of historical excavation produces a conclusion different from that of Brecht or of Barthes, it will not be the first time that a writer's own methodology, exercised on himself by another, will have led to a result different from the one he had hoped for. As the East German dramatist Heiner Müller commented: "To use Brecht without criticizing him is to betray him" (H. Müller 1990, 133).

It is surprising, therefore, that several European Brecht scholars—including East German and western leftist scholars—urge us to avoid such an effort of historical concretization. No doubt there were party-minded critics who called for a literal historicization of the play, but the only one I have read is Alfred Kurella, who wrote that, despite the author's assertion that the setting was imaginary, "the events take place against the perfectly real background of the Chinese revolution" (Kurella 1931, 165). He goes on to exculpate the Young Comrade in light of then-recent revolutionary history, and to characterize the play as opportunistic and idealistic, albeit still revolutionary in its import. My discussion will be in partial agreement with Kurella's, but adds a further dimension.

Although the reasoning of most other Brecht scholars strikes me as an instance of what Russell Jacoby called "social amnesia" (1975), I shall briefly review their positions in order the more clearly to stake out mine. My slogan here is Brecht's abrasive and salutary reminder to the 1935 International Writers Conference. His words were intended to cut through moralistic complacency and classless assertions of unity among 'progressive elements' in the popular front of artists against fascism: "*Kamaraden, sprechen wir von den Eigentumsverhältnisse!*" (Comrades, let's talk about property relations!)[1]

Among the most influential of modern European Brecht scholars is Reiner Steinweg, whose work on the *Lehrstücke* influenced a generation of younger European scholars and practitioners of theater. Steinweg's case against historically specific interpretation of any of the *Lehrstücke* is based on the theory of the genre, whose *Basisregel* (fundamental principle), he claims, is to teach not by being seen but by being performed. These plays aim to revolutionize actors, not an audience. In fact, an audience is not even necessary, though it can be used in discussion with the performers. The point is not to convey a 'message', but to put actors through a process of exercising their dialectical capacities. The *Lehrstück* has no moral; it is only a means to learning. As for *The Measures Taken*, according to Steinweg the conception for it evolved out of Brecht's earlier interest in oriental drama. Moreover, both Brecht and his musical collaborator, Hanns Eisler, claimed in later years that *The Measures Taken* had no historical referent but was merely a kind of fairy tale (see Steinweg 1972). Following Steinweg's lead, Paul Binnerts of Holland, a director, stresses the meaning of the play for actors. The possibility of producing historical drama depends on the function it can have in the present, Binnerts claims. *The Measures Taken*, while offering some "interesting historical information", cannot really apply to contemporary Europe because the Russian revolutionary model is no longer appropriate. Nonetheless it does show the (still-relevant) need for illegal work and for restraint of revolutionary zeal. Brecht's *Lehrstücke* are not performable in post-revolutionary societies such as the DDR; in *The Measures Taken*, Binnerts claims, there is no right and wrong, for the play does not depict real history but rather cultural models (see Binnerts 1976).

Volker Bley confesses to having investigated the actual historical situation in China in the years preceding the composition of *The Measures Taken* (even though, he acknowledges, his mentor Steinweg has repeatedly warned against doing so). And, indeed, the effort turned out to be a diversionary waste of time, just as Steinweg predicted. Did Brecht intend to legitimate Stalin's policies, or does the play offer a hidden critique of Stalinism? Neither one! Bley proclaims, for Brecht intends only to teach the principles of intelligence. Brecht offers no decision, but only suggests the way to a correct decision (see Bley 1976). According to Roland Jost, *The Measures Taken* should not be interpreted

---

1 Several English versions of this exhortation exist; this is my translation. Another can be found in Kuhn 2003, 163.

naturalistically as a play about when and where errant comrades may be liquidated; in reality it is a negative example of how this, in general, can be avoided (see Jost 1983). Although Jürgen Schebera stresses the importance of the period when *The Measures Taken* was written, it is not political history he refers to. Rather, he maintains, the play's plot continues Brecht's working-out of material from Japanese Noh drama. It is set in China because that is an appropriately exotic setting for a parable, and because one of Brecht's friends, Gerhardt Eisler, had recently traveled to China. There is no way, he concludes, that Brecht either wanted to or could write a play about the Chinese revolution (see Schebera 1983).

In a perfect illustration of Harold Bloom's theory of "anxiety of influence" (see Bloom 1973), East German dramatist Heiner Müller's 1970 play, *Mauser*, both imitates formally and trashes ideologically *The Measures Taken*. The editor of Müller's work sees the Brechtian prototype as an allegory, repeating the critical tropes mentioned above: that it

> reflected on the fight of the German Left and its Communist Party against Hitler and Germany's rising Fascism; distancing his fable by way of an East Asian setting, he [Brecht] warned of pitfalls, while pointing out possible strategies in this struggle.
> WEBER 1989, 118

The play itself, *Mauser*, duplicates the Brechtian situation: a revolutionary fighter is examined and punished by a group of comrades for a mistaken execution he has performed. As in Brecht, he is asked to agree to, even praise, his own execution. Brecht's Young Comrade acquiesces for the sake of the struggle; Müller's both does and does not. At first, he refuses the sentence, powerfully asserting his will to live. Nonetheless, he goes to the wall, speaks the command for his own execution, and dies calling out the slogan "Death to the enemies of the Revolution!" The key difference from Brecht's Young Comrade lies in his motivation, for this comrade is not impelled by any of the lofty principles or sympathies revealed by Brecht's character. Simply, he has fallen in love with his Mauser pistol, loves to use it, has become a wanton killer and free-lancer, and, worst, has killed someone without knowing whether the victim was guilty or innocent and without any specific direction from the Party. A more detailed discussion of *Mauser*'s politics and echoes of Brecht isn't called for here, but as a response to and critique of its model, it seems thoroughly disillusioned with the ideology and events that Brecht, like so many intellectuals of his day, was only partly disillusioned by and willing to find reasons for. The change of setting suggests that for Müller, place is irrelevant.

Place, or setting, appears to be equally irrelevant to the prolific theater scholar and Brecht specialist Darko Suvin, who takes a position neither historical nor exoticist. His 'third way', recalling a late-medieval genre, sees *The Measures Taken* as a "great and quasi-religious play" (Suvin 1984, 68), indeed "a kind of Mystery play" with God "laicized into ... the World Revolution" (Suvin 1984, 16) so that the play becomes "a poetical expression of a lay faith whose methodology is fundamentally religious, even though not theistic but political" (Suvin 1984, 127).

Coming to the United States, we may note that Fredric Jameson gives short shrift to *The Measures Taken* in his long book on Brecht. This is perhaps unsurprising for a Hegelian and fan of the Frankfort School wafflers, confronting what is likely the hardest-nosed work by the generally hard-nosed Brecht. In any case, Jameson briefly repeats earlier formulae ("self-sacrifice", "primacy of collective situation over individual ethics": Jameson 1998, 62–63) and even grants vatic powers to Brecht in claiming that the play has "often been taken as an apologia for Stalin's purge trials (to come)" (Jameson 1998, 62)! Again, nothing about the setting or the actual historical moment.

These samples should suffice to give a flavor of some fairly influential Brecht scholarship and the various tactics—indeed, acrobatics—adopted to avoid history. Most frustrating, though, are the East Germans who—precisely because the history of China in the 1920s is part of their own history—maintain the vocabulary of revolutionary struggle while avoiding its most important lessons: the lessons of Stalinism from the mid-1920s to the present, including the post-Soviet era. As an important communist artist, Brecht offers a special problem for these critics. His revolutionary commitment must be maintained, but not in any way that might prove awkward in their own time and circumstances. They do not want to speak of Brecht in connection with Stalin, the individual most prominently responsible for Brecht's specific experience of living revolutionary tradition. The anthology from which several of the above samples are taken includes essays on Brecht and Socrates, Shakespeare, Diderot, Goethe, Marx, Lenin, Korsch, Sartre, and others—but nothing on Brecht and Stalin. To inhabit a non-capitalist and Stalinist society in which Stalin has been partially discredited: that was the paradox for the East German critic. Moreover, to speak of Stalin is to speak of Trotsky and the Left Opposition, a far stricter taboo in the Soviet bloc than the one on Stalin, and one far more troublesome for a bureaucratic regime.

Contrary to the critical views summarized above, I propose that *The Measures Taken* is set in China not simply for the sake of epic distancation or exoticism, nor only because of Brecht's interest in Japanese drama, nor as an allegory of Germany or Russia. Without discounting those factors as interpretive possibilities, I suggest that the play is an imaginative rendering of events that occurred in China during the five years before the play was written. These events were discussed vigorously in the Communist Party of Germany (KPD) and would have been well known to Brecht through several of his close friends. Of course, the Chinese situation becomes morally paradigmatic in Brecht's treatment of it, just as it would become politically paradigmatic in the decades that followed, with devastating consequences for international revolution and world history. In this sense, the play is both *Nachbild* and *Vorbild*, both copy and model; this is why it can be used to test Brecht's reading of history. The relevance for us today, whether as readers, as viewers, or as actors, is that our analysis of the Chinese events, by allowing us to determine possible signifieds for its signifiers, not only influences but constitutes our perception of the play's political morality.

...

My outline of the Chinese events will be necessarily skeletal in foregrounding the issues that reappear in the play.[2] The Chinese Communist Party (CCP) was founded in 1921. From the start, two features were to mark its history. First was its dependence on the Communist International, or Comintern: the Third International founded by Lenin in 1919 but, after 1924, controlled by Stalin. Second was a problematic alliance with the Kuomintang (KMT), a bourgeois nationalist party of landlords, intellectuals, and businessmen led, in the critical period, by Chiang Kai-shek. These two features of CCP history are duplicated in the structure of *The Measures Taken*. In refusing to negotiate with a corrupt merchant, the Young Comrade rejects the Party's policy of alliance with the bourgeoisie. Then his militancy is blocked "on orders from the Party". The Party—centered in Russia, as the opening scene has shown—directs the comrades to postpone armed action. "Do not see with your own eyes!" urge the other comrades: "The individual has two eyes / The party has a thousand eyes". But the Young Comrade refuses this advice, relying instead on his own revolutionary instincts or education. His individualistic breach of discipline results in the flight of all the agitators from the city, and in the Young Comrade's death at the hands of his co-workers.

The Chinese Party's relation with the KMT was constantly at issue from 1921 right up to Mao's 1949 victory over Chiang. It was an issue because China was

---

2 My sources for China include Brandt 1958, Eudin and North 1957, Guillermaz 1972, Isaacs 1938, Peng and Peng 1972, Trotsky 1932 and 1976, and Wilbur and How 1956.

heavily exploited by foreign capital—French, British, American, German, and Japanese—so that the two parties, despite their ultimate hostility, temporarily shared a common goal: to expel foreign capital and overthrow the Peking government. This is why Brecht's agitators approach the corrupt Trader, "the richest of merchants": "Then we heard there was conflict between the merchants and the British, who ruled the city, on account of tariffs. In order to exploit this rulers' quarrel for the benefit of the ruled, we sent the Young Comrade".

Moreover, at the beginning at least, the KMT had far more popular support than did the CCP; it also had press, territories, and an army. The CCP resolved, therefore—not without intense controversy[3]—on entry into the KMT while maintaining an undefined level of independent organizational existence. By 1924, many Communist leaders, including Mao Tse-tung, were also among the KMT leadership, while numerous left KMT had joined the CCP. As one scholar puts it, the CCP "confined itself religiously to building the Kuomintang and propagating its program ... The Communist Party became ... the left-wing appendage of the Kuomintang" (Isaacs 1938, 64). This collaboration, uncomfortable on both sides, continued for several years despite incidents of mutual suspicion and hostility.

Meanwhile, the Chinese labor movement was growing rapidly, and the Communists grew with it. By 1927 the CCP had a hard-core membership of 100,000 including its youth corps. Through its influence in the trade unions, it could count on the support of nearly three million workers in China's key industrial and port cities, especially Shanghai, which contained over half the Chinese industrial proletariat. Ten million peasants could be relied on in the countryside. The CCP ran schools for agitators and for leading cadre; many went to Moscow to study. Party press included theoretical journals, regional newspapers, and a women's journal. Many members and supporters owned guns. Communist cadre held important political positions both within the KMT and in the territories it controlled.

These facts were not lost on Chiang Kai-shek, who realized that his allies soon would be able to lead a genuine workers' revolution. "Raise your left fist to knock down the imperialists and your right fist to knock down the communists" was a slogan of the KMT right wing. Chiang set out to destroy the CCP. He did it rapidly and efficiently, in less than a year and a half, between March 1926 and July 1927. The devastating results were that the labor movement was smashed and disarmed, its leaders and organizers executed in systematic massacres,

---

3 In his introduction to Trotsky 1976, Peng claims that the CCP Central Committee had to be forced into the KMT under threat of Comintern discipline.

Russian advisors driven from the country, and Communists expelled from the KMT. Many tens of thousands died in the terror, and the proletarian social base of the CCP, as well as much of its leadership, was eradicated. One historian writes: "Chiang Kai-Shek's relations with the Shanghai industrial and merchant bourgeoisie, who had to be persuaded to help finance the Northern Expedition [against the warlord Peking government], are said to have had the sole aim of fixing the price of the blood shed by the workers who fell on 12 April [1927]" (Guillermaz 1972, 123). "Do I know what a man is?" asks Brecht's Trader when asked to finance arms for a rebellion: "I don't know what a man is, / I only know his price". Chiang is said to have raised forty-five million yuan from his merchants in exchange for slaughtering China's proletariat.

There were, and are, two interpretations of these events. The first, which predominated, runs as follows. China was a feudal and mainly agricultural nation which had not passed through a stage of full capitalist development. Its proletariat, while militant, were insufficiently numerous to constitute a revolutionary vanguard. Hence China was not ready for proletarian socialist revolution, but only for some progressive variety of bourgeois government. The correct tactic for communists was, therefore, cooperation with and subordination to the so-called 'progressive' bourgeoisie (the KMT), with whom they should seek to govern jointly in a 'bloc of classes'. Workers' revolution should not be encouraged, workers councils (soviets) should not be formed, there should be no attempt to take power. Spontaneous risings, whether urban or rural, should be suppressed as dangerous to the alliance with the bourgeoisie.

We recognize here the agitators' argument against the Young Comrade who, having "put his feelings above his understanding", tries to stir up barge-workers to protest their conditions, textile workers to strike for higher wages, and the unemployed to mobilize a general strike. When the Young Comrade refuses to negotiate with the Trader, "a man he despised", the Control Chorus asks, "With whom would the right-minded man not sit / To help the right?" Their rhetorical question voices the essence of the Comintern's popular-front strategy in China. It is this, the Stalinist interpretation of China, and only this one, that permitted Brecht to present *The Measures Taken* as he did, and only this interpretation that permits us to accept Brecht's representation as 'true' or 'correct'.

This approach was not, even in the mid-1920s, without its history. In 1917 the Mensheviks had precisely this analysis of Russia. So had many Bolsheviks, including Stalin who, as editor of *Pravda* at the time of the February 1917 bourgeois-democratic revolution, ensured that the paper carried that line. It was not, however, Lenin's view and, upon his dramatic return to Russia in April 1917, Lenin was able to dissuade the Bolshevik leadership from its intention to merge with the liberal bourgeois parties and become the left wing of the bourgeois revolution (which had already taken place in February that same year). He won them instead to the perspective of imminent socialist revolution. "We don't want a parliamentary republic", was Lenin's position, tirelessly reiterated from the moment he returned to Russia in April 1917; "we don't want a bourgeois democracy, we don't want any government except the Soviet of Workers', Soldiers' and Poor Peasants' Deputies!" (Lenin 1917, 98–99 passim). Nor was alliance with the bourgeoisie the aim of Trotsky, who already in 1906 had stressed the strategic weight of the proletariat in a backward country rather than its simple numbers, and had insisted on the political independence of the proletariat (see Trotsky 1906). It was because of this common understanding of the task before them that Trotsky and Lenin were able to overcome past disputes and together lead the October Revolution.

With Stalin in power after Lenin's death, however, the Comintern reverted to the old, rejected popular-front line, which remains the hallmark of Stalinist parties to this post-Soviet day. Its constant concern was to placate the ever more hostile KMT leadership by proving its loyalty. This remained the official policy even after Chiang's March 1926 coup against the CCP and its Russian advisors, even after his massacre of workers and peasants in the Shanghai insurrection of April 1927. When Chinese Communist leaders requested arms in self defense, they were ordered instead by Stalin to disarm the workers. "What baseness would you not commit / To root out baseness? / Sink down in the filth / Embrace the butcher", chants Brecht's Control Chorus; and so indeed the Comintern had done. Chiang's nickname was in fact "the butcher".

Only too late did Stalin at last recognize Chiang as an enemy, but the policies that had produced the tragic defeat of a revolution were never repudiated. "Intelligence is not to make no mistakes", Brecht's Chorus advises, "but quickly to see how to make them good". Yet a month after the Shanghai massacre, in May 1927, the Comintern affirmed that the tactics of the bloc with the national bourgeoisie were "absolutely correct". Mao, throughout his sojourn in Yenan, continued steadfastly in the old collaborationist policy. Even on the eve of his entry into Peking in 1949 he offered the olive branch to his old antagonist Chiang Kai-shek, butcher of the Chinese proletariat, proposing a joint government of the "bloc of four classes". Luckily for Mao and the Chinese, Chiang preferred to pursue his fortunes in Taiwan.

The second—oppositional—interpretation of the Chinese events did not prevail historically; it is radically different from the one on which *The Measures Taken* is predicated. In algebraic form, this second interpretation runs, briefly, as follows. China's situation was not qualitatively different from that of Russia in 1917. Its economy had been integrated into that of international finance capital; its proletariat, though small in relation to the peasantry, were extremely militant and played a strategic role in the economy. To collaborate with the nationalist bourgeoisie might be an acceptable short-term tactic while the labor movement and the CCP were weak, but to subordinate the principle of proletarian power to bourgeois nationalists would lead workers to defeat at the hands of their class enemy. In a series of demonstrations, strikes, and insurrections between 1925 and 1927, the Chinese workers, students, and peasants had shown their readiness to act. They required a leadership that would openly fight for a workers' government supported by the peasantry. That the Comintern refused this leadership turned a useful and supposedly temporary united-front tactic into a long-range and suicidal popular-front strategy.

From 1926, this position was elaborated within the Comintern by Trotsky, Zinoviev, and other leaders of the international Left Opposition. Other critics of the official policy were not connected with the Left faction. During 1926, for example, there were two oppositional tendencies within the CCP. One, the Kwangtung Regional Committee, demanded Communist seizure of the KMT; the other proposed immediate withdrawal from the KMT. In 1927, Mao recommended radical policies in the countryside, including expropriation and redistribution of land. In 1926 and again in 1927, Peng Shu-tse, Ch'en Tu-hsiu, and other leaders in Shanghai proposed that the CCP take up arms against Chiang and seize leadership of the revolution so obviously ready to erupt. On the Comintern executive, Treint and Togliatti demanded militant struggle in rural areas. All of these critics were either ignored or suppressed by Stalin, characterized as ultra-left or ultra-right. "We shall fight tooth and nail", pleads the Young Comrade, begging for arms. "Tooth and nail won't suffice" is the reply. The terrible cynicism of this exchange is that, in reality, arms were not unavailable: they were deliberately withheld.

The vocabulary of official polemic was not always confined to political terms. Often it took a peculiarly personalistic tone. A 1925 document drawn up by the Moscow branch of the CCP exhorts its members to

> oppose romanticism. Romanticism is a condition which destroys organization ... Destroy unity based on sentiment—sentimental unity is petty bourgeois unity. ... We must not aim too high ... Absolutely oppose anarchist tendencies. ... We must not have excessive self-confidence. We must have the psychology of thoroughly trusting the organization.
> WILBUR and HOW 1956, 135–37

A CCP Central Committee declaration of July 1926, reiterating the bloc of classes, urges participants to "fight for the common interests, not egotistically defend the interests of their own class" (Trotsky 1976, 117). Such personalistic terminology became part of the artillery with which the Stalinist bureaucracy warded off criticism. When we add to this that the Left Opposition was constantly accused of the sin of "jumping over the petty-bourgeois, peasant stage of the revolution", we begin to appreciate the actual historical resonance of Brecht's romantic, sentimental, anarchistic, class-egotistic, self-confident, and stage-skipping young comrade.

• • •

How would these issues have come to the attention of Brecht? It was just at this period, during 1926, that he began the serious study of Marxism, and it would be natural for him to take a special interest in any revolution occurring at the time, particularly one which aroused so much debate among Marxists and which had such important consequences for the future of international communism.

There are a number of obvious channels for information, among them the bourgeois press which carried news of the Chinese events and, during 1929, interviews with Trotsky in exile. In April 1927, the *Berliner Tageblatt* published discussion of secret Russian and Chinese documents seized in a raid on the Soviet embassy in Peking. One of these, a set of instructions to the military attaché, reiterated the need to "keep all strata of the population ... in the KMT" and warned: "Be careful not to carry through the Communist program at this time".[4] André Malraux's novel *Les conquérants* treats the Chinese events in fictionalized form, clearly describing the Comintern's role. It had been published in French (1928) and English (1929) by the time Brecht began work on *The Measures Taken*; he certainly would have known about the novel whether he read it or not. Besides print, there was film, such as *A Shanghai Document* by the Soviet director Yakov Blok. Brecht announced the 1928 Berlin opening of this documentary in a letter to his friend and theatrical co-thinker Erwin Piscator, in terms that show he had either already seen the film, or was about to do so (Glaser 1981, 142). As for political analysis, to mention only one possible source, Trotsky's critique of the Draft Program of the Comintern, published in German in 1928, is largely devoted to the China question (Trotsky 1932). Walter Benjamin reports that in 1938, Brecht was reading Trotsky (Benjamin 1938, 117),

---

4   Wilbur and How print the document, commenting that it "made a great impact on the public mind both because it was the first Soviet document to be released [after the raid] and because of its sensational character" (Wilbur and How 1956, 15) concerning provocative actions against foreign governments.

so it is likely he was doing the same ten years earlier in light of important international events.

But Brecht did not have to rely on publicly available material, for he had ample access to inner-party discussion through at least three intimates who were virtually inevitable conduits for information and debate. The most important was Hanns Eisler, fellow-traveler of the KPD, who composed the music for *The Measures Taken*. Hanns's brother Gerhard was a Comintern agent who participated in the short-lived Canton commune of 1927 and was sent to China again in 1929 to help liquidate the newborn Left Opposition there (Fischer 1948, xvi, 618; Willett 1984, 162).[5] The intimacy between Brecht and the two Eislers is well known. Moreover, the Eislers' sister, Ruth Fischer, was a party leader and oppositionist, expelled in 1926, so that leftist critiques of Comintern policy would have been part of normal political discussion in the Brecht–Eisler circle. In this light, we may look again at Schebera's attempt, mentioned above, to use the Eisler connection to deny any historical referent for *The Measures Taken*. Schebera cites as evidence Hanns's assertions that the play is nothing but a parable, a fairy tale "like the plays of Shakespeare"(!). But Hanns's comment is every bit as disingenuous as Brecht's testimony before the House Unamerican Activities Committee in 1947; for if Gerhard, Hanns, and Brecht were as close as Schebera himself claims they were, then Gerhard had broken party discipline, or at least had been extremely indiscreet, in discussing his China experience with non-members. Hanns's disclaimer of historicity appears to be an effort to shield his brother from such charges.

Brecht's other two informants for party discussion of China were Karl Korsch and Sergei Tretiakov. Korsch, Brecht's friend and political mentor from the 1920s on, was a KPD leader in charge of ideological affairs. He edited the party's theoretical journal *Internationale* and sat on its Central Committee. Expelled from the Party in 1926, Korsch continued his sharp critique of the Comintern in his teaching and writing. He was always alert to Asian developments, published articles on China in his opposition journal, and wrote an essay called "China in Transition". Brecht's contact with Korsch was especially close in 1929–30, when he was writing *The Measures Taken*.[6]

The poet Tretiakov taught Russian at the University of Peking in 1924–25 and lectured in Germany in 1930, spending a good deal of time with Brecht. His play *Roar China!* Was performed in Berlin that year by the Meyerhold Theatre. Brecht saw it and defended it against the attacks of German critics. The play,

---

5 An anecdote about a bitter confrontation between Brecht and Fischer in Hollywood appears in Hayman 1983, 286.
6 On Korsch, see Kellner 1977, K.-D. Müller 1980, and Schölzel 1983.

set in Hankow, is based on a historical incident which, in the starkness of its moral dilemma, becomes a nearly Brechtian parable of the sacrifice of individual life to protect the collective. It appears, then, that besides helping to familiarize Brecht with avant-garde aesthetic theory, Tretiakov also contributed to the content of *The Measures Taken*. In addition to his play, Tretiakov wrote a book, *Chinese Testament*, based on his experiences in Peking. He called it a "bio-interview": it is the autobiography of one of his students, a revolutionary who became sadly disillusioned with the KMT. The piece was written in 1928 and, although it was not published in Germany until 1932, Tretiakov would obviously have been able to inform Brecht of events and issues of the defeated Chinese revolution.[7]

To summarize: the China question was a critical one for Communists between 1925 and 1930. With his friends and his interests, Brecht cannot possibly have ignored it. When a playwright who is committed to revolutionary politics and to the political education of his audience sets a play in a country which has just experienced an aborted revolution, when he parallels the issues of that revolution in his play, the conclusion would appear inevitable that history is the signified.

On the question posed by the Trader in *The Measures Taken*—"What is a person actually?"—the three persons who interest me here are a fictional one, the Young Comrade; a dead one, the playwright; and an indefinite or collective one, the critic. All of them are, in their various ways, the product of history, for history is that which no one escapes. In *The Measures Taken*, Brecht presents genuine revolutionary opposition in terms derived from polemics of the Stalinized Comintern of the late '20s. Brecht was caught in a dilemma that captured many sincere people, and still does. On one hand, he distrusted Stalin without understanding the social forces Stalin represented. The posthumously published *Me-Ti* suggests the range of his doubts about Stalin.[8]

On the other hand, he continued, as so many understandably did, to support Stalin as an antidote to fascism, and as leader of the first workers' state. That Brecht was unable to develop a comprehensive analysis of Stalinism is an aspect of his thought which permeates his art. It is worth repeating here a line from Müller with which I began, a framing sentiment worthy of BB himself: "To use Brecht without criticizing him is to betray him" (Müller 1990, 133).

Historical knowledge is sometimes a costly form of aesthetic appreciation. In the case of *The Measures Taken*, one's attitude may reverse itself as the

---

7 See Hoover 1973; Tretiakov 1931 and 1934.
8 See Dahmer 1974; H. Müller 1974; Pike 1982; Wirth 1974.

politics of the signified shifts in light of newly acquired knowledge. The play is a powerful and brilliantly constructed work that distorts its subject mercilessly. It perfectly incarnates the terrible duality of Stalinism itself: to be part of the workers' movement and constantly to betray it. History is not necessarily as plastic as Roland Barthes implies. The morality of *The Measures Taken* derives from no comforting "plasticity of history" but from a political understanding inadequate to the all-too-inexorable history it confronted.[9]

References

Barthes, Roland. [1956] 1972. "The Tasks of Brechtian Criticism". In *Critical Essays*, translated by Richard Howard, 71–76. Evanston: Northwestern University Press.

Benjamin, Walter. [1938] 1973. "Conversations with Brecht". In *Understanding Brecht*, translated by Anna Bostock, 105–21. London: NLB.

Binnerts, Paul. 1976. "Die Massnahme von Bertolt Brecht, ein politisch-didaktisches Experiment im Fachbereich Regie-Paedagogik an der Theaterschule Amsterdam". In Steinweg 1976, 299–361.

Bley, Volker. 1976. "Was ist eigentlich ein Mensch? Über die Bedeutung der Lehrstücke fur die politische Bildungsarbeit". In Steinweg 1976, 410–27.

Bloom, Harold. 1973. *The Anxiety of Influence: A Theory of Poetry*. New York: Oxford University Press.

Brandt, Conrad. 1958. *Stalin's Failure in China*. Cambridge: Harvard University Press.

Brecht, Bertolt. 1930. *The Measures Taken*. In Eric Bentley, ed. 1965. *The Jewish Wife and Other Short Plays by Bertolt Brecht*. New York: Grove. 75–92.

Dahmer, Helmut. 1974. "Bertolt Brecht and Stalinism". *Telos* 22, 96–105.

Eudin, Xenia J. and Robert C. North. 1957. *Soviet Russia and the East 1920–1927: A Documentary Survey*. Stanford: Stanford University Press.

Fischer, Ruth. 1948. *Stalin and German Communism*. Cambridge: Harvard University Press.

Glaser, Günter, ed. 1981. *Briefe/Bertolt Brecht*. Frankfurt: Suhrkamp.

Guillermaz, Jacques. 1972. *A History of the Chinese Communist Party 1921–1949*. New York: Random House.

Hayman, Ronald. 1983. *Brecht: A Biography*. London: Weidenfeld.

Hecht, Werner, and Manfred Wekwerth, eds. 1983. *Brecht 83. Brecht und Marxismus: Dokumentation*. Berlin: Henschelverlag Kunst und Gesellschaft.

---

9 This chapter is a revised version of "Politics of the Signified in Brecht's *The Measures Taken*", *Clio* 16, no. 1 (1988): 67–80.

Hoover, Marjorie. 1973. "Brecht's Soviet Connection: Tretiakov". In *Brecht Heute/Brecht Today*, edited by Gisela Bahr et al., 39–56. Frankfurt: Athenaeum.

Isaacs, Harold R. 1938. *The Tragedy of the Chinese Revolution*. London: Secker and Warburg.

Jacoby, Russell. 1975. *Social Amnesia: a Critique of Conformist Psychology from Adler to Laing*. Boston: Beacon.

Jameson, Fredric. 1998. *Brecht and Method*. London: Verso.

Jost, Roland. 1983. "Brecht und Lenin". In Hecht and Wekwirth, 82–90.

Kellner, Douglas. 1977. *Karl Korsch: Revolutionary Theory*. Austin: University of Texas Press.

Kuhn, Thomas, and Steve Giles, eds. 2003. *Brecht on Art and Politics*. London: Bloomsbury.

Kurella, Alfred. 1931. "What was He Killed For?" In Bentley 1965, 163–72.

Lenin, V.I. [1917] 1974. "Political Parties in Russia and the Tasks of the Proletariat". In *Collected Works*, vol. 24, 93–106. Edited by Bernard Isaacs. Moscow: Progress Publishers.

Müller, Heiner. 1970. *Mauser*. In . *The Battle: Plays, Prose, Poems by Heiner Müller*. Edited and translated by Carl Weber. 1989. New York: PAJ Publications.

Müller, Heiner. 1990. "Brecht vs. Brecht". In *Germania*, edited by Sylvère Lotringer, translated by Bernard and Caroline Schütze 124–33. New York: Semiotext(e).

Müller, Klaus-Detlef. 1980. "Me-Ti". In *Bertolt Brecht: Political Theory and Literary Practice*, edited by Betty N. Weber and Hubert Heinen, 43–59. Athens: University of Georgia Press.

Peng Shu-tse and Peng Pi-lan. 1972. *The Chinese Revolution*. New York: Socialist Workers Party.

Pike, David. [1982] "Brecht and Stalin's Russia: The Victim as Apologist (1931–1945)". In *Beyond Brecht: The Brecht Yearbook (1982)*, edited by John Fuegi et al., 1983, 143–96. Detroit: Wayne State University Press.

Schebera, Jürgen. "Die Massnahme-Geschmiedigkeitübung für gute Dialektiker?" In Hecht and Wekwerth 1983, 91–100.

Schölzel, Arnold. 1983. "Korsch, Brecht und die Negation der Philosophie". In Hecht and Wekwerth 1983, 32–44.

Steinweg, Reiner, ed. 1976. *Brechts Modell der Lehrstücke. Zeugnisse, Diskussion, Erfahrungen*. Frankfurt: Suhrkamp.

Steinweg, Reiner. 1972. *Das Lehrstück. Brechts Theorie einer politisch-ästhetischen Erziehung*. Stuttgart: Metzlersche.

Suvin, Darko. 1984. *To Brecht and Beyond. Soundings in Modern Dramaturgy*. Sussex: Harvester Press.

Tretiakov, Sergei. 1931. *Roar, China!* Translated by F. Polianovska and B. Nixon. London: Martin Lawrence.

Tretiakov, Sergei. 1934. *Chinese Testament: The Autobiography of Tan Shih-hua*. London: Gollancz.
Trotsky, Leon. [1906, 1929] 1974. *The Permanent Revolution; and Results and Prospects*, translated by Brian Pearce. New York: Pathfinder Press.
Trotsky, Leon. 1932. *Problems of the Chinese Revolution*. New York: Pioneer Publishers.
Trotsky, Leon. 1976. *Leon Trotsky on China*, edited by Les Evans, translated by Max Schachtman. New York: Monad.
Wilbur, C. Martin, and Julie L. How 1956. *Documents on Communism, Nationalism and Soviet Advisors in China, 1918–1927*. New York: Columbia University Press.
Willett, John. 1984. *Brecht in Context: Comparative Approaches*. London: Methuen.
Wirth, Andrzey. 1974. "Brecht, Writer Between Ideology and Politics". In *Essays on Brecht: Theatre and Politics*, edited by Siegfried Mews and Herbert Knust, 199–208. Chapel Hill: University of North Carolina Press.

CHAPTER 5

Women, Culture, Revolution
Boris Lavrenov's "The Forty-first"

> This conversation took place on a quiet revolutionary evening, on a bench in Martha's garden. A machine gun tick-tocked tenderly somewhere in the distance, calling its mate.
> YEVGENY ZAMYATIN, "X" (1926, 225)

∴

How subversive is revolution, corroding even the descriptive conventions of romantic fiction! Zamyatin's Carrollesque sentences cut two ways, parodying the sentimental pieties of bourgeois romantic fiction, but also those of smug zealotry cloaked in revolutionary rhetoric. Such zealotry would in the next few years bear the sickening fruit of 'socialist realist' art with its ideal stereotypes and petty-bourgeois morality, its dead style and dialogue parroting the regime's latest twist. The story from which the passage above is taken narrates the comical love affair of one of those new village bureaucrats so soon to join party careerists and disgruntled intellectuals in the social base of Stalinism.

The subversion of romantic idealism in Russian art was well under way by 1917 in the critical and creative work of the seething Russian avant-garde: futurists and formalists, Proletkult, imagists, constructivists, rayonnists, suprematists. The Russian Revolutions of February and October 1917 struck many innovative artists and scholars as the social equivalent to their own aesthetic or intellectual concerns. Yet of those who at first embraced or accepted the socialist revolution, few survived its vicissitudes with faculties intact, if they survived at all. Zamyatin early became hysterically alienated from the necessities of national defense and social reconstruction under the Bolsheviks, and eventually left the country, his best work behind him. Mayakovsky could not endure the control and deterioration of creative life in the early Stalin era; he committed suicide in 1930. Isaac Babel was arrested in 1938 and died soon after in a prison camp, as did many other important Jewish writers[1] and the great theater director and producer V. Meyerhold. But the great majority of left-wing artists and intellectuals, whether party members or fellow-travelers, neither killed themselves nor were physically liquidated by the regime. Instead, they went to sleep, to borrow Zamyatin's metaphor of a "hereditary sleeping sickness (entropy)" often afflicting writers and artists who "lack the strength to … walk away into the open field, to start anew" (Zamyatin 1923, 112). To be sure, Zamyatin intended his image as an aesthetic, not a political, category. I have put it to a different use, for the artists I describe accommodated to the bureaucratic regime and produced to its orders, so that, as Trotsky observed: "The art of the Stalinist period will remain as the frankest expression of the profound decline of the proletarian revolution" (Trotsky 1938, 109).

∙ ∙ ∙

Among those who quietly accommodated was the journalist, playwright, and short-story writer Boris Lavrenov (1891–1959). A minor but popular and prolific writer, Lavrenov was twice awarded the Stalin Prize, in 1946 and 1950. His work has been translated into several European languages; it continues to be published in the Soviet Union and elsewhere, including (not surprisingly) Cuba, which in 1966 brought out a Spanish edition of "The Forty-first" (1924), the story I am going to use here as a point of departure for my comments on women, culture, and revolution.

"The Forty-first" is probably the most famous of Lavrenov's civil-war stories, having been filmed twice: in the silent 1920s version of Yakov Protonazov, and in a 1956 color version by G. Chukrai (whose *Ballad of a Soldier* is well known in North America). The story is set during the post-revolution civil war between Red Army and counter-revolutionary White Guards. It narrates the love affair of the ill-educated fisher-girl and would-be poet Maryutka, a sharpshooter in the Red Army, with her prisoner of war, a handsome and cultured White Guard lieutenant. In this way, it knits up the threads of sex, class, and culture. So, too, in its way, does Lavrenov's career, for his accommodation was one small symptom of the bureaucratic degeneration of the revolution itself, a process also visible in the changing position of women during the 1930s and 1940s and in the increasing state control of the arts during the same period. In this way, the story encapsulates a moment in revolutionary history—not the moment

---

1 See Nathan Englander's powerful story about this episode, "The Twenty-Seventh Man" (Englander 2000).

of its setting (1920), but that of its making, some four years later. That moment is, in a sense, the last when the story could have been written as it was. This is the case not simply because in 1925 Dr. Aron Zalkind announced that "sexual attraction to a class enemy is as much a perversion as mating an ape with an alligator" (quoted in Stites 1977, 52),[2] but because its style, its conception of culture, and its heroine would soon become socially impossible.

Like other of Lavrenov's stories from this period, "The Forty-first" shows that in the early 1920s the author knew how to entertain and engage the reader, that he had read the English novel to good effect and was to some extent influenced by various Russian avant-garde literary groups, and above all that he understood the often-contradictory impulses of individuals and of revolution.

Much of this was renounced in subsequent years. In an autobiographical note published in 1930, Lavrenov criticized the breadth of his own reading: "European literary culture is too strong in me. 'Literaturizing'. Too much of an inveterate intellectual. Too much of an un-Russian writer. Bred and brought up on French and English writers" (quoted in Struve 1951, 118). Like many others, Lavrenov belonged to RAPP (the Russian Association of Proletarian Writers). In 1932 Stalin abruptly dissolved RAPP and brutally discredited its leaders, merging all existing writers' groups into the unitary and state-controlled Union of Soviet Writers. Although others protested publicly, Lavrenov's comment on this decisive event was complacent: "I wore the label ['fellow-traveller'] until RAPP's peaceful demise in 1932 when, having escorted the corpse to the cemetery of history, I remained just a Soviet writer. This suited me fine" (quoted in Gasiorowska 1968, 256).[3] In contrast to "The Forty-first" and other early work, Lavrenov's stories from the early 1940s are short, terse, anti-German propaganda pieces with little literary interest, emotional impact, or sense of social complexity (though to be fair they still show considerable narrative skill). Finally, among Lavrenov's cold-war propaganda services to the regime was the play *Lermontov* (1952), in which the life and views of the nineteenth-century poet were knowingly distorted and even falsified in order to recreate the Russian literary past in the desired image of simple, committed national-patriotic militancy (see Roberts 1965).

---

2 Zalkind was professor at Sverdlov University and founder of the Society of Marxist Psychoneurologists. The conservatism and philistinism of his views is representative neither of Marxism nor of Freud's work (though there has been no shortage of conservatives or philistines associated with either movement).
3 On the dissolution of RAPP in context of general state control of literature, see Der Melkonian-Minassian 1978.

It was, of course, an intolerable situation. The image that comes to mind is of a wily Brechtian survivor denying his knowledge in order to stay alive and out of prison. That is the essence of political accommodation, to suppress the 'no' one knows to be true, and there were many who did not accommodate but remained true to the revolution they had fought for. Galileo could recant and rest easy, for *"eppur se muove"* (nonetheless it [the earth] moves). But in politics it committed act is required so that it *will* move. In any case, the accommodations that made the real doesn't: the historical difference were less those of minor artists than of the well-known political figures who, despite their weaknesses, might have helped lead the struggle against bureaucratism but chose not to: the Radeks, Kollontais, Preobrashenkys, Zinovievs, and Smirnovs, who chose capitulation rather than opposition.

> The laboring masses of the whole world immediately showed a readiness to regard the Russian Revolution as a whole, and in this their revolutionary instinct coincided, not for the first time, with high theoretical sense, which teaches that a revolution, with its heroism and cruelty, the struggle for individuality and the suppression of individuality, can only be understood in the material logic of its internal relations, and not by any valuation of its individual phases or separate episodes according to the price list of Right, Ethics, and Aesthetics.
> TROTSKY 1922, Introduction #3

That passage might stand to our story as theoretical gloss to fictional representation, the one asserting, the other showing the empirical/intuitive understanding of revolution by ordinary working people, the contradictions of revolution as translated into desire and necessity, and the view of revolution as an organically integrated whole.

Maryutka's affair with an enemy officer ends, with the story, when Maryutka shoots her lover as he is about to be rescued by other White Guard officers: she had been ordered, near the beginning of the story, not to give him up alive. Thus, the lieutenant becomes the sharpshooter's forty-first victim. On one level, then, the story is about sex and politics—or, as it would have been put at the time, love and duty. But 'love and duty' is inadequate to the story, for in the post-Lenin Soviet context, that phrase generally means 'love versus duty' or 'sex versus politics', with the latter easily and inevitably winning out. While it is true that for Maryutka, political commitment does eventually prevail, the story transcends any sense of easy or mechanical inevitability. It is less 'sex versus politics' than sexual politics: an exploration of how political attitudes might be embodied in complicated individuals, how sexual attitudes and responses are shaped by social factors, including social structures as well as an intensely polarized conflict like the civil war. The ending comes (or came to me, at least) as an emotional shock, for the reader has grown committed to both characters. The act is committed in fear and despair; the story closes with Maryutka's devastated lament for what she has done. That Maryutka falls in love with an enemy officer and gives herself to him; that the lieutenant is capable of generosity, gratitude, vulnerability; that both characters experience moments of ambivalence: all this keeps the story from stereotype or predictability.[4] It is revolutionary propaganda in the very best sense, but propaganda that simplifies nothing, makes nothing easy.

Naturally one's sense of politics affects one's aesthetic response to the story. For a nonpolitical person, or for someone who doesn't intensely desire revolution, it is easy enough to perceive Maryutka and the lieutenant as mere social clichés, and the dénouement as inevitable. Yet part of the cauterizing effect of revolution is to cleanse social clichés of their literary-theoretical accretions: they spring to life again as social reality. To sustain that sense of historical possibility opens in turn the aesthetic possibility of seeing Maryutka and her lover as *real* and indeed as representative of the dimensions in which individuals actually exist during war, revolution, strikes, or other such polarized events—and the ending therefore as one possibility among several.

Besides sex and politics, culture is the other ingredient in the rich mix of "The Forty-first". Maryutka writes poetry, passionately felt but execrably bad verse, old-fashioned and trite, at which not only the cultured lieutenant laughs, but even newspaper editors in small Caucasian towns. (A sample of her doggerel is given in the story.) During the lovers' enforced winter-long sojourn on a deserted island in the Aral Sea, the lieutenant tells the story of Robinson Crusoe, so ironically similar to their own situation. The two debate *Crusoe* and also Maryutka's poetry: content, audience, conditions of production. The discussion of art becomes a mode of characterization and another dimension in which social attitudes are expressed.

The view of culture that emerges from the story is very far from that of high-Stalinist 'socialist realism' or its predecessor, Proletkult. There is no contempt

---

4 In "Such a Simple Thing" (also 1924), Lavrenov gives another variant on the theme of desire and necessity, again permitting his hero a great deal of ambivalence. The hard-nosed young Orlov, Cheka (Soviet secret police) commissar and intelligence agent, trying to save an unjustly arrested peasant from torture at the hands of Whites, foolishly jeopardizes himself, is outwitted by a clever White officer, and is captured. Before going to his execution, Orlov at first declines, then accepts, the handshake of an honorable White Officer who has unsuccessfully interviewed him.

for 'bourgeois culture' or for the lieutenant's book-learning. In fact, his erudition saves their lives, for he has read about abandoned fishermen's huts on islands in the Aral Sea, just as he has read about Forel's hydrographic scale of blueness on which the Aral Sea rates three. Maryutka, on the other hand, knows that dried fat fish can be burned as fuel. Her experience and his education are complementary for survival. The White Guard officer, Govorukha-Otrok, is also an accomplished seaman—a skill Maryutka appreciates on their stormy ride to the island, and which he learned on his luxurious yacht. It is clear where Lavrenov must have stood in controversies about the use of experienced czarist military men—by 1919, 40,000 of them—who were willing to work for the Reds (see O'Ballance 1964, 61).[5]

A few years later Lavrenov would again take up the intertwined themes of sex, culture, and revolution, confirming and developing the attitudes outlined in "The Forty-first". His 1927 *roman à thèse*, *L'Avenir est à nous* (*The Future Is Ours*), has as protagonist Goudrine, a talented artist turned Red Army man and now factory director. Goudrine's wife, a puritanical, uncultured party hack, considers sensuality, comfort, and beauty contrary to the party spirit. The marriage breaks up and Goudrine resigns his position to return to his first love, painting, convinced that he can be more useful in helping to create a vibrant new culture than in performing routine supervisory tasks.

At an art exhibit and lecture Goudrine expresses profound hatred and contempt for the theory and practice of Proletkult and its offspring, socialist realism. The pictures—factory chimneys, workers' demonstrations, parades, red banners, etc.—are joyless and trivial, showing the painters' "misunderstanding of the real nature of the working class and of the party" as well as a "servile desire to serve a new master" (Lavrenov 1927, 23). (Who the new master is, we do not learn.) A young poet–scholar of the "extremist" school—an obvious parody of Proletkult—claims in his lecture that all known literature is dangerous and counter-revolutionary, an opiate of the masses, and should be replaced by factual reportage. This view the hero characterizes as ignorant petty-bourgeois nihilism; the young poet is said to "spit on the party's effort to raise the country's cultural level" (Lavrenov 1927). Now that the civil war is over, he (the philistine poet) is the enemy. The new culture won't be created by such charlatans but by workers saturated in the old culture. A new culture

---

5 Their motive was patriotism: to defend the homeland against foreign invasion. The question of ex-czarist officers provoked one of the earliest Stalin–Trotsky confrontations. At Tsaritsyn, where toward the end of 1917 Stalin was senior political commissar, he ordered the removal of former czarist officers serving the Red Army. Trotsky, as commissar of war, demanded and obtained from Lenin Stalin's transfer to the Ukraine.

can't be forced or legislated into existence, but must grow naturally from the new social milieu that is still being built (Lavrenov 1927, 185–87). A good idea is a good idea, even if it comes from the other side.

But the 'extremist' view is gaining ground all around Goudrine, and so are the dreadful paintings. There are disturbing hints that all is not well in party life. Only with a small group of intimates does Goudrine discuss party affairs "frankly, without those detours that diplomacy requires" (Lavrenov 1927, 33). Moreover, Goudrine's wife denounces him to his boss, and although her attempt fails to discredit him, Goudrine is afraid. The episode evokes a suspicion that such attempts might well succeed in the near future. Nonetheless, laughing and joyful, Goudrine types out his resignation letter: "I too am going to wake the masses so that they can build a culture" (Lavrenov 1927, page). Like a middle-aged Bolshevik Stephen Dedalus, Goudrine wants to "forge in the smithy of [his] soul the uncreated conscience" not of his race but of his class. *The Future Is Ours* is less a gesture of defiance than of revulsion against the tightening net.

The distance Lavrenov would have to travel to reach Stalinist respectability is marked in a pair of his World War II stories. In "The Portrait" (1941), the protagonist, a middle-aged painter enlisted in the Red Army, proclaims of the Germans:

> They are not human beings. They are only images of human beings. ... They've got no soul, only something that stinks like a polecat. And they should be destroyed like mad dogs, without mercy, to the last man. Only then will life flourish again on this earth of ours. Wipe them out, friends! For this land of ours, for our fathers and mother, for the love that you cherish, for the honor of our womenfolk, for everything.
> LAVRENOV 1941, 26

These sentiments are repeated in "Out at Sea": As a nation (i.e., not only the Nazis) the Germans "have not only ceased to resemble human beings but have in every respect proved to be such downright diabolical savages" (Lavrenov 1943, 45–46). Here the hero is an outstanding young naval officer who hopes to write a dissertation on German philosophy. His ship is strafed by a German plane and all aboard are killed. But before he dies the young skipper realizes that his interest in German philosophy is contemptible. His last act is to bring down the German plane—whose pilot's name turns out to be Johann Wilhelm Schelling, that of the famous nineteenth-century German philosopher! All is simple; all is easy. All Germans are evil; German culture is therefore not worthwhile.

To return to "The Forty-first": Maryutka desires to study in order to develop as a poet. The lieutenant has the education Maryutka needs; he is even an amateur philologist who before the war spent his evenings in a book-lined study. More abstractly: his class and its allies monopolize the culture that the rest of the population require, and that they have been systematically denied, but that the revolution had already begun to expropriate (see Fitzpatrick 1970). The lieutenant offers Maryutka his patronage, an offer at once sexual and cultural:

> I've got a little place not far from Sukhumi. That's where we'll go. I'll settle down with my books and let the world go hang. ... And you'll begin to study. You want to study, don't you? You've complained so many times that you had no chance to study. Well, here's your chance. I'll do everything for you. You saved my life and I'll never forget it.
> LAVRENOV 1924, 233

I note a special irony here, for after 1920, as the war journalist Lavrenov would surely know, Sukhumi was a base for Zhenotdel, the Central Committee's Department for Work Among Women, whose primary task was to educate, organize, and recruit women in the remotest areas of the country. "Teams were sent out into the mountain villages and women who had never left their native settlements before were brought down to Sukhumi. Some were shuttled off to Moscow to study, the rest went back to the mountains to organize day nurseries" (Stites 1978, 339–40). The response?

> Men reacted to all this with savage violence. Women coming out of the club at Baku were assaulted by men with wild dogs and boiling water. A twenty-year-old Muslim girl who flaunted her liberation by appearing in a swimsuit was sliced to pieces by her father and brothers because they could not endure the social indignity. An eighteen-year-old Uzbek woman activist was mutilated and thrown into a well. Central Asia witnessed three hundred such murders during one quarter of 1929 alone.
> STITES 1978, 339–40

Angrily, Maryutka rejects the lieutenant's offer with its role of kept woman, its luxury of studying while the war rages, its valorization of individual over collective appropriation:

> So that's what you want me to do, is it? ... Lie beside you on a feather-bed while people are sweating out their life's blood for the sake of justice? Fill

my belly with chocolates when every chocolate is bought with somebody else's blood? Is that what you want?
LAVRENOV 1924, 233

Her denunciation touches off a fight that eventually forces the lieutenant to abandon his escapist fantasies and for the first time to commit himself fully and consciously to class struggle. He embraces the counter-revolutionary cause of his class:

> I can see for myself that it's too soon for me to go back to my books. ... I've come to my senses! ... If we bury ourselves in our books at a time like this and let you do what you like with this old earth of ours, there'll be hell to pay.
> LAVRENOV 1924, 236

So Maryutka does convert her lover—not to revolution (that *would* be a sentimental ending), but to militant reaction.

Again, it is nowhere suggested in these exchanges that bourgeois culture is decadent per se or that what Maryutka needs, rather than *Crusoe,* is images of factory chimneys or simple hortatory verse. There is no hint that people like Maryutka should, will, or can create a new 'proletarian culture' on the basis of their class and commitment. Those were the tenets of Proletkult and, later, of socialist realism, but during the 1920s they were targets of Lenin's and Trotsky's polemics, expressed, among many other places, in Lenin's 1920 "Tasks of the Youth Leagues" and Trotsky's writing on so-called proletarian art (Trotsky 1923, 41–54). Contrary to Proletkult, Maryutka aspires to appropriate the benefits of world culture in order to express her commitment more effectively in art. Her poetry is bad despite its commitment, and to some extent because of her class, which has been excluded from culture and education. To deny the badness of her poetry would be to deny the oppressiveness of oppression. Maryutka is oppressed as a woman and as a rural worker, and one sign of that double oppression is the quality of her verse. For her, decadence is not the possession of culture, but the abandonment of the struggle that will ensure the general and permanent accessibility of culture.

While Maryutka's verse might well qualify for Proletkult's notion of 'worker poetry', Lavrenov's stylistic practice in "The Forty-first" certainly runs counter to Proletkult recommendation. It shows both the influence of bourgeois culture (especially the eighteenth-century English novel, then much in vogue among Russian literary intellectuals) and affinities with certain avant-garde literary groups whose mistrust of politics put them at odds with both Proletkult and the Bolsheviks. Neologisms abound in the story, as in futurist work. The sentence is nervous, economical; imagery frequent and bold. The story has a formal–symbolic structure blocked out in color areas like a canvas: white, red, blue, and yellow are associated with certain characters and objects in the story and, through them, with a cluster of social and ethical values. There is a dream sequence when the lieutenant falls into delirious fever.

As for bourgeois literature, I have already referred to the desert-island motif borrowed from *Crusoe*, and to dialogue about that novel. Also imitated from the eighteenth-century novel is the device of the chapter heading that Lavrenov uses, in the manner of Sterne, as an ironically distancing or (in Brecht's term) alienating technique, in order to emphasize what Viktor Shklovsky and other formalists called the 'literariness' or made, created, quality of the work of art (see Shklovsky 1925). A few samples of these chapter headings:

1. Which was written only because it had to be written.
5. Stolen from beginning to end from Daniel Defoe, except that Robinson has not long to wait for his Friday.
9. In which it is proved that, although the heart defies all laws, one's being, after all, determines one's consciousness.
10. In which Lieutenant Govorukha-Otrok hears the roar of the doomed planet, and the author dodges the responsibility of ending the story.

The headings underscore stylistically a political point made in the narrative itself. They jog the reader out of comfortable received notions of the amenities governing the relations among author, reader, and text; they nudge the reader to interrogate the text just as Maryutka interrogates *Crusoe*. The creation of literature, we are forced to conclude, is artificial, selective, above all conscious; so is the reception of literature (at least it can be); and so is the making of history. The headings assert our capacity consciously to appropriate the past in order to "make it new" (the formalists would say to "make it strange"); indeed, the Bolsheviks were in the process of doing both, not least with respect to the role of women.

⋯

The emancipation of women has been, from 1917 to the present, one of the proudest boasts of Soviet Russia in its catalogue of achievements. … Soviet spokesmen have tended to mask the fact that a reversal in policy has occurred. … The terms set forth in Marxian writings as constituting

> the emancipation of women and the early Soviet steps taken toward their fulfillment are a matter of historical record, as, in part, are later measures toward their abrogation. ... For investigation of widespread attitudes and behavior patterns engendered among Soviet women by the new social organization, Russian literature affords the main accessible source.
> LUKE 1953, 27–28

The figure of the fighting woman comrade or partisan is not unusual in the civil-war literature of the 1920s. In the work of later decades, though, woman's role becomes "increasingly auxiliary": "She accepts her biologically predetermined secondary status in the army, much as the Soviet woman of the 1930's accepted it in civil life, and is rewarded by peace of mind and a sense of duty well done" (Gasiorowska 1968, 156). With this looming shift in mind, I want to turn to the social context in which early readers of "The Forty-first" would have been able to place its heroine. What was the role of women during these early years of revolution and civil war? How did the revolution and its subsequent degeneration affect women? What about the feminist movement?

February 23, 1917 was International Women's Day, commemorating the great strikes of about a decade earlier in New York's predominantly female garment industry, particularly the victorious 'uprising of the twenty thousand' in 1909 and the 1910 cloak strike (the 'great revolt'), which brought 45,000 workers into the streets. At the proposal of Clara Zetkin, Rosa Luxemburg's friend and colleague, in 1911 the Second International adopted the day, which was thereafter celebrated worldwide as an international proletarian holiday.[6]

Fearing premature armed confrontation, none of the political organizations in Russia called for strikes to mark the day. Nonetheless, women textile workers in Petrograd went on strike, joined by about 90,000 workers and soldiers' wives. The momentum generated on Women's Day sped into insurrection, repeated in Moscow and provincial cities. It was the second Russian revolution (the first having occurred in 1905). It transferred state power to a liberal bourgeois parliament (*Duma*), forced the abdication of the czar, and brought into being soviets (elected councils) as organs of workers' power. By autumn

---

6 February 23 was the date in Russia, which at that point kept the Julian calendar, thirteen days behind the Western or Gregorian calendar. The Soviet government adopted the Western calendar in February 1918, so that the date of IWD is now March 8 everywhere. I stress the proletarian and communist origins of the day in order to counterbalance the "sisterhood" celebration often typical of North American feminists, as well as the "sentimental Soviet version of Mother's Day" (Rosenhan 1977, 302) into which IWD has been transformed in Soviet children's books.

the Bolsheviks had gained a majority in the soviets, so that the soviets were able to overthrow the weak coalition government of Kerensky and officially take the state power they already exercised in fact.[7] The civil war—against czarist White Guards, land-owning Cossacks, anti-Bolshevik social democrats, and bourgeois constitutionalists, together with their German, Czech, Japanese, British, French, and North American allies—was more or less won by the end of 1920, although sporadic fighting continued for another year or more in Siberia and the Far East.

Had there been a politically autonomous women's movement in Russia to defend the special interests of women—so 'socialist feminists' often argue— then the revolution would have done more for women, and the bureaucracy would not have been able to reverse such gains as were made during the 1920s. The truth is that there was a lively Russian feminist movement during the revolutionary period, whose inability to affect the course of events was due to its programmatic content. Already during the nineteenth century, the underground non-Marxian revolutionary movement had a significant proportion of female members, activists, and leaders, although none of the groups had a sectoralist vision of social change; that is, they did not imagine that the lot of any single oppressed group could be substantially improved apart from the general liberation of the Russian masses. The issue of female emancipation had occupied the intelligentsia since the 1860s, but not until 1905 did a well-organized feminist women's movement appear, stimulated by the ferment of the 1905 revolution. It is instructive to study the role of the Russian feminist organizations at a time when masses of women were ready to struggle for their rights, and important to know why those women did not see feminism as an appropriate weapon.[8]

The Russian feminist movement was more tactically variegated than its American or British counterparts, not confined to the suffrage issue, and— in the feminist-electoral sense—it was sufficiently developed to include a political party. The male-exclusionist Women's Progressive Party was founded on the premise that none of the existing (male-dominated) parties could be trusted to protect the real interests of women. While its program had several demands intended to attract working women (paid maternity leave, childcare facilities in factories, equal wages for equal work, land rights for peasant women), nonetheless, its general perspective was for sex equality in context of a constitutional-democratic monarchy. The Russian Union for Women's

---

7   See Glickman 1977 on women workers; Trotsky 1930 on the 1917 revolution.
8   On nineteenth-century women radicals, see Engel and Rosenthal 1975; McNeal 1971; Selivanova 1923, chaps. 9–11; and Stites 1978, chaps. 1–6.

Equality called for equal rights in employment and education, abolition of the death penalty, and universal suffrage for a constituent assembly. The union, associated with the Kadet (KD, for Constitutional Democratic) Party, was the largest of the feminist groups, peaking in 1905 with about 8000 members. The Russian Society for the Protection of Women was a patrician–intellectual charity and reform organization that focused on prostitution. The Women's Mutual Philanthropic Society—something like a Russian version of NOW (the National Organization of Women)—devoted itself to lobbying with friends and relatives in government and the professions for suffrage and equal rights. The Russian League for Women's Equality was also a lobbying group, primarily for suffrage; a host of smaller, more specialized student professional groups also addressed conditions in their own areas.

Like its counterparts abroad, Russian feminism was, in Stites's words, "roughly 'middle-class' with an 'upper-class' frosting" (Stites 1978, 227–28). This was true not only of social composition but of program, despite the occasional demand designed to entice working women to join. But by and large the feminist strategy was inadequate to the real lives of working women, whether urban or rural, and nowhere more obviously than on the suffrage issue. Here the feminists did not remain true to their own limited platform. When a period of reaction set in after the short-lived liberalization of 1905, the groups either abandoned their work altogether or adapted to the new climate, no longer calling for universal suffrage but now for sex-equal suffrage by class; hence the women of disfranchised classes would be equally disfranchised with their men! Later, like feminists in all belligerent nations, the Russians greeted the 1914 war as a golden opportunity to display their patriotism and earn the reward of suffrage. But the *Duma* (parliament) continued to disappoint them. Only after the February revolution and three months before its own overthrow did Kerensky's Provisional Revolutionary Government at last, in July 1917, give Russian women the vote. This was not under pressure from the feminists, but from increasingly angry working men and women loyal to the soviets and readier every week to take what they wanted by disciplined force of arms. Feminist issues—inheritance laws for large fortunes, passport laws for travel, admission to professional schools, even the vote—these issues, all of them valid, all of them supportable, all of them important especially to women of the gentry, the intelligentsia, and the professions, had little meaning for impoverished working women whose struggle was for the eight-hour day, for an end to the war in which their men were dying, for literacy, for wages, for food, for housing.

At such a time there could be no 'socialist feminism'. The sharp polarization of issues rendered such a chimera impossible: "Revolution is revolution only because it reduces all contradictions to the alternative of life or death"

(Trotsky 1929, 474). If the oxymoron 'socialist feminism' is possible now, it's in the absence of imminent revolution and expresses the acquiescence of those who are prepared to settle for perpetually unresolved social contradiction.

As for the Communists, their work among women was to address the broad issues with a program that could resolve the contradictions of the old order. They did so by organizing and recruiting working women, by intervening at feminist meetings with Communist politics, and through their journal *Rabotnitsa (Woman Worker)*. On the eve of the February revolution, interestingly, the feminist organizations were operating energetically: their journals appeared regularly, and their membership was on the rise (though not among working women). Three weeks after the October seizure of power, *Rabotnitsa* organized a conference of working women in the Petrograd region. A leader of the feminist League for Women's Equality spoke, concluding her remarks with these words:

> Everywhere women are subjected; everywhere they struggle for their rights. Women from England and America arrive here and are in complete solidarity with us and wish us well in our struggle. Men cannot defend our interests; they do not understand us.
>
> quoted in STITES 1978, 307

The women in attendance booed her down but were persuaded by Alexandra Kollontai, a Bolshevik leader, to let the feminist finish: "The speech marked, practically speaking, the end of Russian feminism" (Stites 1978, 307). Of the movement's leaders, some stayed in the Soviet Union and some emigrated, but there is no record of organized feminist activity after 1920 even by those who stayed: evidently the movement had lost its *raison d'être*.

Almost immediately, the new regime established complete economic equality for working women both in employment and wages, abolished all laws against homosexuality, outlawed the bride price, decreed the absolute right to divorce (free, immediate, and on demand of either party), and promulgated a marriage decree that protected the right of each spouse to separate identity, including name, business, friends, and place of residence. Within a few months they made education and training available to women by overhauling the school system: coeducation at all levels; free and open admissions to all universities, art, and technical schools, and remedial courses; no gender tracking. For mothers, fully paid maternity leave, free pre-and postnatal care, nursing breaks at work, and a network of maternity clinics, mother-and-child homes, and preschool nurseries. The category of illegitimacy was abolished by making the biological father co-responsible with the mother, regardless of marital status, and by giving all children equal legal rights whether born in or out of registered marriages (see Geiger 1968; Schlesinger 1949).

In 1920, abortion was made free and on demand. The Party amalgamated its commissions for work among women into Zhenotdel, a special department or section of the Central Committee whose purpose was to extend organization, education, and health care to women in all regions of the Soviet Union. The Council for Combating Prostitution (founded in 1921) was responsible for medical treatment, education, and job placement for prostitutes; the government's policy was voluntary rehabilitation of prostitutes but severe penalties for pimps and madams. In 1926, a joint property ruling for divorce was decreed, and the validity of common-law marriage confirmed.

In all, it was an astonishing feat of social engineering, unequaled anywhere before or since, and certainly not imagined in the wildest dreams of feminists. It was not accomplished without some ambivalence. For instance, many party members, men and women, deplored even hospital abortions as physically dangerous and as an anti-social act on the mother's part, but they approved its legalization as a necessary health measure. (The abortion issue was dramatized in Avram Room's superb 1927 film, the comedy-drama *Bed and Sofa*.) Some provisions were not immediately enforceable everywhere, as in the most backward Muslim areas. And it was far from perfect; for instance, contraception, so crucial to the equality and independence of women, remained a weak point in the program. As late as 1927, the Health Commissar for the Ukraine, D.I. Yefimov, complained at a conference of gynecologists:

> Fighting abortion means replacing it by contraception ... At present, the production and sale of contraceptives is left to private speculators and quacks. Contraceptives are sold in the streets like any other commodity, without medical control.
>
> quoted in SCHLESINGER 1949, 183

No Bolshevik imagined that law suffices for a revolution in mores, but all understood that law is the necessary prelude.

Naturally women were conscripted into the Red Army, and they volunteered, individually or in factory or village brigades, on equal terms with men. Already in World War I, women in the Imperial Army had served in paramedical, communications, and transport work, with a few in flying and combat. Armed Bolshevik women of the Red Guards fought in September 1917 against the attempted coup by General Kornilov and again in the October insurrection. The Red Army was called into being early in 1918, after the Brest-Litovsk peace treaty had taken Russia out of the World War. Lavrenov's Maryutka would not have been an unfamiliar figure, for although most women made their contribution in industry, by 1920 (when the story evidently takes place)[9] at least 75,000 women were enlisted at every rank and in every capacity: combat, intelligence and espionage, political propaganda, fraternization with the enemy, medical and police work, as well as construction, feeding, and sanitary projects on the home front.[10]

That Maryutka is not a Communist makes her a more representative figure, for most 'Red Armyists' were not. In 1920, about 130,000 of the Army's 5.5 million were party members; like many others, Maryutka is committed to practical social justice, which she sees embodied in the Bolsheviks. That Maryutka is not an urban proletarian also renders her more typical, for most of the Red Army ranks were rurals. Neither, however, is Maryutka a peasant, but rather an impoverished fisher-girl from a tiny village near Astrakhan in the Volga delta, on the north shore of the Caspian Sea. (Astrakhan was one of sixteen major fronts of the civil war; it was the particular target of British shelling and bombs in Britain's 1918 thrust from the south by air and sea.) Certainly unusual are Maryutka's literacy and her poetic aspiration in a country where, at the moment of the revolution, fourteen million of its seventeen million illiterates were women. One could say, with Stites, that "illiteracy was essentially a woman's problem" (Stites 1978, 397) or, more accurately, with Trotsky, that "the 'woman problem' here, then, means first of all the struggle with female illiteracy" (Trotsky 1924, 153). In short, we can see that Lavrenov has made his heroine both typical enough and unusual enough to be an effective model. She has sufficient commitment and culture to focus emulation and aspiration, yet she is not so accomplished as to intimidate the reader, nor so duty bound as to deny sensuality. To fight 'as a woman' would be meaningless for someone like Maryutka; to fight 'for women', an evident idiocy. Her role in the story is consistent with social reality of the revolutionary period. It is gratifying to know that her fictional efforts, and the real efforts of individual women and of Zhenotdel did produce striking results, for by 1926, 43% of Soviet women were literate.

---

9   I have located the story in 1920 because of the reference to Commander Yevsukov's belief in "the Soviets, the International, the Cheka". The Third International was not founded until March 1919; since the story opens in February, it must be February of 1920. Maryutka volunteered into "what was then called the Red Guards", hence before the creation of the Red Army proper in April 1918, so that she has been in the army for about two years.
10   Stites 1978, 278–81 tells the story of the well-known soldier Maria Bochkareva, founder in 1917 of the Women's Battalions, some members of which defended the Winter Palace against the Bolsheviks on October 25. Bochkareva traveled in the United States on a patriotic speaking tour, winding up with the Whites during the civil war. On the Red Army, see Bonch-Bruyevich 1966; Hart 1956; O'Ballance 1964; and Trotsky 1929, chaps. 32–37.

If the heroine of later decades differs from Lavrenov's in "The Forty-first", it is because of a new social milieu: that of the bureaucracy in power. Many examples are provided by Gasiorowska and Dunham; two will have to suffice here. The following exchange occurs in a 1937 novel, *The Village Bruski* by F. Panfyorov, when a woman tractor driver is honored by Stalin:

> "Our feminine hearts are overflowing with emotions", she said, "and of these, love is paramount. Yet a wife should also be a happy mother and create a serene home atmosphere, without, however, abandoning work for the common welfare. She should know how to combine all these things while also matching her husband's performance on the job". "Right!" said Stalin. "How she has grown spiritually!" thought Zhdarkin.
>
> quoted in GASIOROWSKA 1968, 53

In a 1950 novel about agricultural workers, by Y. Kapusto, the wife is a talented agronomist whose husband, her assistant on the job, is studying for a degree. "I can't be the boss forever", she reassures him; "I'll be having children":

> In her there no longer speaks the stubborn agronomist but a woman's ambition. That ambition consists not of a drive to surpass one's beloved but, rather, in being able to consider him superior to anybody else, including herself.
>
> DUNHAM 1976, 223

These passages rather neatly display the reversal of earlier Bolshevik policy on women and the family. Their cynical and philistine sentiments, entirely unironical, would have been treated contemptuously by Lavrenov's heroine; indeed, they seem like a throwback to the consciousness of some Gogolesque pen-pusher, rank #9 of the fourteen bureaucratic degrees.

Where the Bolsheviks aimed to liberate women from the social burdens of maternity (though not necessarily from the biological fact) and ultimately to replace the social and economic functions of the nuclear family with state services and support, the bureaucratic strategy was, on the contrary, to tie women—along with men and children—ever more tightly to the family, while simultaneously encouraging women to participate in industrial labor.

Zhenotdel was abolished in 1929, under the pretext that its job was done. In 1936 abortion was made once again illegal, except in circumstances endangering the mother's life, and divorce was made very difficult to get, through fees, delays, and red tape. Coeducation was ended in 1943, the same year that Stalin obligingly dissolved the Third International as a conciliatory gesture to his allies Churchill and Roosevelt. (Coeducation was restored ten years later, after Stalin's death in 1953, but gender-track curricula and role-biased texts remained.) A ban on paternity suits in 1944, together with denial of the legal validity of common-law marriage and of legal rights to children born out of wedlock, effectively restored the category of illegitimacy with all its injustices to mother and child. The heroine of socialist reproduction might receive a handsome state benefit after her fifth child, but only if the child were the product of a properly licensed marriage. The net effect of this program was to intensify the economic, social, and psychological dependency of women upon men. The ancient mystique of motherhood flourished; it was cultivated in tandem with the new national patriotism that became a major domestic propaganda tool in World War II, replacing the class consciousness so scrupulously maintained in civil-war propaganda and in political education during the 1920s. 'Holy mother Russia', 'the sacred motherland', 'the earth that bore and nurtures us'—this is the familiar message underscored by word and by visual imagery in Soviet literature and film from *Alexander Nevsky* (1938) to *Oblomov* (1980).

∴

Why did it happen? And could it have been prevented? I want to take the long way round in answering these questions. In any society the position of women is one facet of an integrated social structure: so, for the Bolsheviks, as for the bureaucratic regime. Bolshevik family legislation was part of a long-range strategy to construct a material base for eventual communism: an international, classless, stateless society. In 1919, Lenin wrote about the tasks of communist construction, including the necessity to "foster the simple, modest, ordinary but viable shoots of genuine communism". Among these, he writes, are the public restaurants, nurseries, and kindergartens: institutions that were created under capitalism but that, in a collectivized economy and a workers' government, are able to help "really emancipate women, really lessen and abolish their inequality with men as regards their role in social production and public life":

> Notwithstanding all the laws emancipating woman, she continues to be a domestic slave, because petty housework crushes, strangles, stultifies and degrades her, chains her to the kitchen and the nursery, and she wastes her labour on barbarously unproductive, petty, nerve-wracking, stultifying and crushing drudgery. The real emancipation of women, real communism, will begin only where and when an all-out struggle begins (led by the proletariat wielding the state power) against this petty

housekeeping, or rather when its wholesale transformation into a large-scale socialist economy begins.
LENIN 1919, 429

The case of architecture pointedly illustrates the intersection of political program, family legislation and the arts. During the 1920s, architecture was considered both a manifestation of the new family legislation and a means to implement it: a 'concrete expression' (so clichés occasionally come to life again for a moment) of the revolution's intentions toward women. The Moscow Soviet publicized in these words its 1926 competition for the design of a communal dwelling:

> It is the duty of technological innovation, the duty of the architect, to place new demands on housing and to design insofar as possible a house that will transform the so-called family hearth from a boring, confining cell that at present burdens down women in particular into a place of pleasant and carefree relaxation.
> A new life demands new forms.
> The worker does not desire his mother, wife or sister to be a nursery maid, washerwoman or cook with unlimited hours; he does not desire children to rob him and particularly their mother of the possibility of employing their free time for social labor, mental and physical pleasures.
> quoted in ZELINSKY 1976, 6

A contemporary architect wrote:

> The proletariat must at once set about the destruction of the family as an organ of oppression and exploitation. In the communal dwelling the family will, in my view, be a purely comradely, physiologically necessary and historically inevitable association between the working man and the working woman.
> quoted in ZELINSKY 1976, 9

Policies of the 1930s and 1940s were likewise integrated into overall social tasks, such as industrialization and war, but these tasks now included the maintenance of the bureaucracy itself. Programmatically, this required a fundamental revision of Bolshevism because it meant, in practical terms, to not move toward full communism but instead to deliberately preserve a 'transitional' state: a workers' state in its collectivized economic arrangements, but administered by a parasitical privileged caste of managers and technicians, with the political voice of workers stifled by terror, propaganda, and legislation. It was a comprehensive program—not a series of mistakes—and required a variety of tactics for implementation:

- In foreign policy: the 'popular front'—collaboration with the international so-called 'progressive' bourgeoisie.
- In inner-party life: the destruction of the old program and democratic-centralist party structure. This was achieved first by crushing the Left Opposition during the late 1920s, then by exterminating the entire Central Committee of the old Bolshevik Party in the purge trials of the 1930s. Also eliminated were leadership cadre at all levels and rank and file Communists "who had taken any direct part in the Revolution and Civil War, or had participated in party life and knew the party's structure" (Agursky, quoted in Medvedev 1977, 220; see also Medvedev 1971). Finally, the leadership of the Left Opposition in exile were assassinated, including Trotsky in 1940.
- In culture: rigid control of the arts and intellectual life through censorship and the prescriptive aesthetic of 'socialist realism'.
- In family life: to rehabilitate the traditional family as a microcosm of authoritarian relations and a bulwark of conservative values—what Trotsky called "40,000,000 points of support for authority and power", "nests of medievalism, female slavery and hysteria, daily humiliation of children, feminine and childish superstition" (Trotsky 1936, 153, 145).

As reflected in architecture, my exemplary case above, the bureaucratic policy meant that communal housing and the socialization of domestic labor were characterized as 'utopian'; the daring new schemes were shelved for a return to traditional models more appropriate to the privatized nuclear family.

Where would she have to be in, say, 1927: a politically conscious woman who wished to defend what the revolution had accomplished and to extend these accomplishments to full economic and personal liberation? First, she would need to be in the Communist Party, which had initiated these gains but was now supervising their erosion. Moreover, she would need to be with the Left Opposition in the Party, where she would have fought to defend everything that made those gains possible. Had she been there, as numbers of women were, both in Russia and abroad, she would for the time being have lost; victory is not guaranteed to those who are right. But she would have made the best possible fight, and her struggle would have guaranteed—it has guaranteed—the survival of a revolutionary tradition that history continues to test and to vindicate. "Revolution", wrote Rosa Luxemburg, "is the sole form of 'war' … in which the final victory can be prepared only by a series of 'defeats'" (Luxemburg 1919, 304). She was writing shortly after the defeat of the German revolution of 1918–19, known as 'the Spartacus revolt' after the proto-party, the Spartacus League, that led it after its founding by Rosa, Karl Liebknecht, and other comrades who, sympathetic to the Russian Revolution, had split from the German Social Democratic Party. She was writing just before her own arrest and assassination on January 19, 1919:

> The first flaring up of the class struggle, the 1831 revolt of the silk-weavers in Lyons, ended in a heavy defeat. The Chartist Movement in England also ended in defeat. The rising of the proletariat in Paris in June 1848 ended in an overwhelming defeat. The Paris Commune ended in a terrible defeat. ... We stand upon those very defeats, none of which we could have done without, each of which is a part of our strength and clarity of purpose. ... And thus the future victory will blossom from out of this 'defeat'.
>
> LUXEMBURG 1919, 304–6

We recall that "The Forty-first", like many other civil-war stories, is a narrative of military defeat. It opens with the disorderly retreat of Maryutka's unit, the Guryev detachment, from a ruthless Cossack attack. Fewer than one sixth of the unit have escaped; the survivors are starved, desperate, demoralized, ill-disciplined. The story ends as Maryutka confronts the White Guard rescue party; in real life someone in her position would most likely be executed either on the spot or after rape or torture. Thousands of women partisans and comrades died so. To end by saying that their deaths weren't in vain may sound like a cliché, but, like every cliché, it is founded in material truth.[11]

References

Bonch-Bruyevich, M. 1966. *From Tsarist General to Red Army Commander*. Moscow: Progress Publishers.

Delany, Sheila. 1983. *Writing Woman: Women Writers and Women in Literature*. New York: Schocken Books.

Der Melkonian-Minassian, Chaké. 1978. *Politiques littéraires en URSS*. Montreal: Presses de l'Université du Québec.

Dunham, Vera S. 1976. *In Stalin's Time: Middleclass Values in Soviet Fiction*. Cambridge: Cambridge University Press.

---

11 This chapter is a revised version of "Women, Culture, and Revolution in Russia: Boris Lavrenev's "The Forty-first"", chap. 8 of *Writing Woman. Women Writers and Women in Literature*. New York: Schocken Books, 1983, 134–156.

Engel, Barbara A., and Clifford N. Rosenthal, eds. 1975. *Five Sisters: Women Against the Tsar*. New York: Knopf.
Englander, Nathan. 2000. "The Twenty-Seventh Man". In *For the Relief of Unbearable Urges*, 3–23. New York: Vintage International.
Fitzpatrick, Sheila. 1970. *The Commissariat of Enlightenment*. Cambridge: Cambridge University Press.
Gasiorowska, Xenia. 1968. *Women in Soviet Fiction*. Madison: University of Wisconsin Press.
Geiger, H. Kent. 1968. *The Family in Soviet Russia*. Cambridge: Harvard University Press.
Glickman, Rose L. 1977. "The Russian Factory Woman, 1880–1914". In *Women in Russia*, edited by Dorothy Atkinson, Alexander Dallin, and Gail Warshofsky Lapidus, 63–83. Stanford: Stanford University Press.
Hart, B.H. Liddell, ed. 1956. *The Soviet Army*. London: Weidenfeld and Nicolson.
Lavrenov, Boris. [1924] 1967. "The Forty First". In *The October Storm and After*, 179–239. Moscow: Progress Publishers.
Lavrenov, Boris. [1924] 1960. "Such a Simple Thing". In *Such a Simple Thing and Other Soviet Stories*, 10–68. Moscow: Foreign Languages Publishing House.
Lavrenov, Boris. [1927] 1944. *L'Avenir est à nous*. Geneva: Jeheber.
Lavrenov, Boris. [1941] 1943. "The Portrait". In *Stout Heart and Other Stories*, edited and translated by D.L. Fromberg. 20–28. Moscow: Foreign Languages Publishing House.
Lavrenov, Boris. 1943. "Out at Sea". In *Stout Heart and Other Stories*, edited and translated by D.L. Fromberg. 39–56. Moscow: Foreign Languages Publishing House.
Lenin, V.I. 1919. "A Great Beginning". In *Collected Works*, vol. 29, 409–34. Moscow: Progress Publishers.
Lenin, V.I. 1920. "Tasks of the Youth Leagues". In *Collected Works*, vol. 31, 148–66. Moscow: Progress Publishers.
Luke, Louise. 1953. "Marxian Woman, Soviet Variants". In *Through the Glass of Soviet Literature*, edited by Ernest J. Simmons. New York: Columbia University Press.
Luxemburg, Rosa. [1919] 1972. "Order Reigns in Berlin". *Die Rote Fahne*, January 14, 1919. In *Rosa Luxemburg: Selected Political Writings*, edited by Robert Looker, translated by William D. Graf, 300–6. London: Jonathan Cape.
McNeal, Robert H. 1971. "Women in the Russian Radical Movement". *Journal of Social History* 5, 143–63.
Medvedev, Roy. 1971. *Let History Judge*. New York: Knopf.
Medvedev, Roy. 1977. "New Pages from the Political Biography of Stalin". In *Stalinism: Essays in Historical Interpretation*, edited by Robert Looker, 199–235. 1977. London: Routledge.
O'Ballance, Edgar. 1964. *The Red Army*. New York: F. A. Praeger.
Roberts, Spenser E. 1965. *Soviet Historical Drama*. The Hague, Netherlands: M. Nijhoff.

Rosenhan, Mollie Schwartz. 1977. "Images of Male and Female in Children's Readers". In *Women in Russia*, edited by Dorothy Atkinson, Alexander Dallin, and Gail Warshofsky Lapidus, 293–305. Stanford: Stanford University Press.

Schlesinger, Rudolf, ed. 1949. *The Family in the USSR: Documents and Readings*. London: Routledge & Kegan Paul.

Selivanova, Nina. 1923. *Russia's Women*. New York: Dutton.

Shklovsky, Viktor. [1925] 1990. *Theory of Prose*, translated by Benjamin Sher. Normal, IL: Dalkey Archive Press.

Stites, Richard. 1977. "Women and the Russian Intelligentsia: Three Perspectives". In *Women in Russia*, edited by Dorothy Atkinson, Alexander Dallin, and Gail Warshofsky Lapidus, 39–62. Stanford: Stanford University Press.

Stites, Richard. 1978. *The Women's Liberation Movement in Russia*. Princeton: Princeton University Press.

Struve, Gleb. 1951. *Soviet Russian Literature, 1917–50*. Norman: University of Oklahoma Press.

Trotsky, Leon. 1922. *Between Red and White: a Study of Some Fundamental Questions of Revolution*. Westport: Hyperion Books.

Trotsky, Leon. [1923] 1992. "What is Proletarian Culture and Is It Possible?" In *Art and Revolution*, edited by Paul N. Siegel, 41–54. New York: Pathfinder.

Trotsky, Leon. [1924] 1973. "Leninism and Library Work". In *Problems of Everyday Life*, 143–161. New York: Monad Press.

Trotsky, Leon. [1929] 1970. *My Life*. New York: Pathfinder Press.

Trotsky, Leon. 1930. *History of the Russian Revolution*, translated by Max Eastman. 3 vols. London: Sphere Books.

Trotsky, Leon. [1936] 1972. *The Revolution Betrayed*, translated by Max Eastman. New York: Pathfinder Press.

Trotsky, Leon. [1938] 1992. "Art and Politics in Our Epoch". In *Art and Revolution*, edited by Paul N. Siegel, 104–14. New York: Pathfinder.

Zamyatin, Yevgeny. [1923] 1970. "On Literature, Revolution, Entropy, and Other Matters". In *A Soviet Heretic: Essays by Yevgeny Zamyatin*, edited and translated by Mirra Ginsburg. Chicago: University of Chicago Press.

Zamyatin, Yevgeny. [1926] 1966. "X". In *The Dragon: Fifteen Stories*, edited and translated by Mirra Ginsburg, 218–38. New York: Random House.

Zelinsky, Vladimir. 1976. "Architecture as a Tool for Social Transformation". *Women and Revolution* 11, 6–14.

CHAPTER 6

Anti-saints

A Revolutionary's Legendary

Two questions to begin with: Who is the revolutionary of my title? And what is a legendary? When these are answered, a third poses itself: Why would this, or any, modern revolutionary choose to compile a legendary, that relic of the reactionary Middle Ages?

The revolutionary in question is Pierre Sylvain Maréchal (1750–1803), usually known as Sylvain by his own preference, in keeping with the pastoral-erotic verse he composed as a young man; he is Parisian, a prolific author in many genres, an outspoken atheist. A legendary is a collection of saints' lives, known as 'legends' from Latin *legenda*, something to be read. Properly to introduce Sylvain, to place him in context of the French Revolution that he lived through and supported, and to explain his choice of genre, will be the aims of this chapter.

• • •

On Monday, September 14, 1789, the radical journal *Révolutions de Paris* (*RdeP*) covered a local event of some public interest:

> Occupé des intérêts puissans de la nation, nous avions renoncé à parler de ces fêtes militaires, de ces processions, objets d'amusemens & de luxe, que chaque jour on voit renouveller dans cette capitale; car si le pain & les loix nous manquent, du moins le faste & la dévotion nous consolent. Aujourd'hui, cependant, il se présente une de ces processions qui attire l'attention publique: ce sont les citoyens gardes nationaux des districts du fauxbourg Saint-Antoine qui se sont réunis, ayant à leur tête les jeunes vierges de ces cantons, dont le cortége nombreux va faire bénir à Sainte-Genevieve, & mettre sous la protection de cette patrone de la capitale, un modele de la bastille. Ce modele, de la hauteur de quatre pieds ou environ ... rappelle le moment du siege de cette forteresse ... Ici l'on a tout imité, les armes, les hommes, le [*sic*] drapeaux, les canons, & ce modele a produit toute l'illusion que l'on pouvait en attendre.

> Occupied with powerful national matters, we have omitted to speak about those military celebrations and processions, objects of amusement and expense, which are every day seen to proliferate in this capital; for if bread and laws are lacking, at least display and devotion console us. Today, though, one of those parades is presented that draws public attention: it is the national-guard citizens from neighborhoods in the Saint Antoine suburb who have reunited, headed by young virgins of those neighborhoods; their numerous cortège is going to bless Saint Genevieve and place under the protection of this patron saint of the capital a model of the Bastille. This model, about four feet high ... recalls the moment of the siege of this fortress ... Here they imitated everything, the weapons, the men, the flags, the cannons, and this model produced every effect one might expect from it.

Although anonymous, the article was probably written by Sylvain Maréchal, an editor of the journal from late 1790 through its demise in 1794. Maréchal's distinctive style is not hard to spot; it appears he had what we might call 'the women, culture, and religion desk' at the journal. Typical in style and sentiment of Maréchal is the sardonic critique of the current revolutionary government for its attempt to pacify a hungry and impatient working population with elaborate spectacle: this is a recurrent theme in his work. Also typical is the development of the article into an encomium on liberty with its references to Greece, Rome, and *"l'immortel Jean-Jacques"* (Rousseau), its exhortation to citizens to unite fearlessly once again, its denunciation of priests who visited innocent prisoners but did nothing to free them or even to improve their frightful conditions, becoming instead *"les agens du plus horrible despotisme"* (agents of the most horrible despotism)—and, another Maréchal trait—its profuse footnotes.

I choose this anecdote to begin because of its all too evident contradictions. On one hand, the parade features a large mock-up of the Bastille, the medieval fortress–prison hated, assaulted, and taken on July 14, 1789, by the armed population of Paris. This event remains the best known of many revolutionary *journées*, still celebrated annually in France as a national holiday and betokening the explosive beginnings of modern political life and the modern state. On the other hand, the parade also features two oppressive early-medieval institutions: Catholic Church and monarchy. These are combined in the figure of Saint Genevieve, patron saint of Paris, whose prayers were said to have converted the fifth-century Frankish ruler, Clovis, to orthodox Christianity, thus producing the first Christian French monarch. (See Chapter 7 in this collection.)

Such contradictions existed in uneasy equilibrium for years during and after the revolutionary period, and many would say they still do. They characterize the revolution as a whole, or rather in its several phases, and they characterize Sylvain Maréchal, product of and participant in the political culture of his day. The text I shall discuss here—Maréchal's set of saints' lives, his 1790 *Nouvelle légende dorée* or *New Golden Legend*—doesn't by itself illustrate that ambiguity, for its target is Catholicism, and Maréchal was perfectly clear about Catholicism. A militant atheist, he considered all organized religion to be antisocial, exploitative, unnatural, and psychologically damaging. It was therefore an appropriate object of ridicule and rejection, as his legendary amply shows.

Maréchal's prototype for this work was the massive thirteenth-century compilation by the Genoan Dominican bishop Jacob Voragine. Meant as a rich resource for preachers, the original 'golden legend' (*Legenda aurea*) was among the most popular and enduring texts of the Middle Ages (Voragine 1266), with over a thousand manuscripts in Latin alone (omitting translations into other languages) still extant today (see Dunn-Lardeau 1986). The French "*nouvelle*" version was a bold, sardonic, witty, even occasionally nasty parody of what had once been an immensely popular religious genre. Drawing on numerous treatments and documents composed down the ages, Maréchal's new legendary profited from contemporary rationalistic efforts to cleanse the ancient genre of its more obvious bizarreries and fictions. Scholarly clergy from the seventeenth century on labored to present a more convincing image of sainthood and the Church to Catholics and the world at large, especially in confrontation with the Protestant challenge. The monumental *Acta sanctorum (Deeds of the Saints)* project of the Belgian Jesuits (called the Bollandists after their early editor, Jean Bolland, who died in 1665) was one of these scholarly efforts. As a librarian at the prestigious Mazarin Library, Maréchal would have access to a wealth of hagiographical and related materials, many of which he quotes in his *Nouvelle légende*.

In fact, though, much of what Maréchal records is already in the *Legenda aurea* or other unnamed sources, often as minor detail; he foregrounds it, naturalizes it, subjects it to intense linguistic scrutiny, fills in the gaps, or teases the reader by noticing omitted information. "*La sainte chronique ... quelquefois ne diffère pas beaucoup de la chronique scandaleuse*", he remarks (The holy chronicle sometimes isn't much different from a scandalous story: Maréchal 1790, 1:30). As an example: ten years after the death of her beloved confessor, Saint Francis de Sales, bishop of Geneva, Saint Jeanne Frémiot de Chantal has the body exhumed. It is still perfectly whole and fragrant, and so well preserved that one of its "members" extends itself unaided, rising to the lips of the ecstatic Chantal. By omitting to specify which "member" performs this miracle, Maréchal opens the way to an obscene interpretation. Another phallic possibility occurs with "Jacob's staff" in the story of the biblical semi-saints

Leah and Rachel, in which the aged Jacob manages miraculously to produce offspring with two younger wives (Maréchal 1790, 2:22).

Yet despite the similarity in title, Maréchal's *"nouvelle"* strategy differs fundamentally from that of his intellectual hero, Jean-Jacques Rousseau. *Julie, ou la nouvelle Héloïse* (1761) borrows epistolary form and a tutor–pupil love story from the then-recently published correspondence of the twelfth-century couple Héloïse and Abelard. But little of that gritty, tempestuous relationship makes its way into Rousseau's well-behaved, if occasionally melodramatic, novel of upper-class love, marriage, and family life. Maréchal went much further than Rousseau had done; he entered into the spirit of his appropriated genre in order to negate all it stood for, indeed, to negate all it had been devised a millennium earlier to accomplish in the way of religious indoctrination. His imitation was, instead, a de-indoctrination, a tool for unlearning and countering a thousand-year tradition of religious propaganda in its deconstruction of the Catholic master-narrative.

In this sense, Maréchal offers what Amos Funkenstein calls "counter-history":

> A specific genre of history ... [whose] function is polemical. [Its] method consists of the systematic exploitation of the adversary's most trusted sources against their grain ... [Its] aim is the distortion of the adversary's self-image, of his identity, through the deconstruction of his memory ... The adversary's positive self-image is replaced with a pejorative counter-image.
> FUNKENSTEIN 1993, 36, 48[1]

So, instead of a gallery of calm, pious women, as would be typical in an orthodox legendary, we find in Maréchal's text a procession of crypto-lesbians, opportunists, masochists, coerced daughters, disloyal wives and mothers, unruly or disrespectful citizens together with their clerical lovers, incestuous hermit siblings, brutal husbands, and abandoned children. Carla Hesse evokes recent interpretations of the French Revolution that see it "reworking ... public modes of representation and systems of signification" (Hesse 1991, 2). This is what Maréchal had already done with the religious system of signification in two earlier works, his 1784 *Livre échappé au deluge* (*Book that Survived the Flood*) and his 1788 *Almanach des honnêtes gens* (*Almanac of Upright People*), to be discussed briefly below; I propose that it is also what he meant to accomplish in his legendary.

---

1   See Chapter 7 in this collection for further development of this idea.

How, technically, does Maréchal achieve his aim? For he does, in my view, succeed, working within rhetorical as well as genre tradition. "Religious texts are ideal for satire", he wrote in his 1801 Bible commentary (see Chapter 9 in this collection), and he knew whereof he spoke, for satire, parody, and burlesque of religious doctrine, ritual, and discourse had long been known to the French public. The Catholic Church was sometimes able to co-opt subversion by allowing it; hence the parody feasts of the Boy Bishop or of the Ass during the high Middle Ages; the long tradition of Latin poems parodying scriptural or liturgical texts; the *sermon joyeuse* and mock hagiography; the scores of facetious saints—such as *Ste. Andouille* (sausage), *St. Faineante* (do-nothing), or *St. Greluchon* (lover) (see Merceron 2002). More recently, Voltaire, Diderot, and other Enlightenment scholars had ridiculed or satirized the Bible; Voltaire's comparison of hagiography to *The Thousand and One Nights* had already become a rationalists' trope.

As befits an erudite author steeped in ancient classics and modern literature, Maréchal drew on a variety of critical strategies and rhetorical techniques to accomplish his deconstructive aim. Foremost among them, and certainly the one most noticed and disliked by some biographers, is his discernment of an erotic subtext in many of the lives. This is an approach recently taken up by some historians of religion (see Boswell 1994; Burrus 2004). Whether heterosexual, lesbian, or sado-masochistic, whether stated outright or conveyed by broad hints, the erotic dimension allows Maréchal to counteract the traditional notion of asexual holiness. We need to remember, too, that predatory sexuality by clergy, both consensual and not, was a sadly well-known phenomenon of the time, so that bringing to light the historic misbehavior of saints, whether with clergy or with laypeople, reinforced the Revolution's demand for Church reform.

Another favored tactic in Maréchal's legendary is the attribution of apparent devotion to natural causes, especially to diseases such as hysteria, madness, or 'vapors', an imbalance of humors rising to the brain to cause depression or anxiety. Opportunistic motives also serve to undercut traditional ideas about what causes women to join convents: to escape an unwanted marriage or the burdens of childbearing or household labor.

Mocking some conventions of the genre is another technique for undercutting the seriousness of hagiography. For example, rather than the traditional spiritual allegorization of the saint's name that opens many legends, here we are given sardonic commentary on silly-sounding names or on names whose sound or literal meaning might be construed as inappropriate to a saint. The name of Ste. Anne is offered in the misspelled but identically pronounced "âne" (ass or donkey) and followed with a long, faux-erudite commentary which includes these remarks:

> Let the benevolent reader permit this reflection! The Greeks and Romans were assiduous in giving harmonious names to their divinized heroes. Even the god Fart, Crepitus in Latin, is a sonorous word and has an imitative harmony (onomatopoeia) to practised ears. The Church, in reversing the cult of paganism, seems to have taken in everything the opposite step from ancient idolatry: it wanted to confound the pride of scholars, philosophers and people of taste in offering them only bizarre, barbarous and other ridiculous names—as, for example, the one borne by the claimed mother of the mother of Jesus.
> DELANY 2012, 37–38

Besides this sort of 'explanation' throughout, the reader's illusions are punctured in other ways. The monotony of the genre is noted often; there is obvious sarcasm, much double-entendre, frequent wisecracks. The cumulative effect of these devices amounts to what the Russian critic Viktor Shklovsky characterized as "making strange" the hitherto familiar—estrangement, defamiliarization (Shklovsky 1925, chap. 1)—or what Bertolt Brecht, following Shklovsky, would call "alienation" or "A-effect" (Brecht 1936, 91). These make it impossible for the reader simply to accept the work or be caught up in it emotionally; they encourage, even force, him or her to evaluate and judge.

Maréchal's saints are all women. This was an unusual, though not a unique, authorial choice in hagiography. Most hagiographers down the centuries have been men, and something like 75 percent of saints over time have been men as well. To offer an all-female legendary thus skews the genre in a distinctive way. A late-medieval English all-female legendary that I translated into modern English names women patrons of the local nobility and gentry, and, through the gender question, aligns itself with one side in the succession dispute that came to be known as "the Wars of the Roses" (see Delany 1992; Delany 1998). In Maréchal's case, I suggest it is an issue primarily of audience not of patronage. Although both male and female readers are addressed (as is clear in the gender-inflected French original), the all-female tactic makes sense as a special appeal to the devout woman reader, that she might more readily relate to the legends, especially those of the married or maternal women saints, and to the anti-religious message the legends carry in this new version.

To be sure, the *New Golden Legend* wants to free women from the intellectual, emotional, and physical constraints of religion, but for a purpose congenial to the average bourgeois revolutionary: so that they may become good wives, mothers, and citizens. They are to be liberated not in order to pursue their own education or individual gifts, but in order to educate their children in moral values, to perform charitable work and if necessary, to bear arms in defense of their country. This, despite the active participation of women, including organizing and fighting, in key political events, despite the rural and urban labor they performed, despite the presence of women's journals and political clubs,[2] women artists and writers in all genres, and ongoing public debate on the role and education of women in a new *querelle des femmes*.[3] Nor was this ambivalence about women limited to the revolutionary era, for Frenchwomen had to wait until 1944 to achieve the vote. Even for men, suffrage remained a much-debated issue, with property and financial qualifications not resolved until well into the next century.

On the other hand, the revolutionary regime did establish free divorce more or less on demand (a law overturned by Napoleon in 1816), eliminated some of the despotic power of husbands over the person and property of wives, and decreed a range of laws protecting soldiers' wives, single mothers, and their children. Maréchal favored these laws—he believed they would strengthen the marital bond—yet at the same time he deplored the action of a women's delegation petitioning the National Assembly for passage of those same laws (*RdeP* #143:20–24 for March 31–April 7, 1792). This is only one of the many contradictions observable in Maréchal's oeuvre and in the revolutionary process he lived through. To these I now turn, coming back to the notion of contradiction with which I began.

∴

The text that most transparently expresses the personal and political contradictions of the author and the period is a late one, published in 1801, two years before Maréchal's death, and reissued in several further editions during the nineteenth century. It is the *Projet d'une loi portant défense d'apprendre à lire aux femmes* (*Project for a Law Forbidding Women to Learn to Read*), with its 113 reasons supporting that position. Recent interest in this work developed as part of the influence of French feminism and gender studies, particularly surrounding the 1989 celebrations of the two-hundredth anniversary of the beginning of the revolution. Yet despite this obnoxious treatise, Maréchal was married,

---

2   The women's clubs were banned at the end of October 1793, after a series of other decrees against women's political activity and the arrest of several important women leaders.

3   The earlier *querelle des femmes* was a flurry of letters and treatises in the early fifteenth century on the nature and role of women.

apparently happily, to a devout Catholic whom he wed when he was forty-two and she twenty-eight. He had women friends, some of them writers and one of them an editor of his work (Fusil 1936, 221). Two of them responded to the *Projet*, one taking it as a bad joke, the other not; and one of these friends, a feminist, was in the small group at his deathbed (Fraisse 1994, 269). Incongruous as it seems, and is, for someone who considered himself an egalitarian to wish to consign women to illiteracy, even in jest, this was a fairly mainstream attitude. Espousing essentialist concepts of 'feminine nature', no revolutionary government of the time enfranchised women or allowed them to serve in any public function despite various proposals from women and men, including political leaders, to do so; the consensus was that women were simply not made for the rough political life.

The ambiguities observable at many levels of discourse and legislation stem, I suggest, from the multi-faceted nature and needs of the class coming into political power: the bourgeoisie big and small, mercantile and financial, quasi-aristocratic and administrative, land-owning and industrial, judicial, academic, and commercial. For various reasons, this heterogeneous class were not, on the whole, egalitarian in their sentiments. Complicating matters even further is an ambivalent relationship between the new middle-class government and the equally multi-faceted working populations of cities, especially Paris, and other regions of the country. These—the peasants, porters, servants, artisans, small shopkeepers both urban and rural—demanded, initiated, or carried out many components of the revolutionary movement, in its earlier period especially. But their deep needs, surpassing or contradicting those of the middle classes, could not at the time be met; the expression of those needs was soon both legally and militarily suppressed.

Fortunately, the *Projet* doesn't by itself define Maréchal, for he was a prolific author in many genres and with many strings to his bow. Born in 1750 into the Catholic family of a Parisian wine-merchant, he trained and briefly worked in law, but as a stutterer chose instead to devote himself to books as student, writer, and caretaker. Even more important, he had moral reasons for this change, having observed that the legal system was corrupt, weighted in favor of the wealthy (Dommanget 1950, 18; Mannucci 2012, 41). Early on, he became a poet, often imitating classical genres in pastoral-erotic or moral verse. Around the age of twenty, he committed to militant atheism, after a period of intense reflection and reading. Appointed to a position at the prestigious Mazarin Library in Paris, the young scholar–poet gained access to a vast collection of classical, historical, and religious material. His 1784 parody of biblical psalms and prophets, *Le livre échappé au déluge* (*The Book that Survived the Flood*), which denounced the rich, the clergy, hypocrites, royalty, prideful academics, war, and the judicial system, cost him this job.

The book opens with a Rabelaisian *"notice historique"* about the author of these supposedly newly-discovered psalms. It was a difficult birth, he claims, as he didn't want to be born into such a corrupt time and place. At birth he spoke his first words: *"Que ferai-je sur la Terre? J'y arrive beaucoup trop tard"* (What will I do on Earth? I'm arriving much too late). Having spoken too young, he remained a stutterer the rest of his life, a man whose *"idole"* was *"la douce médiocrité"* (sweet/gentle middle-of-the-road). This 1784 work deepened the skeptical-atheistic sensibility already expressed in the 1781 *Fragmens d'un poème moral sur Dieu (Fragments of a Moral Poem about God)*, which overturns any expectations that might be created by its title. The *Fragmens* proclaims Virtue in place of God, offering the Feuerbachian-Marxian notion that *"L'homme a dit: faisons Dieu, qu'il soit à notre image! Dieu fut; et l'ouvrier adora son ouvrage"* (Man said: Let us make God in our image. God was, and the worker adored his work: Maréchal 1781, epigraph). The perspective on God remains materialist:

> Oui, mon Dieu! Tu existes: car j'ai tant besoin que tu existes! J'ai besoin de l'avenir, pour me faire supporter le présent. J'ai besoin d'un père, pour me défendre contre mes frères.
>
> Yes, my God, you exist, for I so much need you to exist! I need the future so that I can tolerate the present. I need a father, to defend myself against my brothers.
> MARÉCHAL 1784, 15–16

His *"Dieu nul ou complice des crimes"* (God worthless or accomplice to crimes) resembles William Blake's "Old Nobodaddy".

Some four years later, another work cost Maréchal his liberty. This was the *Almanach des honnêtes gens (Almanac of Upright People)*, a calendar using the format of an old and at the time still very popular genre. But whereas the usual almanac would start with January, note the Catholic holidays, offer useful information whether astronomical, agricultural, medical, etc., and mark each day with its appropriate saint, this one made innovations. It began with March, in accordance with the author's commitment to nature as norm and with his rejection of a calendrical scheme sponsored by Roman Empire and Catholic Church. It made each month thirty days long. It gave rationalistic numerical names to the months (e.g., June is *"Quartile"*, February becomes *"Duodécembre"*) and proposed, for extra days to make up the full 365, *"solemnités purement morales*" (purely moral rituals): virtuous holidays such as a *"Fête de l'amour"* (Festival of love) in spring or a celebration of *"Reconnoissance"* (Gratitude) in autumn or *of "Amitié"* (Friendship) in winter.

Far worse, in the eyes of civil and ecclesiastical authorities, was that this almanac marked the birth and death days not of Catholic saints and martyrs but of famous people of both sexes from other cultures and religions, many with what a traditional Catholic culture must consider dubious or outright subversive reputations. It was far from being an anti-royalist or anti-aristocratic collection, for numerous nobles, royals, and other rulers appear: Elizabeth I of England, Alfred the Great, several Roman emperors and Ottoman rulers. But first in line, on March 1, is Moses, followed by Saladin on the 4th; Jesus Christ is noted for April 3 and Mahomet for June 7. In this way, Christianity, Judaism, and Islam are given equal status; this, the author explains, is an example of *"un lien commun de fraternité"* (a shared link of fraternity). The presence of Jan Hus, the late-medieval Czech reformer, burnt at the stake for heresy, would further offend religious sensibilities. England, France's great colonial rival throughout the century, to whom vast territories in North America and India had been lost, is well represented with philosophers and poets (Bacon, Shakespeare, Newton, Milton, Dryden, Swift, Pope, and others). Particularly provocative in a colonial context would have been the cartographer and naval commander James Cook, who helped expand England's Pacific territories and had been instrumental in the British victory over the French in Canada. The collection is determinedly internationalist, featuring great artists of other countries—Cervantes, Michelangelo, da Vinci, Tasso, Petrarch, Albrecht Dürer, Handel—alongside such giants of French culture as Descartes, Boileau, Corneille, Voltaire, and Rousseau. The political thrust of this almanac is even more clearly revealed by some of its commemorations: the Edict of Nantes (1588), which granted limited rights to Protestants, a still-controversial issue in 1788; the death of Spartacus, slave leader of a slave rebellion against the Romans; Brutus's assassination of Caesar; the expulsion of King Tarquin from Rome.

Last but not least to offend was the feminine component of Maréchal's new calendar. While a few royal women appear, so do Agnès Sorel, the mistress of Charles VII who set the fashion for bare bosoms at the fifteenth-century court; Héloïse, the twelfth-century nun who refused to repent her passion for her lover and husband, the renowned philosopher–priest Abelard; and Ninon de l'Enclos, the seventeenth-century courtesan and literary lady.

Reaction was rapid and severe: the author was flung into prison, though released after three months through the influence of close friends and relatives. The book was condemned by Parlement to be publicly *"laceré et brulé"* (torn and burnt) as a scandalous, monstrous, miserable, sacrilegious, and blasphemous production; full of impiety, atheism, and folly; tending to destroy religion and good morals (Parlementary document in *Almanach*). Yet despite a ban on sales of the book—or, one might guess, because of it—Maréchal's almanac became a bestseller. Its price rose dramatically, as he relates (*RdeP* #212: 108) and probably made the author rich; it generated many imitations (some of them obscene and incorrectly attributed to Maréchal). The Paris Commune in October 1793 adopted Maréchal's calendar (Fusil 1936, 62), but the Convention—the national governmental body—did not, so a new republican calendar was composed, certainly indebted to Maréchal's (see Perovic 2012).

Two multi-volume scholarly collaborations with artist and engraver François-Anne David occupied some time: the *Antiquités d'Herculanum* (1781–1803), describing artworks in the recently discovered archaeological site near Pompeii, and the self-explanatory *Le muséum de Florence* (1791), for both of which David did the engravings and Maréchal the (often rather prudish) explanatory text. A religious parody, the *Catéchisme du curé Meslier* (1790), deconstructed prayer by ridiculing it in question-and-answer form to yield atheistic answers that Maréchal sardonically associated with the real-life atheist priest Meslier.

Toward the end of 1790, Maréchal took on a co-editorship at *Révolutions de Paris* and helped build it into one of the most influential of the radical journals. This is the year of publication of his anti-religious *Légende*, and although the short-lived 'dechristianization' campaign was still two years in the future, the legendary anticipated it, much as the *Almanach* had anticipated the new official calendar. There was significant anti-clerical, though not necessarily anti-religious, sentiment in Paris and elsewhere, due to obvious moral and financial abuses by clergy. Though Catholicism remained the dominant and, pragmatically though not legally, the official religion in France, nonetheless this same year saw the start of the appropriation and sale of ecclesiastical property; Latreille comments that the government lived for ten years on this transfer of wealth, and fought the war as well, against the several powers that invaded or tried to invade the country (Latreille 1970, 1:92). Also in 1790, new religious vows were made illegal, although monks were permitted to remain in their establishments until death, and hospitals or teaching institutions remained; small establishments were combined; nuns who left their convents were given pensions. In November, the Civil Constitution of the Clergy was decreed this was a set of regulations meant to eliminate abuses by reorganizing clerical structures and procedures. It was followed by the loyalty oath required of all clergy, to support *loi et roi* (law and king). It was thus a propitious year for the appearance of such a text as Maréchal's subversive legendary.

1793 might have seemed a similarly propitious year for a writer of Maréchal's pro-revolutionary, anti-royalist (indeed tyrannicidal) and atheistic convictions, for it opened with the execution of King Louis XVI on January 21 and continued with other events suiting a radical perspective. In June, the moderate Girondin party were expelled from the Convention (the governmental body) and subsequently executed, leaving the more radical Jacobins in control and their leader, Maximilien Robespierre, with considerable influence. A new constitution was approved;[4] the new revolutionary calendar was introduced; price controls were decreed as the Parisian working people had demanded. The Terror officially began in September, defined by Robespierre as "prompt, severe, inflexible justice" for internal enemies (Robespierre 1794, 115). Hundreds of hoarders and speculators in foodstuffs or other essentials, people with noble or royalist connections or sympathies, and many others denounced for, or simply suspected of, anti-revolutionary behavior or sentiments, went to the guillotine or to prison. The 'dechristianization' movement, though unofficial and unevenly manifested across the country, was implementing anti-clerical or anti-religious events in many places during the winter. On November 7, the Jacobin bishop of Paris, J.-B. Gobel, abdicated his office in a spectacular renunciation before the Convention. On November 10, the festival of Liberty and Reason was celebrated in Notre Dame Cathedral in Paris; Maréchal helped organize it and spoke at it (Fusil 1936, 145). Counter-revolutionary revolts amounting to civil war in the north-west and south-east were suppressed during the winter, and in December, the British were driven out of Toulon, on the Mediterranean, by an artillery commanded by the young Napoleon Bonaparte. Although at first the revolution had aimed at a constitutional monarchy, the intervening three years had produced intensifying polarization and indeed treasonous behavior on the part of the royal couple, particularly the queen, who hoped to crush the revolution and regain absolute power with the help of foreign invaders. She was executed on October 16, 1793.

Two days later, Maréchal's play, *Le jugement dernier des rois* (*The Last Judgment of Kings*), opened at the Théâtre de la République (formerly the Variétés-Amusantes) in Paris. It portrays the shipwreck of a group of squabbling European royalty plus the pope and the Russian czarina on a small volcanic island, and culminates in their death when the volcano erupts. The play was met with wild enthusiasm both by audiences and the radical press

---

4 The 1793 constitution guaranteed private property, provided for universal education, work and relief for the poor, and some level of popular legislative power. It was suspended by the government nominally because of war on several fronts; but after the government was ousted, no new one brought back this constitution even when the wars were over.

as "a fit spectacle for republican eyes" (Carlson 1966, 177; Root-Bernstein 1984, 222). It was strongly supported by the government, which donated gunpowder to be exploded at the end of each performance in imitation of the volcanic eruption (Carlson 1966, 177) and paid for several thousand copies to be distributed throughout the country (Rodwell 1990, 165). In defending the Revolution against the coalition of European powers determined to destroy it, Maréchal's play seemed, and for the moment was, perfectly in tune with the spirit of its time and the will of people and government.

But an abrupt turn was about to take place and a new strategy would be implemented in short order. The dechristianization campaign, led by radicals to the left of the government, constituted a potential power base for rivals to Robespierre and his followers. Also, to get rid of religion meant getting rid of what most intellectuals and politicians of the time saw as a necessary restraint on popular emotions as well as a powerful force for national unity, especially among the still-devout French peasantry. Moreover, France's international reputation as an atheistic country could turn populations in allied countries (Switzerland and the United States) against what might be interpreted as barbaric excess. For hostile countries, meanwhile, Robespierre was always careful to insert a wedge between populations and rulers. He thus effected a surprising turn. The dechristianization campaign—always scattered and uneven—was ended and its leaders were imprisoned. Maréchal's play was taken off the stage in February 1794 after twenty-two successful performances (Kennedy et al. 1996, 4); parody of Catholic ritual, a staple of revolutionary theater, was now forbidden. On May 7, 1794, Robespierre's report to the Convention proposed a new official policy against atheism, although Robespierre had been arguing for some time already in other venues, especially the Jacobin Club, against this 'aristocratic vice'. No longer was atheism a respectable intellectual option; now it was an aristocratic, counter-revolutionary offense, and an atheist, however supportive of the Revolution, was simply a traitor. The Convention was asked to declare that *"le peuple français reconnaît l'Être Suprême et l'Immortalité de l'âme"* (the French people acknowledge the Supreme Being and the immortality of the soul: Rudé 1967, 72). Robespierre proposed a new Festival of the Supreme Being as well as thirty-six other ten-day festivals, for which Maréchal, perhaps surprisingly, composed hymns. This took place on June 8, 1794, celebrated with all due pomp, ceremony, and expense (Ozouf 1988, chap. 5), designed and supervised by the pro-revolutionary painter Jacques-Louis David. The new Festival was a conciliatory effort that radical revolutionaries must have viewed with dismay as an ignominious concession and a retreat from revolutionary principles. Given Robespierre's sharp warnings, it was doubtless lucky for Sylvain that the *Révolutions de Paris* had already published its last issue, in February 1794.

In this new scenario it is scarcely surprising that the subversive *Nouvelle légende dorée*, Maréchal's anti-Catholic legendary, could neither thrive nor come to further printings. Truth to tell, even during its two-to three-year history before the reversal of 1793–94, it was no bestseller, for readers preferred novels and amusing fare (Hesse 1991, 4); even Maréchal's good friend, the atheist astronomer Jérôme Lalande, omitted it from his obituary essay and bibliography (1803). An early scholar, Jules Gay, referred to it as *"livre rarissime, inconnu aux principaux biographes"* (an extremely rare book, unknown to the main biographers: quoted in Karmin 1911, 266; Dommanget 1950, 454). Although no longer unknown, the satirical legendary has been dismissed with few and unflattering words.[5] Could Maréchal have hoped or expected otherwise? Was it pointless, mere tilting at windmills, to try to win the French reader, especially the devout woman reader, away from Catholic values and for those of the Revolution?

I think not, for two reasons. One is that the current of revolutionary thought in the first couple of years, 1789–90, looked promising in this respect because of anti-clerical legislation and because of popular anti-clerical feeling, particularly in Paris. The other is that hagiography was a popular genre in city and countryside alike. Itinerant booksellers, the *colporteurs*, brought religious and secular materials into every part of the country, and literacy rates were fairly good for both men and women (Roche 1987, 199–204); saints' lives sold well. The average person would encounter saints in many other formats as well: popular calendars and almanacs that featured a saint per day, place names and street names, the Sunday sermon, statues and shrines in churches and other public places. For those who anticipated social change, the lessons associated with saints and their lives would have to be confronted and rejected: humility, acceptance of persecution, above all the supervaluation of Catholic doctrine

---

5 Some Sylvain scholars have been embarrassed by the *Légende*. Fusil gave it a page (the pages of his book are very small) with the snide comment that *"Il fallait soulever le coin de la tapisserie. Laissons-la retomber. ... C'est par cette littérature de club et de bouge que Sylvain Maréchal travaillait à chasser le mauvais air des croisades et des cathédrales gothiques"* (A corner of the curtain had to be lifted. Let us drop it again. ... It's with this literature of club and dive that Sylvain Maréchal worked to get rid of the stench of the crusades and the gothic cathedrals: Fusil 1936, 70–71). Dommanget has a short paragraph coyly noting *"plaisanteries qu'on devine"* and *"ces traits communs à l'amour mystique et à l'amour charnel qui n'échappent point à Maréchal"* (jokes that one may guess; those features shared by mystical love and carnal love that did not escape Maréchal: Dommanget 1950, 165). Aubert (1975) neither mentions nor lists the book, nor does Perrot (2007).

and clerical authority over the duties of family and citizenship. Two years later, during the dechristianization campaign, "it was above all the saints who bore the brunt of this operation" as wood or plaster saints were smashed and gold or silver ones melted down. "They have gone off to work miracles", was the popular joke (Vovelle 1991, 55). Thus in choosing this genre as a vehicle for his ideas, Maréchal need not have meant to produce a mere rhetorical curiosity with erotic undertones; he could, not unreasonably, have hoped that his propaganda might reach a responsive audience and in some small way do its part for the Revolution, perhaps even achieve the popularity of his 1788 *Almanach*.

⋯

How, then, might we characterize Sylvain's politics, in a more granular way than the rather vague 'pro-revolutionary'? The most sharply politicized moment in Maréchal's life was not, in my view, his editorship of the *Révolutions de Paris*, important as that journal was, but rather his association with François-Noël Babeuf and the so-called conspiracy that Babeuf eventually organized and led, between 1793 and 1797. A feudal law specialist and popular legislator in the Picardy region, Babeuf witnessed and understood the legalized oppression of peasants, artisans, and small shopkeepers. He became a leader and spokesman in their struggles against feudal taxes and restrictions, articulating in speeches and writing the widespread anger and desires of rural populations. For this reason, he adopted the first name Gracchus, after the Roman brothers (about 130 BCE) who fought for agricultural reform. Babeuf established a connection with Maréchal, whose work he knew, in March 1793 (Rose 1978, 138; Dommanget 1970, chap. 10); they became friends and collaborators. After moving to Paris, Babeuf published his own journal, the nationally popular *Le tribun du people* (*The People's Tribune*). In 1796 the Society of Equals was formed, a rather loosely defined body of people committed to the 1793 constitution, to the overthrow of what they saw as the tyranny of the prosperous classes (who in 1794 had got rid of Robespierre and the more radical elements in the legislature), to land redistribution, and to universal education, along with other social reforms. Babeuf himself, at least according to his close friend, colleague, and belated biographer Philippe Buonarroti, had further goals that together can legitimately be considered proto-communist: an armed coup; a revolutionary state apparatus serving the needs of workers and peasants; abolition of private property; land redistribution; universal suffrage; a planned and centralized economy; the disappearance of class difference. He opposed inheritance, extreme wage differentials, and the antagonism of intellectual and manual work (see Buonarroti 1828). But this complete program did not appear in all the group's propaganda, and many who attended meetings would not necessarily agree with all of it, not even those in its leadership. The group evidently had over 2,000 members and several thousand sympathizers including workers, soldiers, police, and professionals.

Sylvain was among the leadership of the Babeuf group, part of what we might call its Central Committee, whose job was to discuss principles, strategies, and tactics, and to prepare the uprising. His leaflets and songs expressing its views were sung and postered all over the city and the country. He wrote a "Manifesto of Equals" for the group (somewhere between 1794 and 1796), addressing the people of France. It calls not for agrarian reform but for something *"plus sublime et plus équitable, le bien commun ou la communauté des biens! Plus de propriété individuelle des terres"* (more sublime and more equitable: the common good or community of goods! No more private property in land; Maréchal 1795, 4). It envisions universal education and an end to repulsive distinctions of rich and poor, master and servant, governing and governed—evidently a classless society. Nonetheless, other of its formulations caused the other committee members to table the leaflet (Dommanget 1970, 235).

What were Sylvain's own politics? He considered himself an "egalitarian"; this label provided the title for Maurice Dommanget's magisterial and detailed 1950 biography. But the label leaves a lot undefined, and it seems to me that if the planned coup had succeeded, Maréchal might not have been content with the Babouvian revolutionary regime either. To be sure, in his journalism Maréchal is a constant and vitriolic critic of the 'new tyrants' who have hijacked the revolution; however, this critique is not in the direction of a protocommunist program but rather toward an idealized 'state of nature'. If we consult other works, earlier and later, we find little in common with the Babouvian model; the labels that must supplement "egalitarian" are, in my view, 'anarchist' and 'agrarian-utopian'. He did not approve of a state, any state, however revolutionary its intent; he deplored laws, civil society, cities and international commerce, despite his commitment to international revolution (yet another contradiction!); he wanted people to be organized in familial clan structures with the oldest male as patriarchal ruler. His *Correctif à la révolution* (1793) elaborates these ideas at tiresome length.

The earlier (1791) and more interesting *Dame Nature à la barre de l'Assemblée Nationale* (*Lady Nature at the Bar of the National Assembly*) is a brilliant, bitterly impassioned denunciation of the government's newly enacted constitution which—Sylvain's lawyerly spokeswoman maintains—has preserved all the gangrene-producing seeds of corruption: royalty, commerce with its base passions, religion with its errors, law with its subterfuges (Maréchal 1791a, 14). Nature despises mass society, cities, and redistribution of property. She deplores its now-falsified words (e.g., brother, nation, liberty, people) and its pompous new rituals. In short, Maréchal deconstructs the verbal and visual semiotic of the new regime; but his solution is the same as it would be years later: *"l'homme en famille isolée, propriétaire d'un champ"* (man in a separate family, owner of a field), with a community of perhaps 100 *"du même sang"* (of the same blood), leading a life of *"douce médiocrité"* (gentle/sweet mediocrity [i.e., avoiding extremes]: Maréchal 1791a, 40, 37).

Yet if Maréchal did not share all of Babeuf's or Buonarroti's vision, he shared some of it. Above all he shared the commitment to a real social revolution— the *"grande belle révolution"* invoked by Dame Nature but not yet achieved, the great and final future revolution to which 1789 was *"avant-courrière"* (forerunner: Maréchal 1795, 3). He cared deeply about ameliorating the condition of the working masses urban and rural, a passion evident well before 1789, as is clear from even a work as apparently removed from polemic as his 1788 *Costumes civils actuels de tous les peuples connus* (*Current Local Costumes of All Known Peoples*). This beautifully illustrated survey starts with Paris, opening with a scathing, heart-wrenching visual and verbal portrait of the Paris poor. It then moves step by step up the social ladder, showing the dress typical for each class in a sharply pointed social commentary. As to colonialism and color, Maréchal welcomed the three Haitian delegates who were seated in the Convention (Aubert 1975, 111–12). It is surely not irrelevant that one of his colleagues at *Révolutions de Paris* was L.F. Sonthonax, who, as representative of the revolutionary government in Saint-Domingue (now Haiti) abolished slavery there in 1793, even before the government officially did so.[6]

In Paris, major popular revolts against the Convention had occurred in May and October 1795; both were harshly suppressed, the second by the young general Napoleon Bonaparte. Given the people's temper, there was nothing utopian about insurrection at this moment. Meticulous plans for the uprising were, according to Buonarroti, nearly ready to be implemented when a member of the organization betrayed them to the government on May 10, 1796. It isn't entirely clear how Maréchal managed to escape arrest; Dommanget adduces evidence that the informer simply didn't know his name (Dommanget 1970,

---

6 There was also a colonial motive: abolition would strengthen loyalty to France rather than to England or Spain, which were competing with France for influence in the Caribbean and North America. However, Sonthonax was personally and politically committed to abolition; he worked in the *Société des amis des noirs* (*Society of Friends of Blacks*) and wrote defending the rights of people of color. In 1802 Napoleon sent a large army to re-establish slavery in the colonies and end the independence of Haiti, but this campaign ended in defeat for the French.

chap. 10). Babeuf, Buonarroti, and several others were arrested. Buonarroti was sent into exile, and Babeuf, denied legal representation, defended himself in a magnificent speech that lasted three days; he was executed on May 27, 1797.

While Babeuf sat in prison awaiting trial, Maréchal published the most—perhaps the only—deeply poignant of his works: *L'Opinion d'un homme* (*A/One Man's Opinion*), first as an article in the *Tribun*, then as a widely distributed pamphlet. Here Maréchal bids farewell to a friend and comrade, and to his last hope, incarnated in the now obviously guillotine-bound Babeuf, of the true revolution, the one that might have offered at least the possibility of moving to genuine "liberty, equality, fraternity". After the "*érudition et plaisanteries*" (erudition and witticisms: Maréchal 1796, 2) with which the piece opens, the bitterness sets in: three million people in six years have died, and there is still tyranny in France; there is still poverty and inequality. 1789 was a magnificent moment, but it lacked the leadership that Babeuf could have provided to take it to the next level (4–5). France is not ruled by virtuous men in the tradition of Lycurgus, Rousseau, or the Gracchi, but by trivial, corrupt hypocrites, insects, worms in ordure. The piece not only pays homage to Babeuf and their shared, defeated vision—"*ta sublime théorie*" (your sublime theory)—but encourages and counsels the imprisoned leader in his approaching martyrdom.

After this tragic episode, Maréchal took up his habitual themes. Was the Babeuf interval merely, in Françoise Aubert's striking image, merely a parenthesis in Sylvain's life (Aubert 1975, 5)? Was he lost or led astray ("*égaré*") by Babeuf, as François Furet patronizingly suggests (Furet 1988, 201)? More cynically, did the will to survive stifle a political vision? I think it is more complicated than any of these interpretations. I 15believe that Sylvain recognized the futility of further activism or propaganda and, while maintaining his worldview, gave up hope of completing the revolution in his lifetime.

In 1797 Maréchal published the *Culte et loix d'une société d'hommes sans Dieu* (*Ritual and Laws of a Society of Men without God*), a model for an elite club of patriarchal atheists with its own insignia, processions, and motto: "*A-t-on besoin d'un dieu, quand on a la vertu?*" (Do we need a god when we have virtue?). The HSD (*Hommes Sans Dieu*) are patriotic but apolitical (yet another Sylvain paradox); their only concern is the regeneration of morals (chaps. XC, XCI). Spinoza is mentioned as a model, but Sir Thomas More's *Utopia* seems the more relevant text. In 1800 came the *Dictionnaire des athées anciens et modernes* (*Dictionary of Ancient and Modern Atheists*), a heterogeneous compilation of some 800 names of skeptics, atheists, doubters, heretics, provocateurs, and people whose words or ideas were close enough to materialism or atheism to be nearly the same thing (Lalande 1803, 14): these included Maréchal himself, Jesus, Job, Mahomet, and Moses. The "*Discours préliminaire*" sketches an idyllic bygone age, much the same as that recommended a decade earlier in *Dame Nature*.

Besides the *Projet*, discussed above (which definitively put paid to the egalitarian notion of "*une seule éducation*" [universal education]), 1801 saw publication of an epistolary novella, *La femme abbé* (*The Woman Priest*), and *Pour et contre la Bible* (*For and Against the Bible*), a book-by-book 'Bible as literature' analysis of Hebrew and Christian scriptures. The novella recounts the story of a cross-dressing Parisienne in love with a handsome young priest, while the long Bible commentary broadens the anti-religious project begun in the legendary, extending it into the Urtext of the Judaeo-Christian tradition. (See Chapters 8 and 9 in this collection.)

In 1803, Maréchal died of natural causes in his own bed, surrounded by friends and family. Ironically, he was given a Christian burial, though there is no information as to whether he got the epitaph he had written for himself over twenty years earlier:

> Cy repose un paisible Athée.
> Il marcha toujours droit, sans regarder les cieux.
> Que sa tombe soit respectée:
> L'ami de la vertu fut l'ennemi des Dieux.
>
> Here rests a peaceful Atheist.
> He walked upright [or: straight ahead], without regarding the skies
>   [or: heaven].
> May his tomb be respected.
> The friend of virtue was enemy of the Gods.

• • •

The critical reception of Maréchal's legendary makes it clear that some readers will find it offensive. I saw this contrarian, deconstructive appropriation of a medieval genre as a phenomenon important for us—not only medievalists—to understand as an example of the extension of medieval literature and ideas into the modern period, and as a special instance of hagiography: what I've elsewhere called the "afterlife" of a medieval genre (Delany 1998, 185). The image of "afterlife" is slightly exaggerated in this case, for in important ways the Middle Ages wasn't entirely over when the French Revolution began. A central task that delegates to the new National Assembly set themselves was to end or at least manage the three major institutional legacies of the Middle Ages: the feudal system, the Catholic Church, and the monarchy. Medieval chateaux were still occupied by families ennobled in medieval times, and the peasantry still lived and labored under feudal obligations and proscriptions. In August 1789, feudalism was formally abolished, although *"le projet féodal"* as a whole took much longer to dismantle. The absolute monarch, figurehead of the system, ruled as a constitutional monarch for three years before the Republic was proclaimed on September 22, 1792. As for the Catholic Church, the mainstream revolutionaries' impulse was to purge its obvious corruption and render it a constitutional, national church. For these reasons, then, when Maréchal's legendary appeared, the social-institutional context made both the medieval genre and its specific Maréchalian treatment equally appropriate.

I write this at a moment when religion has penetrated North American public life to an unprecedented (and to many, an alarming) degree. I saw Maréchal's work as a valuable entrant in the public conversation and was pleased to have the opportunity to translate it. For me, it's especially gratifying to be in accord with Lenin's observation in his 1905 article "Socialism and Religion": "We shall now probably have to follow the advice Engels once gave to the German Socialists: to translate and widely disseminate the eighteenth-century literature of the French Enlightenment and atheism" (Lenin 1905, 86). Some will want to make the banal and incontrovertible observation that it is no longer 1905. Sylvain proclaims in his heart-rending address to the imprisoned Babeuf, that

> la Révolution ne sera faite, tant que les hommes ne partagerent pas les fruits de la terre, comme ils partagent les rayons du soleil ... Ces trois grands principes ... te servent de texte: Oter à celui qui a trop, pour donner à celui qui n'a rien. Le but de la Société est le bonheur commun. Les fruits sont à tous, la terre n'est à personne ... C'est un beau crime que de conspirer pour le bonheur commun! ... La revolution n'est pas finie.

> the Revolution will not be complete until people share the fruits of the earth as they share the rays of the sun ... These three great principles were your text: Take away from the one who has too much, in order to give to the one who has nothing. The goal of Society is general well-being. The fruits belong to all, the land belongs to no one ... It's a fine crime to conspire for the general well-being ... The revolution is not finished.
> MARÉCHAL 1796, 3, 4, 5, 8

If this is the case, and if the Middle Ages wasn't entirely over in 1789, then we may need to think—along with Sylvain—the possibility that the French Revolution isn't, either—or, if over, not necessarily complete.[7]

References[8]

Aubert, Françoise. 1975. *Sylvain Maréchal: Passion et faillite d'un égalitaire.* Pisa: Goliardica; Paris: Nizet.

Boswell, John. 1994. *Same-Sex Unions in Premodern Europe.* New York: Villard.

Brecht, Bertolt. [1936] 1964. "Alienation Effects in Chinese Acting". In *Brecht on Theatre: the Development of an Aesthetic*, edited and translated by John Willett. New York: Hill and Wang.

Buonarroti, Philippe. [1828] 1836. *Buonarroti's History of Babeuf's Conspiracy for Equality*, translated by Bronterre O'Brien. London: Hetherington.

Burrus, Virginia. 2004. *The Sex Lives of Saints: an Erotics of Ancient Hagiography.* Philadelphia: University of Pennsylvania Press.

Carlson, Marvin. 1966. *The Theatre of the French Revolution.* Ithaca: Cornell University Press.

Delany, Sheila. 1992. *A Legend of Holy Women.* Notre Dame: University of Notre Dame Press.

Delany, Sheila. 1998. *Impolitic Bodies: Poetry, Saints and Society in Fifteenth-Century England; The Work of Osbern Bokenham.* New York: Oxford University Press.

Delany, Sheila, trans. 2012. *Anti-Saints. The New Golden Legend of Sylvain Maréchal.* Edmonton: University of Alberta Press.

Dommanget, Maurice. 1950. *Sylvain Maréchal, l'égalitaire: Vie et œuvre.* Paris: Spartacus.

Dommanget, Maurice. 1970. *Sur Babeuf et la conjuration des égaux.* Paris: Maspero.

Dunn-Lardeau, Brenda, ed. 1986. *Legenda aurea: Sept siècles de diffusion.* Montreal: Bellarmin.

Fraisse, Geneviève. 1994. *Reason's Muse: Sexual Difference and the Birth of Democracy*, translated by Jane Marie Todd. Chicago: University of Chicago Press.

---

7 This chapter is a revised version of the introduction to my translation of Maréchal's legendary: *Anti-Saints: The New Golden Legend of Sylvain Maréchal.* Edmonton: University of Alberta Press, 2012, 1–24.

8 In the eighteenth century, books were often printed without a date, without a publisher's name or place of publication, or with a false name or place of publication; all information available has been provided. These features were precautions due to fear of censorship or legal prosecution. Many of Maréchal's works have been reprinted in modern editions or are available online. I was able to consult most of them in original editions at the various libraries in which they are held.

Funkenstein, Amos. 1993. *Perceptions of Jewish History*. Berkeley: University of California Press.
Furet, François. 1988. "Babeuf". In *Dictionnaire critique de la Révolution Française*. F. Furet and Mona Ozouf, eds. Paris: Flammarion.
Fusil, C.A. 1936. *Sylvain Maréchal, ou l'homme sans Dieu*. Paris: Librairie Plon.
Hesse, Carla. 1991. *Publishing and Cultural Politics in Revolutionary Paris, 1789–1810*. Berkeley: University of California Press.
Karmin, Otto. 1911. "Essai d'une bibliographie de Sylvain Maréchal". In *Revue historique de la Révolution française* 2, 262–67 and 437–43.
Kennedy, Emmet, et al., eds. 1996. *Theatre, Opera and Audiences in Revolutionary Paris*. Westport: Greenwood.
Lalande, Jérôme. 1803. "Notice sur Sylvain Maréchal". Privately printed.
Latreille, A. 1970. *L'Eglise Catholique et la Révolution française*. 2 vols. Paris: Cerf.
Lenin, V.I. [1905] 1972. "Socialism and religion". In *Collected Works*, vol. 10, edited by Andrew Rothstein, 83–87. Moscow: Progress Publishers.
Mannucci, Erica Joy. 2012. *Finalmente il popolo pensa: Sylvain Maréchal nell'immagine della Rivoluzione francese*. Naples: Guida.
Maréchal, Sylvain. 1781–1803. *Antiquités d'Herculanum, gravées par F.-A. David avec leurs explications par P. Sylvain M*. 12 vols. Paris: F.-A. David.
Maréchal, Sylvain. 1781. *Fragmens d'un poème moral sur Dieu*. Athéopolis [Paris].
Maréchal, Sylvain. 1784. *Livre échappé au déluge, ou Pseaumes nouvellement découverts*. Paris: Chez P-Sylvain Maréchal [Imprimerie de Cailleau].
Maréchal, Sylvain. 1788. *Costumes civils actuels de tous les peoples connus*. 3 vols. Paris: Pavand.
Maréchal, Sylvain. 1788. *L'Almanach des honnêtes gens, l'an du premier regne de la raison, pour la présente année*. [Paris].
Maréchal, Sylvain. 1790. *Catéchisme du curé Meslier ... l'an premier de la raison & de la liberté; de l'ère vulgaire 1789*. Paris.
Maréchal, Sylvain. 1790. *La nouvelle légende dorée ou dictionnaire des saintes*. 2 vols. Rome [Paris].
Maréchal, Sylvain. 1791a. *Dame Nature à la barre de l'assemblée nationale*. Paris.
Maréchal, Sylvain. 1791b. *Le muséum de Florence*. Paris: M. David.
Maréchal, Sylvain. 1793. *Correctif à la révolution*. Paris: Cercle Social.
Maréchal, Sylvain. 1793. *Le jugement dernier des rois*. Paris: C.-F. Patris.
Maréchal, Sylvain. 1795. "*Le Manifeste des Egaux*". Accessed May 23, 2023. https://libertaire.pagesperso-orange.fr/portraits/egaux.htm.
Maréchal, Sylvain. 1796. *L'Opinion d'un homme, sur l'étrange procès intenté au tribun du peuple, et à quelques autres Écrivains Démocrates*. Paris.
Maréchal, Sylvain. 1797. *Culte et loix d'une société d'hommes sans Dieu*.

Maréchal, Sylvain. 1800. *Dictionnaire des athées anciens et modernes*. Paris: Grabit. 2nd edition 1833. Brussels: Chez l'editeur [Balleroy].

Maréchal, Sylvain. 1801. *La femme abbé*. Paris: Ledoux.

Maréchal, Sylvain. 1801. *Pour et contre la Bible*. Jerusalem [Paris].

Maréchal, Sylvain. 1801. *Projet d'une loi portant défense d'apprendre à lire aux femmes*. Paris: Massé.

Merceron, Jacques. 2002. *Dictionnaire des saints imaginaires et facétieux*. Paris: Seuil.

Ozouf, Mona. 1988. *Festivals and the French Revolution*, translated by Alan Sheridan. Cambridge: Harvard University Press.

Perovic, Sanja. 2012. *The Calendar in Revolutionary France: Perceptions of Time in Literature, Culture, Politics*. Cambridge: Cambridge University Press.

Perrot, Michelle. 2007. "Les paradoxes du berger Sylvain". In *Projet d'une loi portant défense d'apprendre à lire aux femmes* (1801), by Sylvain Maréchal, edited by Michelle Perrot, 93–105. Paris: Mille et une nuits.

Robespierre, Maximilien. 1794. "On the principles of political morality". In *Virtue and Terror*, edited by Jean Ducange, translated by John How, 108–125. Verso: London.

Roche, Daniel. 1987. *The People of Paris: An Essay in Popular Culture in the Eighteenth Century*, translated by Aubier Montaigne. Berkeley: University of California Press.

Rodwell, Graham E. 1990. *French Drama of the Revolutionary Years*. London: Routledge.

Root-Bernstein, Michèle. 1984. *Boulevard Theater and Revolution in Eighteenth-Century Paris*. PhD diss., Princeton University, 1981. Ann Arbor, MI: UMI Research Press.

Rose, R.B. 1978. *Gracchus Babeuf, the First Revolutionary Communist*. Palo Alto: Stanford University Press.

Rudé, George. 1967. "On the cult of the Supreme Being". In *Robespierre*, edited by George Rudé, 68–73. Englewood Cliffs, N.J: Prentice-Hall.

Shklovsky, Viktor. [1925] 1998. *Theory of Prose*, translated by Benjamin Sher. Normal, IL: Dalkey Archive Press.

Voragine, Jacobus. [1266] 1993. *The Golden Legend: Readings on the Saints*, translated by William Granger Ryan. Princeton: Princeton University Press.

Vovelle, Michel. 1991. *The Revolution Against the Church: from Reason to the Supreme Being*, translated by Alan José. Columbus: Ohio State University Press.

CHAPTER 7

St. Genevieve in the Revolution
Sylvain Maréchal's Counter-History

St. Genevieve was by no means without a presence in revolutionary France. Nor were all the other saints, whether local or national, ancient or modern, real or fictional. This is because the high Middle Ages—golden age in the making and worship of saints—was not quite dead by 1789 but survived in three dominant institutions of French life: the monarchy, the nobility with its feudal powers and privileges, and the Catholic Church.

Not only by force did all three maintain their power within the population at large but also by indoctrination. Among the most popular and most effective means of indoctrination was hagiography: stories of saints that inculcated the 'virtue' of submission to divine will, the redemptive value of suffering and humility, the moral beauty of poverty, the superiority of faith over family ties and citizenship, and belief in eventual reward for the virtuous, punishment for the wicked oppressor. These stories were kept before the rural and urban population in every medium: oral, textual, and visual. Statuary and paintings in churches and in public places, the church edifice itself often dedicated to a saint, the weekly sermon, names of cities and streets, the cheap *bibliothèque bleue* blue-paper–covered versions of hagiographical legends that were peddled throughout the country, familial or neighborhood reading circles in which these legends were repeated, the ubiquitous household almanacs with a saint for each day: all affirmed the importance of saints and their cults, their anniversaries, their influence.

The French Revolution, we need to remember, did not begin as an anti-royal, anti-Catholic or even anti-religious movement. Its original aim was constitutional monarchy on the British model, along with a constitutional Catholic Church that would eliminate the most blatant abuse and corruption in the clerical hierarchy. It need not surprise us, then, that St. Genevieve was a prominent presence in a notable public event reported in *Révolutions de Paris*, one of the most widely read radical journals in the country:

> Occupé des intérêts puissans de la nation, nous avions renoncé à parler de ces fêtes militaires, de ces processions, objets d'amusemens & de luxe, que chaque jour on voit renouveller dans cette capitale; car si le pain & les loix nous manquent, du moins le faste & la dévotion nous consolent.

Aujourd'hui, cependant, il se présente une de ces processions qui attire l'attention publique: ce sont les citoyens gardes nationaux des districts du fauxbourg Saint-Antoine qui se sont réunis, ayant à leur tête les jeunes vierges de ces cantons, dont le cortège nombreux va [se] faire bénir à Sainte-Genevieve, & mettre sous la protection de cette patrone de la capitale, un modele de la bastille. Ce modele, de la hauteur de quatre pieds, rappelle le moment du siege de cette forteresse ... Ici l'on a tout imité, les armes, les hommes, le [sic] drapeaux, les canons, & ce modele a produit toute l'illusion que l'on pouvoit en attendre.

Occupied with important national affairs, we have ignored those military celebrations and processions, objects of entertainment and expense, which daily are seen to proliferate in this capital; for if we lack bread and laws, at least splendor and devotion console us. Today, though, one of those parades appears which draws public attention: it is the national guard citizens from neighborhoods in the Saint Antoine suburb who have reunited, headed up by young virgins of those neighborhoods. Their numerous cortège is going to be blessed by Saint Genevieve and to place under the protection of this patron saint of the capital, a model of the Bastille. This model, four feet high, recalls the moment of the siege of this fortress ... They have imitated everything, the weapons, the men, the flags, the cannons, and this model produced all the effect one might have expected.

Révolutions de Paris #10, Monday, September 14, 1789

To be sure, such a juxtaposition of revolution and piety would be impossible a few years later, when anti-religious sentiment was more pronounced, especially during the short-lived and ill-organized 'dechristianization campaign' of late 1793–94. But that is precisely what strikes the modern reader: that the Bastille, symbol of popular revolt, is not only associated with but blessed by the symbol of combined Church and monarchy, for among St. Genevieve's accomplishments is said to be her role in helping convert Clovis I, the first Christian king of France and founder of the Merovingian dynasty.

Although anonymous, the notice in *Révolutions de Paris* is likely to have been written by Sylvain Maréchal, who worked for the journal as writer and editor throughout its short life from late 1789 through early 1794. The style of the passage distinctly resembles Maréchal's and the remainder of the piece in which it occurs reiterates his central concerns and tastes. He would continue to report on events concerning women, culture, and religion: these were his

special interests, on which he had already written and would continue to write until his death in 1803.

Unlike most revolutionaries, Maréchal was a militant atheist, having converted to this position around the age of twenty, after a period of reflection and research; religion in general—not only Catholicism—was his constant *bête noire*. The *Fragmens d'un poème moral sur Dieu* (*Fragments of a Moral Poem about God*, 1781), claiming to be printed at "Athéopolis", is a collection of scattered quotations and aphorisms about atheism. The collection includes an epitaph for the author, who identifies himself as *"un paisible Athée"* (a peaceful Atheist) who, loving virtue, was the enemy of the gods.

In 1784, Maréchal lost his position as assistant librarian at the prestigious Mazarin Library upon publication of his *Livre échappé au deluge* (*The Book that Survived the Flood*), a parody of biblical genres that expressed rationalistic views on religion, royalty, war, and other topics. This was defiantly followed with the explicitly anti-religious "Noël anacréontique", a mock Christmas song, which proposed Eros as a superior deity to God (Mannucci 2012, 50). Two later texts, his *Dictionnaire des athées anciens et moderns* (*Dictionary of Ancient and Modern Atheists*, 1800) and his rationalistic-literary study of Hebrew and Christian scripture, *Pour et contre la Bible* (*For and Against the Bible*, 1801), continued this theme into the early Napoleonic era as propagandistic interventions against the revival of Catholicism after the defeat of the Revolution's radical phase. (See Chapters 9 and 10 in this collection.)

If Maréchal was indeed the author of the journal notice cited above, he would already have been at work on the text I shall foreground in this paper: the satirical legendary *La nouvelle légende dorée* (*New Golden Legend*), published in 1790. Thanks to his ardent support of the Revolution, Maréchal had regained his position at the Mazarin Library, a vast collection of materials old and new relating to philosophy, religion, and many other subjects. There he would have had the opportunity to explore the literature of hagiography, much of it incorporated into his *New Golden Legend*. The title, of course, pays ironic homage to Jacob Voragine's *Legenda aurea* (*Golden Legend*, 1266: see Ryan, 1993) the great thirteenth-century compendium made for the use of priests in composing their sermons, but many other sources find their way into Maréchal's text as well. What is new about his legendary? A number of things, and to illustrate them I shall focus on his treatment of St. Genevieve.

Not unique but unusual was Maréchal's choice of the all-female legendary. Few hagiographers have made this choice, as is understandable considering that only about a quarter of saints, and few authors, were women. For Maréchal, this format was audience-driven, for I believe he meant his legendary as a propagandistic intervention into the revolutionary movement, targeting the devout woman reader in order to disabuse her of religious illusions and replace them with the modern values of family and citizenship. In 1790, when anti-clerical and anti-religious sentiments were not uncommon in Paris, and were spreading to the provinces, this doubtless seemed a realistic hope. But many rural women (and men) clung to their faith with its miracles, saints, and local priests. Maréchal would address this social issue again in his one-act opera, *La fête de la raison* (1793), performed at the National Opera (as its title page boasts), with music and dance. Set in a village, the piece fully acknowledges and enacts the rural woman's resistance to the new regime and to the new rationalistic approach to the Church. The village's patron saint is Saint Anne; the older women cling to their Catholic rituals. But the *curé* (priest) renounces his calling, removes his robe to reveal a *sans-culotte*[1] outfit, "retakes his dignity as a free and thinking man" claiming that he will go to Rome and convert the pope to *sans-culottism* (Maréchal 1793, scene 7). The chorus of women then burns the missal, crosses, and church ornaments, and the piece ends with a chorus and a ballet.

But such expressions of anti-religious or seriously rationalistic views fell out of vogue soon afterward; they proved dangerous after the government's 1794 turn against atheism. Accordingly, the new Festival of the Supreme Being of June 8 that year replaced the previous year's Festival of Reason. In this climate it is easy to see that Maréchal's legendary could have little effect, doomed almost from the start to remain *"livre rarissime et même inconnu aux principaux bibliographes quoique fort curieux"*[2] (an extremely rare book, unknown even to the main bibliographers despite being quite unusual: Karmin 1911, 266; Dommanget 1950, 454).

The major innovation of Maréchal's legendary was, of course, its appropriation of a medieval genre to negate all that that genre was meant to do. This was accomplished with a variety of rhetorical devices (to be elucidated below); their purpose to exhume the social realities buried between the lines of official versions of saints' lives. That is why I frame the text as a "counter-history", using the theory of David Biale and Amos Funkenstein. In studying the work of Gershom Scholem on kabbala, the Jewish mystical tradition originating in the thirteenth century, Biale wrote that Scholem's recovery of the irrational side of Jewish tradition, which had been more or less ignored or devalued by rationalistic Jewish scholarship, was a source of renovation, a reordering of

---

1 The *sans-culottes* were the radical wing of the urban workers, so called because they proudly did not wear the tight-fitting knee-length pants (*culottes*) of the more prosperous classes.
2 In the eighteenth century, 'curious' was often used as a euphemism for 'erotic' or 'pornographic'.

priorities. Counter-history, Biale writes, is "the belief that true history lies in a subterranean tradition", producing a revisionist historiography that "transvalues" old theories and facts (Biale 1979, 11). Funkenstein generalized this idea to historians and other writers whose function is polemical. Their method consists of the systematic exploitation of the adversary's most trusted sources against their grain. Their aim is the distortion of the adversary's self-image, of his identity, through the deconstruction of his memory (Funkenstein 1993, 36). The adversary's self-image is replaced "with a pejorative counter-image" (Funkenstein 1993, 48). In all, there could hardly be a more accurate definition of Sylvain Maréchal's strategy in his legendary, as he replaces the usual gallery of chaste virgins and pious matrons with a parade of lesbians, cruel mothers, alienated wives and spoilt daughters, sensual masochists, selfish wasters of family fortune, gullible victims, purveyors of lies and illusions, wasted lives.

I have avoided referring to our text as a 'mock' legendary, because it does not simply employ the conventions of hagiography to a comical end. Alexander Pope's *Dunciad* or *Rape of the Lock*, for example, are considered 'mock epic' because they deploy the conventions of epic for trivial and clearly non-epic events; Maréchal does not practice that technique. On the contrary, his legends are drawn from numerous authoritative sources, often with direct quotation. In this he differs from the centuries-old French tradition of mock legends amply documented by Jacques Merceron, in which such figures as *St. Jambon* (ham), *St. Andouille* (sausage), *St. Fainéante* (do-nothing) or *St. Greluchon* (betrayed lover) make their appearance in mock sermons, jokes, or amusing stories (see Merceron 2002). How, then, does Maréchal achieve his desired effect of undermining the traditional saint's life and converting it into a counter-history; how does he read 'against the grain'? We may use the story of St. Genevieve as a paradigm for several techniques in his repertory.

Of the approximately 350 saints and 'semi-saints' (blessed or beatified but not canonized) in Maréchal's alphabetically ordered collection, Genevieve is an especially difficult target for ironical debunking. Unlike some major saints, she was not a fictional character but—despite the *"guerres génovéfaines"* (Genevievan wars: Poulin 1986, 116) of a century ago—is now accepted as historically real, attested by several ancient documents. So, although fictional and religiously edifying material (such as miracles) would be added to her biography, the main outlines cannot be attributed only to unbridled imagination or ideological zeal. Unlike many saints, Genevieve was unmarried, so that she did not abandon a husband and children to follow her vocation. Although a committed virgin, she did not spend her life immured in a convent. Nor was she a martyr, so, despite ascetic practices, she cannot be blamed for extreme masochism, lack of citizenship, or compulsive anti-authoritarianism as is the case with numerous of Maréchal's other saints. On the contrary, as a wealthy, educated land-owner and businesswoman, Genevieve was much engaged in public life in the Paris-Tours region, traveling, undertaking architectural projects, counseling royalty in the persons of Clovis and Clotilde, and playing a significant, if minor, role amid the complex relations of Romans, Gauls, Franks, Catholic administrators, and the local population in Lutèce (later Paris) during the convulsive years of the dying Roman empire. (See Schmidt 1990 and 1996.)

A skeletal version of Genevieve's life tells us that she was born at Nanterre, near Paris, about 423 or slightly earlier (Heinzelmann 1986, 26) and may have herded sheep; that at the age of seven she heard a sermon by Bishop Germain of Auxerre and on the spot consecrated herself to a life of chaste devotion. Later she moved to Lutèce, living with such austerity that some found her self-denial excessive. In 451, when the town was threatened by the army of Attila the Hun, she persuaded the population not to abandon the city but to pray; Attila diverted his troops from the city and attacked Orléans instead. In 464, when Lutèce was besieged by the Franks under Childeric, she procured food for the population; the Franks treated the population mercifully. Genevieve thus established herself as a great benefactress of her city. She was also said to have been instrumental in the conversion of Clovis, Childeric's son, who became France's first Catholic king; he founded a basilica in which the saint was buried along with Childeric and his queen, Clotilde.

How, then, does Maréchal meet the challenge of Genevieve? Here is his treatment of the narrative:

> Vers l'an 429, Germain et Loup, tous deux évèques et tous deux saints, s'arrêtent en passant, à Nanterre. Germain remarque une petite fille de onze ans, la prend à part, la fait diner avec lui, et au dessert lui fait jurer de mourir vierge. Il n'étoit peut-être déjà plus tems. Cette petite fille, c'est la bienheureuse Geneviève. Une maladie dont on ne dit pas le genre, lui survint quelque tems après avoir fait son voeu et sa consécration à la virginité. Elle fût trois jours évanouie. Nous regardons cette évanouissement de trois jours, comme un des plus signalés miracles dans la vie de cette sainte. Tout le monde ne prit cependant pas ces vapeurs en bonne part. Le lecteur remarquera que Geneviève séjournait alors à Paris.
>
> Cette circonstance peut jetter un coup de lumière sur la nature de ses indispositions. Germain revint à Paris dans ce tems, et l'on ne doute pas qu'il ne prit vertement la défense de celle qu'il avoit mise au nombre de ses vierges. L'évèque étant parti, les mauvaises langues recommencèrent leur caquet contre sa protégée. On alla si loin, que le bon prélat fut obligé

de lui envoyer un diacre chargé d'agnus, qui appaisa les mécontents et délivra G.

Les Parisiens ne connoissoient pas le trésor qu'ils possèdoient en sa personne. Childéric, père de Clovis, dont on connoit la conversion conditionnelle, assiégea la capitale des Gaules, et s'en étant rendu maître, voulut en massacrer tous les habitans; pour cet effet, il avoit fait clore les portes; elles s'ouvrent à la présence de G. Cette autre Esther sort des murs de Paris et sans en être attendue, s'offre, pour le disarmer, aux désirs du prince, qui apparemment eut pour elle les yeux d'Assuérus; et les Parisiens durent leur salut au pieux abandon de leur patrone.

Un miracle plus difficile à croire que celui que nous venons de rapporter, fut la reconstruction de l'église de saint Denis, que Geneviève fit avec la même facilité que Dieu, quelques milliers d'années plus haut, bâtit le monde, ouvrage d'un souffle.

About the year 429, Germain and Loup, both bishops and both saints, stopped while passing through Nanterre. Germain notices a little girl of eleven, takes her aside, has her dine with him, and at dessert makes her swear to die a virgin. Maybe it was already too late. This little girl is the blessed Genevieve. An illness of unspecified type comes over her sometime after having made her vow of consecration to virginity. She was unconscious for three days. We view this fainting spell as one of the most outstanding miracles in this saint's life. However, not everyone took these vapors in a good way. The reader will observe that Genevieve lived at the time in Paris.

This circumstance can shed a ray of light on the nature of her illnesses. Germain returned to Paris at this time and there is no doubt that he undertook the lively defense of her whom he had placed in the number of his virgins. The bishop gone, evil tongues recommenced their cackle against his protégée. They went so far that the good prelate was obliged to send her a deacon carrying a blessed candle, who pacified the complainers and rescued Genevieve.

The Parisians didn't know what a treasure they possessed in her. Childeric, father of Clovis, whose conditional conversion is known, besieged the capital of the Gauls and, having vanquished it, wanted to massacre all the inhabitants; to that end he had had the gates closed; they opened in the presence of Genevieve. This other Esther exits the walls of Paris and, without being expected, offers herself, in order to disarm him, to the desires of the prince, who apparently had eyes for her as Ahasuerus did [for Esther], and the Parisians owed their salvation to the pious abandon of their patron saint.

A miracle more difficult to believe than the one we have just reported, was the reconstruction of the church of saint Denis, which Genevieve did with the same ease that God, a few thousand years earlier, built the world, a breath's effort.

DELANY 2012, 79–80

Let us pause here to analyze the preceding. We note, first, that Maréchal does not begin with Genevieve herself, but opens her story with the two bishop-saints responsible for her consecration. His concern throughout the legendary is not simply the individual saint but rather the entire institutional environment in which she lives; thus, we are often told of the (usually baneful) role of confessors, spiritual advisors, monastic communities, preachers, nuns, missionaries, bishops, etc. For this pair of ecclesiastical travelers (who in 429 were en route to Britain to combat the Pelagian heresy there), the treatment hints at a scenario of child molestation or even seduction; at the very least, a scenario of lecherous adult men with a little girl. The details chosen from official versions, and the details omitted, produce a particular impression. Nothing is said of a sermon entrancing the girl, or of a spontaneous vow. Instead, initiative is transferred to the bishop. Germain notices the child (why would he?), takes her aside (again, for what reason?), has her dine with him (apparently alone, without her parents) and even provides dessert. Her conversion is now no product of an inspiring sermon but rather of an enticing dinner plus dessert, at the end of which the generous sugar-daddy extracts a promise. As for the child, her age is increased from the usual and rather sentimentalized seven to eleven, transforming her from an innocent small child into a pre-adolescent 'nymphet'—who may, moreover, already have had some sexual experience, as the narrative voice hints in a snide aside. Later, we hear that she is only one among "*ses vierges*" (his virgins): the community of local virgins, but here made to sound like a virtual harem of nubile girls. With or without the salacious skew, Genevieve is being diverted from what Maréchal, along with most revolutionaries and intellectuals of the day, considered her 'natural' role: to marry and reproduce.

Lest this beginning be considered gratuitous slander of the Church, we need to remember that sexual impropriety was far from unusual among clerics, then or at any other time. Elsewhere (Maréchal 1790, s.v. "Chantal"), Maréchal refers to the sensational case of Father Girard, in which an influential Jesuit in Toulon was brought to trial for seducing, impregnating, and giving an abortion to the young woman, Marie Cadière, whose confessor and advisor he was. Although the lengthy trial took place in 1731, its proceedings were printed and reprinted in French and in English; it gave rise to numerous literary treatments down the century (ballads, novellas, etc.) and was known throughout Europe. It was only the tip of the iceberg, though, and in Maréchal's day the misbehavior of clergy, especially the highly placed, was notorious. The story of the Blessed Mother Jeanne-Françoise Frémiot de Chantal and her very devoted confessor, the Blessed Francis de Sales, is one of the longest and juiciest in the collection, and it can hardly be coincidental that this is where Maréchal chose to insert a retelling of the Girard case. Such relationships, real and fictional, form a tradition extending from the Middle Ages (think of the *fabliau* priest–lover) to our own day, unfortunately.

Sometime thereafter, Genevieve falls ill. The author directs our attention to the unknown type of this illness, thus raising a question the reader might not have had on his or her own. He refers to her three-day faint as "vapors": a medical term denoting a nervous condition such as hysteria or melancholy caused by the emanation of humors (fluids) from a diseased organ. Connected as it is with the consecration that just precedes it in the narrative, we are invited to see this illness as one of sexual frustration: again, for Maréchal, a violation of nature. This suggestion is reinforced by the comment just afterward that she lived at the time in Paris, for 'the vapors' was considered an affliction of frustrated society ladies, so that residence in that city helps to explain the saint's indispositions.

The saint is apparently not popular in Paris, and people gossip about her. Her mentor, Germain, arrives to mount a vigorous defense. Again, this is an issue of selectivity, for in an orthodox version of this saint's life, the populace is shown to be wrong, but for Maréchal their gossip may be well founded. Later, Germain sends a substitute priest armed with a candle blessed by the pope and bearing the image of a lamb (*'agnus'*). Another more clearly eroticized candle will appear later in the narrative, but even here we may suspect a phallic image in the large, white taper that aids in the deliverance of Genevieve from a quasi-hysterical torpor.

Eroticization continues in the account of a major alleged achievement of the saint, in which her influence on Childeric, Merovingian king of the Salian Franks, is represented as a seduction modeled on that of Esther and Ahasuerus. In the biblical story, the Jewish Queen Esther uses feminine wiles and trickery to get the uxorious King Ahasuerus to punish her people's enemy, Haman, and thus to save the Jews from persecution. Here, a similar tactic is attributed to Genevieve, with the added irony of a married Jewish analogue for this virginal Catholic saint. At a time when the issue of Jewish emancipation was much in the public eye through debates, treatises, newspaper articles, and speeches in the National Assembly (see Chapter 10 in this collection), the analogue would have had special bite. Whether for or against emancipation, everyone accepted the concept of supersession: that Judaism had been replaced or superseded by Christianity. Figuralism, the notion that Christian events replicated Jewish ones but with different meaning (e.g., baptism as a new, spiritual version of Noah's flood, or Jesus's cross as the spiritualized version of the Tree of Knowledge, etc.) was part of this discourse. What Maréchal gives us in his use of the Hebrew Bible here is thus an ironically pointed figuralism that works to the detriment, not the advantage, of the saint.

The skepticism in the last sentence cited above, about Genevieve's role in building a basilica for St. Denis, first bishop of Paris and martyr buried there, is echoed by modern historians (see Heinzelmann 1986, 96): no miracle, but rather the support of municipal institutions would have enabled this wealthy woman to initiate and supervise such a project. Maréchal deflates the supernatural pretensions of some orthodox versions of the legend with a hyperbolically ironic comparison to God's instantaneous creation of the world—which, of course, as an atheist he would also have rejected.

At this point Maréchal's parodic *vita* turns away from the legend, introducing the narrator in his own voice with a direct (albeit still heavily ironic) address to the reader about methodology in this genre:

> Nous ne nous sommes attachés qu'aux faits certains et peu connus. Quant aux autres, nous nous ferions un scrupule d'en conserver la tradition. Nous copierons seulement ici quelques couplets de chanson addressés à une aimable veuve, pour montrer à nos bénins lecteurs, jusqu'à quel point on s'est permis la license d'écrire sur les choses les plus respectables. Pour réfuter les incrédules libertins, il suffit de les citer.
>
> We are committed only to certain and little-known facts. As for others, we would hesitate to maintain their tradition. We will copy out here only a few couplets of a song addressed to a friendly widow, to show our kind readers the point to which one is permitted the freedom to write on the most respectable things. To refute libertine disbelievers, it suffices to cite these couplets.
>
> DELANY 2012, 80

The stanzas that follow are certainly by Maréchal himself; he was well known as a composer of both erotic and political songs. Insertion of lyric or other poetry into a narrative was not uncommon in French medieval literature of various genres, both prose and verse, as Maureen Boulton has shown (although her list does not include any saints' lives: Boulton 1993, 95–97). Given the eighteenth-century vogue for medievalism (see Gossman 1968 and Montoya 2013), it is likely that the scholarly Maréchal would be aware of this practice. Here, the song continues the eroticization already prominent as a technique of demystification. This is done in a particularly medieval way, appropriating the vocabulary of religion for the purpose of amorous pursuit, much as in troubador love lyric or the Italian *stilnuovisti*. Imagery in the last stanza recalls the final scenes of Jean de Meun's portion of the *Roman de la rose* with its architectural allegory of the female body; indeed, the word *"enceinte"* (enclosure/pregnant) in that stanza may point to the finally impregnated heroine of that famous work. This was clearly a favorite metaphor for Maréchal, providing the conceit of another, earlier, song of his, "Une fin" (Marion 1911, 140–41), which develops the image in much greater detail. There the narrator presents himself as a chaplain serving a lovely chapel located in a protected woods shrouded in mystery. This well-concealed chapel has a double altar of white marble at which the devoted chaplain performs his office day and night with two little acolytes and never more than one candle. In the same vein, here is the lyric attached to our legend, "addressed to a friendly widow who had Genevieve for her patron saint" (Delany 2012, 81–82):

Adressés à une aimable veuve, qui avoit G pour patrone.

Courez en diligence,	Run promptly [or: in a carriage],
Trop crédules Badauts!	Too credulous passersby!
Pour gagner l'Indulgence	To win the indulgence
Que l'on prodigue aux Sots.	Wasted on fools.
D'une autre Geneviève	By another Geneviève
Nos coeurs se sont épris	Our hearts are captured,
Qui nous feroit mieux qu'Eve	Who, better than Eve,
Chasser du Paradis.	Would get us chased from Paradise.
De Paris la Patrone	The patron saint of Paris
Est vierge, nous dit-on.	Is a virgin, they say.
Cependant on lui donne	Nevertheless she is given
Marcel pour Compagnon.	Marcel as companion.
Même champ les rassemble	The same field joins them
Auprès de leurs moutons;	Near their sheep;
Mais étoient-ils ensemble	But were they together
Toujours en oraisons?	Always in prayer?

Choisis donc, ainsi qu'elle,	Choose, therefore, as she did,
Un Compagnon d'amour.	A companion of love.
Prends-la pour ton modèle;	Take her for your model;
Tu feras Sainte un jour.	You'll be a saint someday.
L'almanach de Cythère	The almanac of Cythera
Fera place à ton nom;	Will include your name;
À veuve qui fait plaire	To a widow who pleases
On a dévotion.	One has devotion.
À ta chapelle sainte	To your holy chapel
Avec zèle on ira;	With zeal we will go;
Dans son étroite enceinte	In its narrow enclosure
Un cierge on brulera.	A candle will be burnt.
De nos Vierges tremblantes	Of our trembling virgins
Geneviève est l'appui,	Genevieve is the support,
De nos Veuves souffrantes	Of our suffering widows
Tu calmeras l'ennui.	You will calm the nerves.

Details drawn from various versions of the life are turned to sexual innuendo: the boy who helps little Genevieve herd sheep, the community of Nanterre virgins, and of course the phallic candle. This object appears twice in orthodox versions of the legend: once in the hand of a priest sent to calm the saint's detractors, again in a miracle associated with the dedication ceremony at the new basilica, when Geneviève's candle could not be extinguished by wind and rain (Schmidt 1990, 164). To commemorate these incidents in her life, the saint has often been depicted holding a long white taper.

Let me, then, review the rhetorical devices deployed by Maréchal in re-creating the legend as an anti-religious tract. Eroticization is a primary tactic, and lest we think it far-fetched, we may note that some contemporary scholars, such as Virginia Burrus (2004) and John Boswell (1994), have done exactly what Maréchal did in reading 'between the lines' so to speak, in order to extract the erotic possibilities of hagiographical texts. Naturalization of the supernatural is another favored approach: the visionary trance is nothing but the 'vapors'. In a similar vein, modern scholars, following the lead of Caroline Bynum (1987), have noted the social advantages and personal liberties accruing to women who chose the cloistered life. Biblical reference to a Jewish analogue, normal in Catholic figuralist interpretation of the Hebrew Bible and common enough in eighteenth-century religious discourse, in this case twists figuralism in a way unflattering to the Catholic saint. Direct address to the reader, appealing to his or her judgment, along with ironic comments in the first person, help to remind the reader that any written text—any version of a saint's life—is a human effort, subject to authorial motive and to a reader's evaluation. A related technique of distanciation—what Viktor Shklovsky called "defamiliarization" (1924)—is the faux-naïve narratorial voice in which Maréchal recounts much of the tale. *Occupatio*, a favorite classical and medieval rhetorical trope, creates doubt in a reader's mind by claiming ignorance on questions the reader would not have thought of otherwise. Pun and homophonic wordplay are scattered throughout. A similar arsenal of devices occurs throughout Maréchal's legendary: no surprise for an author steeped in classical, medieval, and early modern cultures through the literatures made available to him by an elite education and by his profession as librarian at the Mazarin Library.

Maréchal could have witnessed, and doubtless would have approved, the fate of Genevieve's monuments in his own day. The saint's relics were publicly burnt in 1793 and dispersed. The reliquary, like many others, was melted down for the war of defense against counter-revolutionary foreign powers and internal rebels: ordinary metals were used for cannon, gold or silver for money to ransom prisoners. Can we be sure the saint would have objected to such use of her wealth for the protection of her city once again? The basilica itself, founded by Clovis, where Genevieve was buried along with the royals, went through renovations and repurposing down the centuries. In 1791 it was renamed the Pantheon, designated as a mausoleum for French cultural heroes. As such, it too went through several turns from religious to secular and back again during the nineteenth century; today it combines lay and secular functions.

My contact with the cult of St. Genevieve came in the Mediterranean village of Cassis, where I spent the autumn of 2009. One day, passing the usually deserted little church, I heard a choir from within, and the square outside was crowded with uniformed and decorated officers. When I inquired as to the occasion, I was told that it was the feast of St. Genevieve. She is the patron saint of Paris, I replied, why is she being celebrated in Cassis? Because, came the answer, she defended the city and now she is the patron saint of all police in France. And, indeed, the church was filled with police from the region and their families and friends; the choir sang; a sermon followed. I didn't discover why the ceremony was being held in advance of January 3, the saint's official feast day, but it sufficed for me to know that the ancient cult still survives.[3]

---

3   This chapter is a revised version of "St. Genevieve in the Revolution: Sylvain Maréchal's Counter-History". *Conserveries mémorielles* 14 (2013). *Les saints et la sainteté*. https://journals.openedition.org/cm/1645.

References

Biale, David. 1979. *Gershom Scholem: Kabbala and Counter-history*. Cambridge: Harvard University Press.

Boswell, John. 1994. *Same-sex Unions in Premodern Europe*. New York: Villard.

Boulton, Maureen. 1993. *The Song in the Story*. Philadelphia: University of Pennsylvania Press.

Burrus, Virginia. 2004. *The Sex Lives of Saints: an Erotics of Ancient Hagiography*. Philadelphia: University of Pennsylvania Press.

Bynum, Caroline Walker. 1987. *Holy Feast and Holy Fast: the Religious Significance of Food to Medieval Women*. Berkeley: University of California Press.

Delany, Sheila, trans. 2012. *Anti-Saints: the New Golden Legend of Sylvain Maréchal*. Edmonton: University of Alberta Press.

Dommanget, Maurice. 1950. *Sylvain Maréchal, l'égalitaire*. Paris: Spartacus.

Funkenstein, Amos. 1993. *Perceptions of Jewish History*. Berkeley: University of California Press.

Gossman, Lionel. 1968. *Medievalism and the Ideologies of the Enlightenment*. Baltimore: Johns Hopkins University Press.

Heinzelmann, Martin. 1986. *Les vies anciennes de sainte Geneviève de Paris*. Geneva: Slatkine; Paris: Champion.

Karmin, Otto. 1911. "Essai d'une bibliographie de Sylvain Maréchal". In *Revue historique de la Révolution Française* 2, 262–67 and 437–43.

Mannucci, Erica Joy. 2012. *Finalmente il popolo pensa: Sylvain Maréchal nell'immagine della Rivoluzione francese*. Naples: Guida.

Maréchal, Sylvain. 1781. *Fragmens d'un poème moral sur Dieu*. Athéopolis [Paris].

Maréchal, Sylvain. 1784. *Livre échappé au déluge, ou Psaumes nouvellement découverts*. Paris: Chez P-Sylvain Maréchal [Imprimerie de Cailleau].

Maréchal, Sylvain. 1790. *La nouvelle légende dorée ou Dictionnaire des saintes*. Rome [Paris].

Maréchal, Sylvain. 1793. *La fête de la raison*. Paris: C.-F. Patris.

Maréchal, Sylvain. 1800. *Dictionnaire des athées anciens et modernes*. Paris: Grabit. 2nd edition 1833. Brussels: Chez l'editeur [Balleroy].

Maréchal, Sylvain. 1801. *Pour et contre la Bible*. Jerusalem [Paris].

Marion, Paul, ed. 1911. *Choix de Chansons Galantes d'Autrefois*. Paris: H. Daragon.

Merceron, Jacques. 2002. *Dictionnaire des saints imaginaires et facétieux*. Paris: Seuil.

Montoya, Alicia. 2013. *Medievalist Enlightenment from Charles Perrault to Jean-Jacques Rousseau*. Suffolk: D.S. Brewer.

Poulin, Joseph-Claude. 1986. *Les cinq premières vies de sainte Geneviève*. In Heinzelmann 1986.

Ryan, William Granger, trans. 1993. *Jacobus de Voragine: The Golden Legend, Readings on the Saints*. 2 vols. Princeton: Princeton University Press.
Schmidt, Joël, 1990. *Sainte Geneviève: La fin de la Gaule romaine*. Paris: Perrin.
Schmidt, Joël. 1996. *Le baptême de la France: Clovis, Clotilde, Geneviève*. Paris: Éditions du Seuil.
Shklovsky, Viktor. [1924] 1965. "Art as Technique" and "Sterne's Tristram Shandy". In *Russian Formalist Criticism: Four Essays*, translated by Lee T. Lemon and Marion J. Reis. Lincoln: University of Nebraska Press.
Voragine, Jacobus. [1266] 1993. *The Golden Legend: Readings on the Saints*, translated by William Granger Ryan. Princeton: Princeton University Press.

CHAPTER 8

The Woman Priest
Obsession, Cross-Dressing, and Canada in an Eighteenth-Century French Novella

Cross-dressing: surely, we may think, a contemporary phenomenon, a product of our mixed-up times. But far from it: there it is in indigenous North American tribal culture with the berdache or two-spirit person; in European medieval saints' lives and high-medieval French *contes* and *fabliaux*; in Arabic cultures; in the Indian 'third-sex' *hijra* communities[1]—and in the social reality of Sylvain Maréchal's day in France and elsewhere, as we will see below. Before and after Maréchal's time, some girls and women passed as men in order to serve as sailors or soldiers or even pirates. Even today, stories continue to surface of women passing as men to acquire enhanced opportunities, and girls dressing or being dressed as boys for protection.[2]

It may be difficult for us to imagine the shock value of his title—*La femme abbé* (*The Woman Priest*) —at a time when the Catholic ban on women's ordination was accepted by a majority of France's population and indeed that of Europe, and when other denominations had not yet opened the way for women officiants as they have in recent years, when we see women rabbis, cantors, ministers, and bishops. Maréchal's epistolary tale of a cross-dressing girl was probably less scandalous to its contemporary audience than what he has her do: study Latin on her own, apply to and be admitted into an elite Parisian seminary, take minor orders, and serve as private clerk–secretary to the handsome young priest, Saint-Almont, with whom she is obsessed. Indeed, so efficiently does the star-struck Agatha perform her duties that the next step in her successful ecclesiastical career can only be admission to full priesthood

---

1   For French medieval tales about cross-dressing, see Heldris's *Le roman de silence* and the anonymous *conte* "*Le roi Flore et la belle Jehane*" (Moland and d'Héricault 1865); both are thirteenth century, and both are treated by Dietzman (2005). See also Delany 1981 and the version of "*Flore et Jehane*" in Jacob 1972. For *berdache* or two-spirit people, see Lang 1998 and Roscoe 1998; for Oman, see Wikan 1982; for Europe, see Friedli 1987, and Dekker and van de Pol 1989.

2   See Cordingly 2001, especially chapters 4 and 5; Stark 1996; and Wheelwright 1989 on women (mostly British, some American) at sea. For a mid-nineteenth-century American instance, see the "Narrative" of Lucy Ann Lobdell (Lobdell 2012). For current instances, see Attenberg 2015; and Nordberg 2014, on girls raised as boys in Afghanistan.

with all its sacerdotal obligations, such as hearing confession or performing marriage and the other sacraments. All of this, of course (except the learning of Latin), was forbidden to women by centuries-long policy of the Catholic Church. It still is as I revise this in 2023, though not without protest from many in the Church, both men and women, lay and ordained.

Although raised as a Catholic, Sylvain Maréchal (1750–1803) in early manhood became a militant atheist, enemy not only of the Catholic Church (the dominant religious institution in the France of his day) but of all religion—or, as he would have it, "superstition", whether Christian, Jewish, Muslim, or other. His own faith was in nature and reason. He left law school for ethical reasons and because his stutter would disqualify him from the oratory required in that profession. Instead, he devoted himself to literature both as reader and writer in many genres ranging from classicizing erotic lyric to impassioned political treatise. Committed to domestic harmony, he married an observant Catholic woman considerably younger than himself in a religious ceremony, wrote erotic verse to her, and apparently lived happily with her until his death in 1803, when he was buried by a priest in a church cemetery. His nickname for his wife was Zoé—Greek for 'life'—the same name he gives to Agatha's sensible, happily married correspondent and confidante.

Maréchal's sardonic anti-establishment writing, as expressed in his *Almanach des honnêtes gens* (*Almanac of Upright People*, 1788), landed him in prison for a short time; the volume was publicly burnt by order of Parlement as an offense to morals and taste. It had, however, a *succès de scandale* and earned him a modest fortune. Moreover, its calendrical format, typical of the almanac genre, along with its rationalist–humanist content, made it a model for what a few years later would become the new revolutionary calendar. Maréchal welcomed the great French Revolution of 1789 and, as editor of and writer for the influential Parisian journal *Révolutions de Paris* from about 1790 to its demise in early 1794, he was able to spread the news across the country. His play *Le jugement dernier des rois* (*The Last Judgement of Kings*, 1793) depicted the ignominious deaths of a group of tyrannical kings and a pope; it was a hit in Paris and other major cities and was supported by the revolutionary government.

As an employee of the prestigious Mazarin Library in Paris, Maréchal had access to a vast treasury of manuscripts and books from every period; even before taking up this position, he had been well schooled in the classics. The fruit of his study, whether while employed at the Mazarin or before or afterward, is obvious in the breadth of reference in his many works, ranging from classical Greek and Roman through medieval and renaissance, and international in scope. He would have encountered the phenomenon of cross-dressing in many texts, some of them rare, some readily available. When his heroine,

Agatha, remarks in Letter XIII that she has several antecedents for her daring transgressive project, she may well have in mind—Maréchal certainly did—some of the cross-dressing saints whose stories, well known over the centuries, disseminated in sermons, almanacs, and popular pamphlets, were also amply represented in the Mazarin holdings of hagiographical literature. Those who appear in Maréchal's 1790 set of women saints' lives, the satirical *Nouvelle légende dorée* (*New Golden Legend*) include Eugenia, Euphrosyne, Hildegonde, Marina, and Pelagia (see Delany 2012).

But the phenomenon was far from merely literary, especially during the revolutionary years. Every French person would know of Joan of Arc who, although not canonized until the twentieth century, was a national heroine for her military leadership of French forces against the English in the fifteenth century. She had, of course, dressed as a man; this was one of the offenses for which she was tried and executed. So, too, did some Frenchwomen dress as men to perform military service in Maréchal's day. Despite being excluded from the franchise and from holding office (an injustice against which many women and men strongly protested), women had political discussion clubs (until these were shut down by the Robespierre government late in 1793), newspapers, and magazines; and they played a leadership role both verbally and physically in many major struggles. When women joined the ranks of the revolutionary army or of its counter-revolutionary enemies, they often did so dressed as men or passing as men, sometimes to be unmasked only when taken to hospital wounded or dead (Bouvier 1931, 198–215). Even apart from the military instance, women sometimes found it convenient and liberating to wear trousers, much as Agatha does in her first forays into transvestism; enhanced employment opportunities might well play a role, especially in Holland and England (see Dekker and van de Pol 1989). In Paris, the well-known revolutionary and feminist Théroigne de Méricourt dressed as a man in her daily peregrination around the city (Yalom 1993, 21); the theater critic Mme. de Beaumer did so in order to enter the cheap seats that were restricted to men (Gelbart 1987, 95), and it is likely that, especially given the wide range of heavy-work jobs filled by women, others did the same. At the other end of the social spectrum from working women, some fashionable Parisiennes in 1799 enjoyed the thrill of donning menswear. The tendency was not ignored by the authorities, and in 1800 a new law made the fad illegal (Douthwaite 2012, 50). Thus, Agatha's disguise, playfully endorsed by her indulgent grandmama, would, by the time of the novella's publication, be not only culturally transgressive but illegal.

• • •

By 1801, when *La femme abbé* was published, Maréchal was a severely disillusioned revolutionary. He saw the cause he had embraced halted partway through, unable to complete its trajectory toward the fully egalitarian society he and others had hoped for in 1789, despite the loss of millions who had died to achieve and defend the revolution. The brave new constitution of 1793— imperfect, but a step in the right direction—had been suspended, permanently, as it turned out. Atheism, Maréchal's abiding conviction, had been declared an aristocratic vice by the 'incorruptible' Robespierre, and Robespierre himself was sent to the guillotine in 1794. Maréchal's friend, the radical lawyer François-Noël ("Gracchus") Babeuf, leader of a planned insurrection against the new bourgeois government, had been betrayed and executed in 1797. Through mere coincidence, Maréchal escaped arrest (Dommanget 1970, chap. 10), but it was clearly time to keep a low profile. The government had turned the revolutionary army, led by Napoleon, against a still more revolutionary urban working population whose needs and demands it refused to meet. Counter-revolutionary priests and aristocrats flocked back into France from their exile in England as earlier attempts to reform the Catholic Church were abandoned or reversed; even the once-despised Pope Pius VII was invited to preside over the coronation of the new Bonaparte monarch. Clearly, the revolution (as Napoleon had already proclaimed in 1797) was over.

In such a context, the two works that Maréchal published in 1801 represent a kind of farewell to the hopes and possibilities that had sustained him since young manhood. *Pour et contre la Bible* (*For and Against the Bible*) is a close reading of Hebrew and Christian scriptures from a critical-rationalistic perspective that combines literary, moral, and historical approaches in a massive critique of Judaeo-Christian tradition (see Chapter 9 in this collection). Having often written on specific institutional abuses, especially in his *Nouvelle légende dorée*, here Maréchal analyzes the foundational scriptural writings that he sees as responsible for every subsequent institutional and theological abuse. As he observes in his life of the Virgin Mary, without her acquiescence to the angelic annunciation, we might have had "no popes, no cardinals, no priests, no masses, no councils, no indulgences, no inquisitions, no crusades, no Saint Bartholomew's Day Massacre, no Carmelites, no little nuns"[3] (quoted in Delany 2012, 103). His biblical reading thus becomes a mordant message to

---

3 On August 24, 1572, the feast day of St. Bartholomew, Protestants in Paris were massacred by Catholics. Only in 1598 with the Edict of Nantes was freedom of worship allowed; this was revoked in 1685 until civil rights were restored over a century later during the Revolution. Carmelites were an order of nuns and mendicant friars, taking their name from Mt. Carmel in Palestine.

his countrymen in the new century just begun, a century from which he and many others had hoped much more but which now Maréchal sees as, dismayingly, little improvement on previous ones.

La femme abbé, published the same year, may be taken as something of a companion piece in a less academic vein. Although taking the more accessible form of an epistolary novella, it displays many of the same opinions both through its plot and through the opinions of the character of Timon (clearly named after the eponymous misanthrope of Shakespeare's play). Although Agatha has succeeded brilliantly in her disguised effort to be near the man she loves, eventually she feels compelled to confess and to reveal all, for she cannot proceed to the next step in the profession: that of full priesthood. She leaves the academy intending to drown herself in the nearby river, but instead loses her way and collapses in a cave. There she is found by Timon. Introduced late in the story, he becomes Agatha's caretaker during her last days hiding in the cave. Timon serves as something close to authorial *porte-parole*, for, like the author, he is bitterly anti-clerical, anti-religious, author of a book that brought him fame and trouble, and weighed down by blasted hopes for a society governed by reason and nature. Yet Timon is capable of the most delicate charitable gestures and perceptions in his relationship with the depressed Agatha, making her comfortable, attempting to cure her broken heart, offering her a new life with him in the new world across the Atlantic.

Timon lives, and Agatha dies, in a vast subterranean cave system, actually a disused quarry located south of Paris between the villages of Ivry and Vitry-sur-Seine, as the narrator specifies. Such quarries are common beneath and around Paris, some of them now used as chic underground restaurants, mushroom farms, bomb shelters, or wine cellars. From the late Middle Ages, these quarries were a source of limestone, clay, and gypsum used to build the edifices and streets of Paris; by the later eighteenth century, most of them were exhausted. Agatha stumbles across the entrance to Timon's cavern while wandering, shell-shocked and lost, in search of the River Seine, where she plans to end her life. Having at last revealed the secret of her sex, she has been expelled from the seminary by the priest she is obsessed with and whose private secretary she has become. This seminary, located near Paris and only two or three hours' walk from the above-named villages, possesses a country retreat where the seminarians often go for recreation, and where Agatha makes her fatal confession. There was such a seminary in the vicinity: the well-known Parisian seminary of Saint-Sulpice with its country house at the village of Issy, a major site of chalk quarries only a few miles southwest of central Paris. Once the royal pavilion of Queen Marguerite, it was later donated to the Sulpicians as a branch of their Paris house; its luxurious grounds and copses correspond well to the description Maréchal gives of the landscape surrounding the seminarians' outing and the disastrous final interview of Agatha and Saint-Almont.

This is an area that Maréchal knew well. Having lived in Paris his entire life, first in the center and then, after his marriage in 1792, in the more rural *faubourg* Saint-Marceau, he later retired to the rural village of Montrouge "*pour mieux voir le soleil*" (the better to see the sun: Fusil 1936, 271). This was close to the other sites mentioned above and itself the site of quarries used, from the fifteenth century on, for construction in Paris. Here Maréchal died of natural causes in the company of his wife, his good friend the writer Mme. Gacon-Dufour, and a few other close friends.

The geographical specificity of setting is not duplicated in temporal specificity. We are told by the fictional editor or publisher of the Agatha–Zoé correspondence that the action takes place "well before 1789" (quoted in Delany 2016, 3) but we are not told how long before. Saint-Almont's first Paris mass is said in Letter II to be an elaborate affair, with Miroir at the organ. Miroir was prominent as a Parisian organist from about 1780, skilled in "special effects, tonal contrasts ... and ways to arouse and gratify sensual instincts ... Miroir enjoyed a great reputation for that kind of wizardry" (Fétis 1856), so it is tempting to think that the events are not far removed from the author's lifetime; but other details suggest that he may have had an earlier period in mind.

•••

France's colonial empire figures prominently in Maréchal's novella, especially toward the end of the story. The intense correspondence between the two best friends Agatha and Zoé is interrupted when Zoé must accompany her husband to a post overseas, as she reports in Letter XV; thus the correspondence is replaced by Agatha's diary, which she addresses to the absent Zoé. In Letter XVII, Agatha refers to her friend's "departure for the islands", even though no destination was specified in Zoé's previous letter. These islands might be the French-dominated Antilles off the Americas, between Florida and Venezuela; or the archipelago colonies of Mauritius or Seychelles, both in the vicinity of Madagascar off the southeast coast of Africa.

This represents an inconsistency that Maréchal did not correct, for later we discover that the posting was to North America, which seems to have occupied a special place in Maréchal's imagination. Timon, having allowed affection for Agatha to overcome his anti-social tendencies, suggests to her "a happy future according to his principles": he proposes that they emigrate to form a little colony "in the forests of North America ... in the vicinity of the good Quakers". This would likely be Pennsylvania or Rhode Island, where Quakers established significant colonies, and could refer to any time after 1681, when William Penn received his land grant and Quakers began to emigrate to the British colonies. On returning to Paris, Zoé manages to locate her friend and attempts to administer to her—too late, as it turns out—a medicine made by Canadian "savages" and well known for its miraculous cures. At the very end, all of the other characters beside Agatha—Timon, the priest Saint-Almont, and Zoé with her husband—wind up in "Canada". This geographical designation (as distinct from "Acadia", "Newfoundland", or "Nova Scotia") was not the entire country of Canada as we know it today; rather, it was, and had been since the late sixteenth century, the northern part of New France, *"la nouvelle-France"*, the vast French colonial empire in North America extending from the Gulf of Mexico northward almost to Hudson Bay, and from the Appalachians westward nearly to the Rockies—roughly half the continent. However, the French empire in North America ended with their defeat at the Battle of Quebec (1759), also known as the Battle of the Plains of Abraham, and the subsequent Treaty of Paris (1763), which ceded control to the English. If we may assume that a French colonial administrator such as Zoé's husband would not be posted to an area under English control, then we may imagine the action taking place before this period.

The "Indian" population mentioned as targets of Saint-Almont's conversion efforts are the Iroquois, who were indigenous to this territory (as opposed, for instance, to the Mi'kmaq in the Acadia region). The Iroquois, a confederation of five and then, after 1722, six nations, had largely withdrawn from the St. Lawrence valley by the seventeenth century, driven out and replaced by the Algonquin (Champlain 1603, 22). Although the often-shifting loyalties and complex alliances among French, English, and numerous native nations of the period make dating difficult, it does appear that during the first half of the eighteenth century in the Lake Erie region and elsewhere, Iroquois were allies of the French (Eccles 1987, 81, 174–75). This may allow a general periodization of the novella's setting to a half century or somewhat more before date of publication.

We are told little about how or where the immigrants live in Canada; there is no mention of a city such as Quebec or Montreal; of church, school, or Jesuit seminary such as those long established there; or of social organization at any level. Saint-Almont abandons the priesthood and becomes tutor to Zoé's son (we hear nothing of other children). They might well live in Montreal or Quebec, where they would be able to enjoy a relatively pleasant and sophisticated urban life, with the husband perhaps in an administrative post befitting his previous colonial experience, perhaps as a wealthy land-owning *seigneur* owing fealty to a commercial fur-trading company. Or they might become *habitants*, freehold farmers, perhaps quite prosperous ones. Timon is adopted into an indigenous tribe, living and hunting with them in the state of nature to which he has long aspired. Adoption was not uncommon among the northeastern First Nations, especially with captives and the children of enemies; indeed, many *coureurs de bois* (fur hunters and traders) adapted to indigenous culture as their best means of survival in the wilderness, and many intermarried. Maréchal's point appears to be that the characters end up free and content, able to make of their lives more or less what they please in a place where nature has not yet been tamed or depleted by commerce.

How would Maréchal have learned about North America and, more especially, about Canada, France's former colony? Reading would be an obvious way. In his personal library of 354 items, catalogued for sale just after his death, we find *La vie de Guillaume Penn, fondateur de la Pennsylvanie* (*The Life of William Penn, Founder of Pennsylvannia*, 1791) and *Nouveau voyage dans l'Amérique septentrionale* (*New Voyage to Northern America*, 1781) by Abbé Robin, among numerous other travel accounts describing the Orient, Europe, and the Americas (Aubert 1975, 156–74). Popular novels might also have been a resource, particularly one by the well-known English writer Frances Brooke, whose novels were frequently translated and republished in France. This was not untypical for the period, which Lorraine McMullen claims "was a period of French Anglomania" (McMullen 1983, 64) during which hundreds of English novels were translated for an enthusiastic French audience. As Harold Wade Streeter points out, thousands of French Protestants had emigrated to England after revocation of the Edict of Nantes in 1685 and the consequent return of official religious intolerance. Many settled in London, where "they constituted themselves the interpreters to Europe of the great controversial English writers" (Streeter 1936, 11), and although these works may not have centered on novels, the project would have created the environment in which a taste for translated novels could thrive. McMullen's observation about anglomania occurs in her study of Frances Brooke, whose best-known epistolary work, *The History of Emily Montague* (1769), tells the story of several British colonials living in Quebec, including two young women friends of contrasting personalities. Brooke's detailed portrait of Canada, and the relationship between the two friends, might well have influenced Maréchal's novella.

A more personal connection was probably the Montréalais Jacques Grasset de Saint-Sauveur, whose five-volume *Encyclopédie des voyages* (1796) was on Maréchal's shelves. This author was also a friend and collaborator. Saint-Sauveur's father was an official in Montreal; the Canadian-born Saint-Sauveur became an artist and engraver in Paris. In that capacity he was one of several illustrators of the magnificent multi-volume *Costumes civils actuels de tous les peuples connus* (*Current Local Costumes of All Known Peoples*, 1788) to which Maréchal provided the text; volume four includes several pages on the Nootka of Canada's west coast, probably derived from Captain James Cook's account of his voyage to the Pacific northwest (see Mannucci 2012, chap. 5). Indeed, Saint-Sauveur seems a kindred spirit. Like Maréchal, he was a prolific writer in varied genres, with a philosophical, political, and erotic bent. Perhaps he related to Maréchal the *"très fantastique"* (Roy 1930, 147) story of Esther Brando or Brandeau, the Jewish girl from Bayonne who, disguised as a Christian boy, spent two years in Quebec until she was discovered and sent back to France in 1739 (see Varin 1738).

Why Canada for this happy ending rather than one of France's Caribbean or South American colonies? In refusing to offer a clear sketch of his characters' lives in Canada (whether under French or British rule) or a clear date for the narrative, Maréchal is able to draw on the quasi-utopian representations of early colonists, explorers, and missionaries such as Marc Lescarbot (1604–7, 1606), Chrestien Leclercq (1691), and Samuel de Champlain (1603), whose accounts were frequently reprinted and widely read from the moment of their publication down through the eighteenth century. Closer to his own day, reports from Canada made it clear that in many respects, the settlers were far better off than those working people who remained at home. They enjoyed minimal taxes, free land, none of the violent slums and grinding poverty of major French cities, no feudal remnants under which French peasants suffered until the Revolution ended them, a good social support network of hospitals and charities, little corruption, and some democratic institutions (see Eccles 1965 and 1968). Thus, the Canadian setting would enable the simpler, more wholesome life for his characters that would have been impossible in a place like Haiti (then known as Saint-Domingue) or any other sugar-or coffee-producing colony worked by African slaves, hence in a condition of severe immorality (as Maréchal would have seen it). Daily displays of horror in the treatment of slaves would have been part of his characters' experience, along with frequent slave revolts, rather than the healthful 'natural' life of Canada's indigenous. As editor of the prominent radical journal *Révolutions de Paris* between 1790 and 1794, Maréchal followed colonial events closely. Indeed, one of his associates at the journal, the admirable Sonthonax, as a colonial administrator in Haiti amidst the constant warfare there, was the first to abolish slavery in his corner of the empire, even before freedom and independence were won from the revolutionary government at home. Moreover, the indigenous Caribbean populations, the Taino and others, had been exterminated earlier on by Spanish colonists, so these territories lacked a substantial population of 'noble savages' to adopt Timon or to form alliances with immigrant families. The tropics also,

THE WOMAN PRIEST   143

of course, lacked a climate sufficiently similar to that of Europe to permit physical comfort; even the long, snowy Canadian winter, deplored by early writers, was more readily tolerable than suffocating tropical heat.

Is there a political point to the Canadian setting for the novella's end? Perhaps there is, if by sending his characters to a still-French North America Maréchal reminds his audience of what France had lost only a few decades earlier and was still losing. In 1801 and the several years preceding, terrible events were unfolding in France's Caribbean colonies as Toussaint Louverture led black armies in their battles for personal freedom and political independence. Emancipation of slavery in the colonies had been declared by the French National Assembly in 1794, but there was no easy transition and much resistance from planters, merchants, and conservatives. The fate of these colonies was high on the public agenda during these years both in France and abroad; American land-owners in particular feared Haitian emancipation as a threat to their own slave system and lucrative slave trade, as did the British in connection with Jamaica. In 1800, Napoleon Bonaparte—now consul and soon to be emperor—began the process, at first legal, then military, of rolling back the achievements and aspirations of Toussaint's revolution. Only near the end of 1803 did the Napoleonic army surrender to the new leader, Jean-Jacques Dessalines, of the country henceforth to be called Haiti. It is an ending Maréchal would have applauded had he survived another few months; perhaps the Canadian ending of his novella is a quiet allusion to the fragility of imperial ambition.

•••

Of course, the elephant in the room when discussing this text is the woman question in early revolutionary France. What positions did, and could, women occupy, and what were Maréchal's views on the matter? The issue was central to political discourse and public life of the day. A thorough discussion of the topic is beyond the scope of this discussion of Maréchal's novella, and it has generated an enormous bibliography. Yet it is important to observe that the novella presents a fundamental paradox with respect to this question. On one hand, the heroine displays an adventurous—even ambitious—spirit; she writes eloquently, teaches herself Latin, moves into an apartment of her own before gaining admission to seminary, fulfills her ecclesiastical duties outstandingly well, and succeeds in the rather difficult seminary curriculum well enough to be invited to proceed to full priesthood. On the other hand, she dies a stereotypically melodramatic death, of a 'broken heart' (or, as we might say, of anorexia, shame, and despair) in a cave, rejecting any opportunity to lead a fulfilling life whether as a single working woman like so many others, or as partner with Timon, or with someone she has not yet met. Her punishment is self-inflicted, true; yet as a consequence of her transgression she suffers and is punished. It will be up to the reader to decide whether these two representations of the heroine contradict one another.

Perhaps most telling in the characterization of Agatha is the contrast with her best friend, Zoé. Not only do their names begin with letters at opposite ends of the alphabet, as a kind of visual reminder of their opposed attitudes and psychologies, but the meanings of these names also, I suggest, play a role in the reader's response. This would be particularly the case for a French reader, for whom the Greco-Latin root of Zoé's name (meaning 'life') is a loving literary compliment to Maréchal's wife, an allusion to his beloved, long-lost classical era, and a constant reminder of life itself, hence nature, maternity, and all that promotes and protects life. By the same token, the name Agatha (in French, *Agathe*) sounds like the root of the verb *agacer*: to irritate, upset, or provoke. Moreover, Agatha was one of the early Christian virgin saints, martyred because of her religion; it might be said that Maréchal's Agatha is martyred by her religion as well, albeit in a very different way from that of the saint. Interestingly, the breast plays a central role in both stories: the saint's breasts are torn off and then miraculously grow back; the disguised girl is recognized as such by Timon when her breast is revealed through torn clothing—a moment commemorated in the single illustration to the novella. Hagiography—a genre with which Maréchal was of course deeply familiar, as a Catholic, a scholar, and a satirist—frequently opens a saint's life with a brief exposition of the meaning of his or her name, so the resonance of a name was ready at hand for Maréchal as a literary device. Lastly, at a time when many novelists used quasi-allegorical names for their characters, based on either meaning or sound, the two young women's names clearly help to produce the moral structure of the novella, a function borne out by the values the young women explicitly embrace in their correspondence. And, since authorial choices often have multiple causes, another possible influence might be an English novel, translated in 1797 as *Agatha, ou la religieuse anglaise* (*Agatha, or the English Nun*: Streeter 1936, 176). It portrays the conflict of love and religion, but unlike Maréchal's Agatha, the English one is "mistress of herself—of her reason—and triumphed over every propensity not warranted by the strictest duty".

Zoé constantly exhorts her friend to think things over, to be logical and rational, to accept reality and allow herself to be guided by Zoé's advice and example as a happily married homemaker. 'Prudence' is the term often used by and associated with Zoé. She reprimands Agatha for her lack of this virtue: that is, for her imprudence, a characteristic to which Agatha herself admits more than once. For Agatha, on the other hand, the constant theme is her heart, her desire, her 'sensitivity'. In French, the word is *sensibilité*, and it or its cognates occur several times throughout the story, predicated of Agatha and, in her letters, of Saint-Almont as well. But during the eighteenth century, this word did not have the positive valence that it does today in English, for at the time it was not necessarily a virtue. Rather than indicating perceptivity, keen awareness of others, or even fragility, it denoted a tendency to be unduly excited by or susceptible to physical phenomena and impressions, so that the word carried overtones of emotionality, even irrationality. We may think of Jane Austen's novel *Sense and Sensibility* (1811) as a fuller and much better-known novelistic exploration of the binary represented here by Zoé and Agatha.

At the same time, though, Agatha's character is far from simple. Talented and ambitious, resourceful and ruthlessly honest, she is restricted by the values of her culture, even though those values are only partially internalized. Is she a heroine or an anti-heroine? Again, this is the reader's decision.

Agatha is, of course, the fictional female creation of a male author, so it is interesting to observe that he foregoes many of the slanders and insults that some of his contemporaries might have leveled at a woman who dresses as a man—indeed, did level at the occasionally cross-dressing Olympe de Gouges or other women activists regardless of costume. At no time are we encouraged to think of Agatha as someone who is insane, who wants to be a man, who is lesbian, or who is confused about her sexuality; on the contrary, she is portrayed as all woman, all the time. She takes on a man's outfit for specific practical reasons: at first, to explore Paris easily and safely (a serious challenge at the time, as Arlette Farge's meticulous documentation shows [see Farge 1979]); then, to be near her beloved. Unlike the cross-dressed heroine of the thirteenth-century romance *Silence* (Heldris of Cornwall 1996), whose parents raise her as a boy to ensure her inheritance, Agatha is entirely autonomous. Her masquerade is her own decision, not that of parents, and it has nothing to do with inheritance, for she has inherited a comfortable sum from her grandmother. Nor, since she does not have to work for an income, is she in the same situation as the real-life cross-dressers whose stories were told in the eighteenth-century press and biographies or autobiographies, so she does not place herself in a dangerous or morally questionable situation. Her project is carefully planned and successfully executed. Indeed, the name she chooses for her life as a seminarian echoes that of her beloved. He is Saint-Almont; she becomes Sainte-Alba, a feminized version. That the names differ only in their last syllables is perhaps emblematic of authorial subversion of the character's intent (*mont* as a height, *ba* pronounced the same as *bas*, or *low*).

What can be said, though, is that paradoxical as Agatha's story may be, the pros and cons just noted do reflect not only Maréchal's attitude toward women but the mainstream attitude of the Revolution itself. Women worked; women led popular uprisings; women wrote, spoke, and demonstrated publicly, including in the National Assembly; they fought in the revolutionary army; yet they were denied full citizenship rights such as the vote and the right to hold public office, attendance at university, and so on. Full enfranchisement was a constant topic for debate over the years, supported by many men as well as women, but the famous 'rights of man' were not fully applied to women; indeed, it was only in 1946 that French women won the vote! Those who opposed full citizenship for women did so on the basis of what we would now call an essentialist view of 'feminine nature' or of 'Nature' herself, who, they thought, had designated women to the honorable roles of motherhood and wifehood, creator and manager of a happy household, teacher to new generations, fighter when necessary to defend the Revolution—but not suited to the rough-and-tumble of active political life. These are attitudes to which Maréchal subscribed. It is, in my view, the underlying problem in the plot of his novella and in the society from which it emanates.

I am reminded here of Fredric Jameson's description of a cultural artifact as "a symbolic act, whereby real social contradictions, insurmountable in their own terms, find a purely formal resolution in the aesthetic realm" (Jameson 1981, 79). A self-willed death and a far-off utopian colony are, in this case, aspects of "aesthetic or narrative form ... with the function of inventing imaginary or formal 'solutions' to unresolvable social contradictions" (Jameson 1981, 79). Yet if we return to the text by Claude Lévi-Strauss from which Jameson derived this idea, we find a somewhat differently angled perspective, perhaps somewhat less pessimistic. Discussing facial and body decorations in several Brazilian tribes, Lévi-Strauss writes:

> On the social level, the remedy [for resolving social contradictions among the Mbaya] was lacking ... but it never went completely out of their grasp. It was within them, never objectively formulated, but present as a source of confusion and disquiet. In fact, they dreamed of it ... present only in their art, it seemed harmless.
> LÉVI-STRAUSS 1955, 179

There is no mention of unresolvability or insurmountability, and one might infer from Lévi-Strauss's careful formulation that the issue of social resolvability is not absolute but relative, not a human lack but a social one.

•••

For me, the author's retreat from his daring premise doesn't detract from the pleasure of reading his skillfully written novella. What might have been the literary influences? Maréchal's personal library held a recent edition of *L'art épistolaire par Jaufret* (*The Art of Letter Writing, by Jaufret*, 1798), doubtless useful in the composition of an epistolary narrative. We infer, too, that Maréchal admired the epistolary novels of Samuel Richardson, whose name appears in the *Calendrier des républicains* (1793) for July 1, along with those of other English writers (e.g., Shakespeare, Milton, and Addison) for other dates. His *Almanach des honnêtes gens* displays a similar anglophilia, with listings for these and others such as Pope, Dryden, Prior, Gay, and Swift, and I have mentioned above the possible influence of Frances Brooke—all or most of these English writers known in translation, to judge by the contents of Maréchal's library.

Another layer of influence can be found, I suggest, in medieval literature. Through his years as an employee of the compendious Mazarin Library in Paris with its thousands of printed and manuscript volumes (see Molinier 1885–98),[4] Maréchal had access to a great deal of medieval material. He refers to some of this material in various works, particularly those modeled on, and revising, the traditional almanac or calendar, which would normally feature a saint for each day. Replacing the Catholic saints in Maréchal's version is a range of early-and late-medieval figures, both men and women. In the *Almanach des honnêtes gens* we find Héloïse (May 17); she reappears in the *Calendrier des républicains* under the same date. The *Almanach* has Czech reformer Jan Hus (July 16), Petrarch (July 18), the chronicler Jean Froissart (October 7), Abbé Suger (January 13), Mahomet (June 7 and in the *Calendrier*, same date). Dante appears in the *Calendrier* (November 27), as do the philosopher Roger Bacon (September 18) and John Wyclif "martyr" (December 29).

As with the fad for English novels from which Maréchal clearly benefited, medieval literature was also much in vogue, and its traces are visible in his novella. French medievalism emerged in the seventeenth and even sixteenth centuries with concerns about cultural patrimony that arose from civil wars, as well as international "competition for cultural hegemony in Europe" (Zezula 1987, 15); Nathan Edelman adds several further socio-political motives for the development of medieval studies (Edelman 1946, especially chap. 2). The *Roman de la rose* was edited as early as 1526 by the court poet Clément Marot;

---

4 Despite the title of Molinier's *Catalogue des manuscrits de la Bibliothèque Mazarine*, most of the items in his catalogue are not in manuscript form, and many are nearly contemporary with the compilation.

other editions, collections, and linguistic studies followed, with special interest in chivalry and court spectacle, queens, genealogy, epic, and romance heroes. During the seventeenth and eighteenth centuries, not only creative writers but academicians and scholars debated the meaning of the medieval, as Alicia Montoya (2013) shows. And throughout the eighteenth century there was, of course, the *bibliothèque bleue*, the library of blue paperbound modernized versions of medieval stories peddled around the country by itinerant booksellers; these acquainted much of the rural and urban population with the medieval literary heritage both religious and secular.

Most prominent in popularity was the correspondence between the twelfth-century ecclesiastical lovers and spouses Héloïse and Abelard. Their epistolary story, translated from Latin several times during the seventeenth and eighteenth centuries, generated selections, revisions, and even fabricated new letters (Cizewski 1987, 75). A modern translation found a place in Maréchal's library, and indeed it had influenced one of his heroes, Jean-Jacques Rousseau, for the latter's epistolary tale of a tutor and pupil who, like Abelard and Héloïse, fall in love: *Julie, ou la nouvelle Héloïse* (1761). Maréchal also owned a manuscript Book of Hours; an illustrated Boccaccio; a history of Joan of Arc and another of the fictive Pope Joan (another story of cross-dressing and ecclesiastical success!); several accounts of early French kingship and chivalry; general histories of France, England, Scotland, and other countries including Russia; a biography of Mahomet; and histories of the University of Paris, founded in the twelfth century, and the Sorbonne College, founded in the thirteenth (see Aubert 1975, 156–74).

How is this background, both personal and cultural, evident in *La femme abbé*? I've discussed above the influence of hagiography on some of Maréchal's choices in the representation of his protagonist, which are not surprising given his Catholic upbringing and education, as well as his decade-earlier publication of a satirical legendary, the *Nouvelle légende dorée* (1790). But other reminders of the medieval matrix surface throughout, and it is well to remember that the three dominant institutions of the Middle Ages—feudal law, monarchy, and the Catholic Church—lived on even after 1789; the first was finished within a few years, the second in a few decades, the last is still with us. If we read through Maréchal's novella with a medievalist's eye, we spot a number of familiar medieval motifs.

In Letter XVIII, Agatha writes that she is torn between two desires: Zoé's image, like that of a good angel, is at her right, while an evil spirit seems to be at her left. This ancient topos, the *psychomachia* (battle of/for the soul) goes back to early Christian personification allegory. Its later manifestations appear in Romanesque church architecture as well as late medieval and renaissance morality plays, most memorably for English drama in Marlowe's *Faust* (1592). In early French moralities, the prototype is likely the twelfth-century "*Jeu d'Adam*" (play of Adam) with its arguments by *Figura* (image of God) and *Diabolus* (Satan) for influence over Adam. Further on in the same letter, Agatha writes that her heart and imagination are allied against her reason. Again, this image of psychic warfare partakes of the allegorical morality-play tradition as well as that of personification allegory best represented in the great thirteenth-century allegory of love, the *Roman de la rose* with its externalized and embodied psychic faculties of both the lover and his lady. In Letter XXI, Agatha notes that most people believe that leisure (*oisivité*) is the cradle of love. Here the allusion is to Oiseuse, an important character in the *Roman de la rose*. Later, in the quarry when Timon offers her a new life in North America, Agatha replies: "A doe that carries in her flank the spear with which she's been wounded, can go no further" (Delany 2016, 54). Marie de France's *lai* "Guigemar", probably composed in the late twelfth century, features a mortally wounded speaking doe. (Oddly, this female deer is also a cross-dresser as it were, her head carrying a stag's antlers.) Both Marie and Sylvain might have had in mind an even earlier wounded doe, the one that Dido compares herself to in *Aeneid* 4:69–72, although in both earlier instances the weapon is an arrow, not a spear. In Letter XXII, Agatha justifies her profanation of sacred things by asserting the purity of her intentions; this may allude to the Abelardian theory of intentionalist ethics.

Perhaps most telling of the medieval matrix, though, is the eroticism that Agatha disguises or expresses as religious fervor and on account of which she undertakes her short-lived ecclesiastical career. The nexus can doubtless be traced to late-Jewish and early-medieval allegorization of the explicitly sensual biblical Song of Songs as a devotional hymn. This exegetical tradition continued down the Middle Ages in religious lyric, sermon, and prayer depicting or addressing Jesus as bridegroom or lover, the Church or the worshiper as bride, suitor, or beloved. Not least important in this tradition are the numerous Bible commentaries by French scholars of the previous two centuries that Maréchal consulted for his own thorough study of Hebrew and Christian scripture, *Pour et contre la Bible*, published the same year as the novella. The writing of French and English medieval women visionaries gives ample attention to this trope. Among writers known for it, whom we know Maréchal read, and whose names appear in his various *almanachs*, we may cite Dante and Petrarch, particularly Dante's *La vita nuova* and Petrarch's *Canzoniere*. Indeed, Agatha implements the program of much Italian lyric poetry: the beloved as adored saint and source of salvation, Eros as new deity, the practice of erotic desire as pilgrimage or ritual of worship, importuning as prayer, etc. Maréchal had already, in his satirical legendary, expressed the view that many women become nuns or practice intense lay devotion from non-religious motives, whether to escape the burdens of housework and childbearing, like the blessed Raingarde; to pursue a lesbian friendship (e.g., Saint Guiborat or Saints Sabina and Serapia); to indulge a taste for sadomasochistic 'discipline' (Saints Delphire and Elzear, Saint Catherine of Sweden); or to develop an especially close and sexualized relationship with a spiritual advisor, such as that between Jeanne Frémiot de Chantal and her spiritual director, Francis de Sales. Maréchal's effort to foreground the erotic subtext of some hagiographical writing is particularly noticeable in his version of the life of Saint Genevieve, patron saint of the city of Paris (see Chapter 7 in this collection).

Given his broad literary background, and his youthful experience in Parisian salon culture, it is no surprise that Maréchal is able to portray with considerable art and insight the progress of a sheltered young woman's rapid slide into obsession. Although it is clear where his moral convictions ultimately lie, the author refuses to turn his characters—even the doting grandmother, even the unhappy priest—into mere caricatures. Only Zoé, who bears his wife's pet name, remains, as Agatha admits, all good. The author's earlier success as a playwright is surely echoed in the tense emotionality of Agatha's terse dialogues with Saint-Almont, creating suspense as to whether and when she will be discovered. The complex personality of Timon, with whom the author shares opinions and some personal history, emerges with all the contradiction of a real individual, as do the rationalizations Agatha produces to justify herself as a good Catholic despite her real blasphemies, which go well beyond the "imprudence" to which she confesses. I hope that others will enjoy the story as much as I have done.[5]

References

Attenberg, Jami. 2015. "Track Changes". *New York Times Sunday Magazine*, January 25, 2015, 54.

Aubert, Françoise. 1975. *Sylvain Maréchal: Passion et faillite d'un égalitaire*. Pisa: Goliardica; Paris: Nizet.

Bouvier, Jeanne. 1931. *Les femmes pendant la Révolution*. Paris: Figuère.

---

5 This chapter is a revised version of the introduction to *The Woman Priest: A Translation of Sylvain Maréchal's Novella*, La Femme Abbé, translated by Sheila Delany. Edmonton: University of Alberta Press, 2016, ix–xxxii.

Champlain, Samuel. [1603] 1993. *Des sauvages*, edited by Alain Beaulieu and Réal Ouellet. Montreal: Typo.

Cizewski, Wanda. 1987. "From Historia Calamitatum to Amours et infortunes". In Heather, Arden, ed. 1987. *Medievalism in France, 1500–1750*. Special issue of *Studies in Medievalism* 3, 71–76.

Cordingly, David. 2001. *Women Sailors and Sailors' Women: an Untold Maritime History*. New York: Random House.

Dekker, Rudolf M., and Lotte C. van de Pol. 1989. *The Tradition of Female Transvestism in Early Modern Europe*. New York: Palgrave Macmillan.

Delany, Sheila. 1981. "Flore et Jehane: A Case Study of the Bourgeois Woman in Medieval Life and Letters". In *Science & Society* 45. Reprinted 1983 in *Writing Woman: Women Writers and Women in Literature, Medieval to Modern*, 22–35. New York: Schocken Books.

Delany, Sheila, trans. 2012. *Anti-Saints: the New Golden Legend of Sylvain Maréchal*. Edmonton: University of Alberta Press.

Delany, Sheila. 2016. *The Woman Priest. A Translation of Sylvain Maréchal's La Femme Abbé*. Edmonton: University of Alberta Press.

Dietzman, Sara Jane. 2005. "En guize d'omme: Female Cross-Dressing and Gender Reversal in Four Medieval French Texts". PhD. diss., University of Virginia.

Dommanget, Maurice. 1970. *Sur Babeuf et la conjuration des égaux*. Paris: Maspero.

Douthwaite, Julia. 2012. *The Frankenstein of 1790 and Other Lost Chapters from Revolutionary France*. Chicago: University of Chicago Press.

Eccles, W.J. 1968. *Canadian Society During the French Regime*. Montreal: Harvest House.

Eccles, W.J. 1987. *Essays on New France*. Toronto: Oxford University Press.

Eccles, W.J. 1965. *The Government of New France*. Ottawa: Canadian Historical Society.

Edelman, Nathan. 1946. *Attitudes of Seventeenth-Century France toward the Middle Ages*. New York: King's Crown Press.

Farge, Arlette. 1979. *Vivre dans la rue à Paris au XVIIIe siècle*. Paris: Gallimard.

Fétis, F.-J. 1856. "L'orgue mondaine et la musique érotique à l'église". *Revue et gazette musicale*, April 6.

Friedli, Lynne. 1987. "'Passing Women': A Study of Gender Boundaries in the Eighteenth Century". In *Sexual Underworlds of the Enlightenment*, edited by G.S. Rousseau and Roy Porter, 234–60. Manchester: Manchester University Press.

Fusil, Charles. 1936. *Sylvain Maréchal, ou l'homme sans Dieu*. Paris: Librairie Plon.

Gelbart, Nina Rattner. 1987. *Feminine and Opposition Journalism in Old Regime France: "Le journal des dames"*. Berkeley: University of California Press.

Heldris of Cornwall. 1992. *Silence: a Thirteenth-Century French Romance*, translated and edited by Sarah Roche-Mahdi. East Lansing, MI: Colleagues Press.

Jacob, Eliane, ed. 1972. *"Le conte du roi Flore et la belle Jehane"*. PhD diss., University of Strasbourg.

Jameson, Fredric. 1981. *The Political Unconscious: Narrative as a Socially Symbolic Act*. Ithaca: Cornell University Press.

Lang, Sabine. 1998. *Men as Women, Women as Men: Changing Gender in Native American Cultures*. Austin: University of Texas.

Leclercq, Chrestien. [1691] 1999. *Nouvelle relation de la Gaspésie*, edited by Réal Ouellet. Montreal: Presses de l'Université de Montréal.

Lescarbot, Marc. [1606] 2006. *Spectacle of Empire: Marc Lescarbot's Theatre of Neptune in New France*. Edited by Jerry Wasserman. Vancouver: Talonbooks.

Lescarbot, Marc. [1604–1607] 2007. *Voyages en Acadie, suivis de la description des mœurs souriquoises comparées à celles d'autres peuples*, edited by Marie-Chrisine Pioffet. Quebec City: Presses de l'Université Laval.

Lévi-Strauss, Claude. [1955] 1967. *Tristes Tropiques: An Anthropological Study of Primitive Societies in Brazil*, translated by John Russell. New York: Atheneum.

Lobdell, Bambi. 2012. *A Strange Sort of Being: the Transgender Life of Lucy Ann/Joseph Israel Lobdell*. Jefferson, NC: McFarland.

Mannucci, Erica Joy. 2012. *Finalmente il popolo pensa: Sylvain Maréchal nell'immagine della Rivoluzione francese*. Naples: Guida.

Maréchal, Sylvain. 1788. *L'Almanach des honnêtes gens, l'an du premier regne de la raison, pour la présente année*. [Paris].

Maréchal, Sylvain. 1793. *Calendrier des républicains*. Paris: Gueffier.

Maréchal, Sylvain. 1793. *Le jugement dernier des rois*. Paris: C.-F. Patris.

Maréchal, Sylvain. 1788. *Costumes civils actuels de tous les peoples connus*. 3 vols. Paris: Pavand.

Maréchal, Sylvain. 1790. *Nouvelle légende dorée, ou Dictionnaire des saintes*. 2 vols. Rome [Paris].

Maréchal, Sylvain. 1801. *Pour et contre la Bible*. Jerusalem [Paris].

McMullen, Lorraine. 1983. *An Odd Attempt in a Woman: the Literary Life of Frances Brooke*. Vancouver: University of British Columbia Press.

Moland, Louis and Charles d'Héricault, eds. 1856. *Nouvelles françoises en prose du XIIIe siècle*. Paris: P. Jaunet.

Molinier, Auguste, ed. 1885–98. *Catalogue des manuscrits de la Bibliothèque Mazarine*. 4 vols. Paris: Plon.

Montoya, Alicia C. 2013. *Medievalist Enlightenment from Charles Perrault to Jean-Jacques Rousseau*. Cambridge: D. S. Brewer.

Nordberg, Jenny. 2014. *The Underground Girls of Kabul: In Search of a Hidden Resistance in Afghanistan*. New York: Crown Publishers.

Roscoe, Will. 1998. *Changing Ones: Third and Fourth Genders in Native North America*. New York: St. Martin's Press.

Roy, Pierre-Georges. 1930. "La demoiselle Esther Brandeau à Québec". In *La ville de Québec sous le régime français*, vol. 2, 147–48. 2 vols. Quebec City: Service des Archives du Gouvernement de la province de Québec.

Saint-Sauveur, Jacques. 1796. *Encyclopédie des voyages*. Paris: Lescoure et Labotière.

Stark, Suzanne J. 1996. *Female Tars: Women Aboard Ship in the Age of Sail*. Annapolis: Naval Institute Press.

Streeter, Harold Wade. 1936. *The Eighteenth-Century English Novel in French Translation: a Bibliographical Study*. New York: Institute of French Studies.

Varin de la Marre. [1738] 2012. "Report from Varin de la Marre to the Authorities in France, September 15, 1738". In *The Tale-Teller*, by Susan Glickman, 213–15. Markham, ON: Cormorant Books.

Wheelwright, Julie. 1989. *Amazons and Military Maids: Women Who Dressed as Men in Pursuit of Life, Liberty and Happiness*. London: Pandora.

Wikan, Unni. 1982. *Behind the Veil in Arabia: Women in Oman*. Baltimore: Johns Hopkins University Press.

Yalom, Marilyn. 1993. *Blood Sisters: The French Revolution in Women's Memory*. New York: Basic Books.

Zezula, Jindrich. 1987. "Scholarly Medievalism in Renaissance France". In Heather Arden, ed. 1987. *Medievalism in France, 1500–1750*. Special issue of *Studies in Medievalism* 3, 10–20.

CHAPTER 9

An Atheist Reads the Bible in Revolutionary France

On February 23, 2017, American Vice-President Mike Pence spoke passionately and reverentially about the Bible on which he had been sworn into office a month before, for it was the very same Bible on which, in January 1981, the 40th president of the United States, Ronald Reagan, had also been sworn in and, in Pence's words, had "actually used"; indeed, Pence claimed to have uncannily opened that Bible at the very same verse to which Reagan had opened it.[1] The book had acquired an aura. It had become what a medieval priest, or a medievalist nowadays, might think of as a relic: an object touched by a holy person and which therefore confers special healing power—or, in this case, prestige, an aspect of political power—on whoever touches it next.

This is exactly the sort of religious fetishism Sylvain Maréchal despised. He denounced it in much of his writing throughout his life, and especially in *Pour et contre la Bible* (*For and Against the Bible*, 1801), his lengthy commentary on Jewish and Christian scriptures. The title suggests an even-handed approach to this monumentally influential text, or set of texts. But such balance is not quite the case, for although Maréchal took pains to praise the literary beauties and spiritual profundity of some scriptural writing, his real theme is "*contre*": to demonstrate that this book stands at the origin of age-old oppressive and destructive practices as their theological justification and practical example; that it should no longer be read, much less venerated; that, far from being 'the good book', it is a harmful book. Maréchal was no mere skeptic but claimed with pride the title of atheist; he didn't merely doubt, he denied.

The title alone is provocative enough—for and against the Bible—in a society for which, on the whole, there ought to be no 'against' in this case. We need to remind ourselves that there was as yet no Darwin, and the notion of the extinction of species was only just being hypothesized by Cuvier on the basis of gigantic skeletons discovered in several distant lands. For a medievalist, Maréchal's title recalls the equally provocative *Sic et non* (*Yes and No*) of

---

1 Although Pence didn't cite the verse, it was 2 Chronicles 7:::14; nor did he cite it quite accurately, and he managed to transmute it into a preface to the American Pledge of Allegiance (as revised in 1954 to include the phrase "under God"). The speech was given at the Conservative Political Action Conference in National Harbor, Maryland. Alter documents "this American biblicizing impulse ... the pervasiveness of the Bible in American culture from the colonial period onward" (Alter 2010, 1).

Peter Abelard, whose work Maréchal acknowledged in his own *Dictionnaire des athées anciens et modernes* (*Dictionary of Ancient and Modern Atheists*, 1800); indeed, Abelard takes pride of place as first entry in this alphabetical collection.[2] The great twelfth-century philosopher and teacher presented contradictory opinions by Christian *auctores* on various theological questions, showing how they might be argued in dialectical logic and suggesting methods of possible resolution. Maréchal owned a copy of a French translation of the letters Abelard exchanged with his wife, the nun Héloïse; the philosophical tracts were available at the Mazarin Library, where Maréchal worked for several years as a young man. But Sylvain had already used, or seen, this meme in the 1794 *Fable de Christ dévoilée* (*A Fable About Christ Revealed*), a fictional letter presenting an imaginary history of how certain priests invented the Bible, Judaism, and Christianity, an effort for which they required *"le pour et le contre"* (Maréchal 1794, 44, 47) in order to appear authentic. Clearly it was a common phrase both before and after Maréchal used it,[3] albeit not about the Bible.

Living as an atheist in a predominantly believing culture, Maréchal confronted some of the very issues we do now. For some of us, the Bible guides behavior: no work on Saturdays, honor your parents, avoid and denounce homosexuality, tell the truth, pay your taxes, etc. Others take the Bible as a portrait of historical reality a few thousand years ago when dinosaurs, human beings and every other life form were made *ex nihilo*, out of nothing, in a magical moment of creation. For most scholars it is a literary anthology compiled by various hands over a period of several centuries, reflecting evolving social forms and political events. Maréchal's Bible commentary, despite its two-sided title, is not motivated by a desire to bridge such gaps, for his hatred of all organized religion and of theology itself remained steady and intact throughout his life. Nonetheless it can speak to both sides of the divide: to atheists

---

2 This is not to say that Abelard, or indeed most of the figures populating Maréchal's *Dictionnaire des athées*, were actually atheists. Maréchal spread his net extremely wide, to include skeptics, deists, rationalists, heretics, and doubters of any kind from every historical period, including his own. Some cannot have been pleased, in this oppressive environment, to find themselves included; indeed, Kors (1976, 297) writes that the inclusion of Naigeon prevented the latter's appointment to important positions. The low-set bar was, however, normal throughout the previous two centuries' discourse in theology and morality (Febvre 1982; Kors 1990). The *Dictionnaire* had a *succès de scandale* upon publication and was reprinted twice during the nineteenth century (Karmin 1911, 439).

3 A London literary journal (1733–40) was published by the Abbé Prévost under the title *Le pour et contre*, and a polemical correspondence between Diderot and the sculptor Falconet, from 1766–7, was published under the title *Le pour et le contre*, but not during Maréchal's lifetime (Benot 1958, 37–38). Authorship of the *Fable* is uncertain.

confirming their rejection of dogma, clergy, and what Richard Dawkins calls "the God delusion" (Dawkins 2006); and to believers in affirming the (intermittent) poetic value, literary skill, and occasional moral sublimity of Jewish and Christian scriptures.

Maréchal was a prolific author in many genres: poetry, journalism, drama, treatise, novella. *Pour et contre* is unique in his œuvre in that it is not a primary original work like the others, but an extended commentary on another text known to Maréchal only in translation. And this not only in one translation but many, for the Bible came down to Maréchal, as it comes to us, as a palimpsest incorporating layers and layers, translations of translations reflecting different cultures, histories, and religions. Some versions try to be faithful to a source while others consciously revise according to current taste or doctrine. Maréchal had several versions of biblical material at his disposal. There were individual books of scripture such as Psalms; dramatic or poetic treatments of specific episodes or figures such as Susanna, Judith, and Esther; along with the entire corpus. Any of these sources might display a Catholic or a Protestant scholarship in its translation into current French, with greater or less fidelity, the earlier French or the Latin of its source. Generally, the Latin source would be St. Jerome's Vulgate, which in turn translated earlier Greek material which relied on Hebrew or Aramaic sources. When working with biblical material, then, one might replace Umberto Eco's image of "translation as negotiation" (Eco 2003) with "translation as *mise-en-abîme*".

A major difference that readers might note between their own Bible and another is the order of texts and texts included. This is largely because of the Apocrypha: texts whose divine inspiration has been doubted and debated down the ages at various religious councils. The Apocrypha are usually considered canonical by the Roman Catholic Church and therefore included in and as scripture. Most Protestant or Jewish authorities have not agreed, so in their Bibles the Apocrypha will be excluded or attached in an appendix as useful, historical, but not of equal authority to canonized scripture. That said, there are many more texts—other gospels, other apocalypses, other letters, other mystical treatises—that have not qualified as official (see Barnstone 1984) but that can considerably enhance the reader's appreciation of religious life and belief before, during, and after the life of the literary figure we refer to as Jesus.

This layering of biblical translations is something that Maréchal himself clearly found frustrating, as he makes clear both in his commentary and in the handwritten marginalia in his personal Bible, held at the International Institute for Social History in Amsterdam. Often, he is contemptuous of a translator's lack of fidelity to Latin biblical language, whether because of the translator's prudishness or his fear of offending contemporary sensibilities with a crude but striking biblical metaphor. In other cases, the French translator may interpret a terse Latin phrase rather than giving an exact literal equivalent. In Ecclesiastes, for instance, where the Latin reads "*laudavi magis mortuos quam viventes*" (I have praised the dead more than the living), the French translator writes the French equivalent of "I have said that it is better to be dead than to live", bringing the sentiment down to a more prosaic level.

"'What are the two major inventions of French and British culture?' 'Where France is concerned: the language of the eighteenth century, and soft cheese.'" Muriel Barbery's endorsement—or that of her narrator and heroine, the discerning concierge Renée—of the linguistic "invention" is well supported in Maréchal's work (Barbery 2008, 266). Although not a premier stylist of the age, his writing displays a command of rhetoric not surprising in a former law student; this is coupled with a passionate—and, as we will see, sometimes disconcerting—flow of ideas and language, allowing a glimpse into the culture at large and the depth of his own personality.

• • •

Maréchal was distinctive in his day, but neither unique nor as thoroughly radical in his views as others. Atheism had long been an issue in France and elsewhere: the great dramatist Molière was accused of it; well-known writers hypothesized about its origins or debated the possibility of a virtuous atheist. During and after the seventeenth century, the Church carried on a constant struggle against atheism—albeit broadly defined—with the paradoxical result, according to Kors, that it had to raise arguments in order to refute them, thus serving as a source or conduit for the very arguments it hoped to defeat (Kors 1990, 79). Some of Maréchal's friends and collaborators were atheists, among them the eminent astronomer Jérôme Lalande, the scholar Jacques-André Naigeon, the rebel aristocrat and utopian scholar Pierre Antoine Antonelle—Maréchal's co-member in a Parisian club during 1799 (Serna 1997, 416)—and others less well known (see Dommanget 1950, 383). Another class traitor, the revolutionary Marquis de Sade, renounced his title to become a leader in a section of the Paris Commune; his 1795 novel *La philosophie dans le boudoir* (*Philosophy in the Bedroom*) incorporates a passionate defense of atheism. King Frederick of Prussia was known to be an atheist. One acquaintance, the physiocrat Fréville, debated with priests in cafés, like a "public professor of atheism" (Mannucci 2012, 52 n51). Maréchal knew the work of other free-thinking contemporaries such as the scholarly atheist and best-selling author Baron d'Holbach (Darnton 1995, 194–96), whose biweekly salon has been described as an "enormous and clandestine atheism factory" (Curran

2019, 235); the Prussian-born atheist and political writer J.-B. "Anacharsis" Cloots, *"millionaire et sans-culotte, baron et jacobin"* (Mortier 1995, 13); British-American radical Thomas Paine, elected to the National Assembly in 1792 and author of *The Age of Reason*. Maréchal may have known some of these luminaries in person: Cloots notes in 1790 that he dined every Saturday with M. de Lalande amidst *"une société choisi"* (Mortier 1995, 255); the famous astronomer was one of Sylvain's closest friends and collaborators, so it is not impossible that Sylvain might have been among that chosen group. Much of this pathbreaking work was inspired by even earlier writing: the deistic philosophy of the rationalist Dutch Jewish scholar Benedict Spinoza (1632–1677), the work of encyclopedist Denis Diderot, and the posthumously discovered "Testament" of the atheist priest Jean Meslier, the latter two earlier in the eighteenth century.

Most of these figures, admired by Maréchal, appear in his *Dictionnaire des athées* and other of his writings.[4] Many of these men (and some women) met regularly to discuss their ideas on the arts, religion, science, and politics, frequently with distinguished guests from England or Italy. As a young man, Maréchal participated in similar if less-exalted groups, whether artistic salon or masonic lodge, as Mannucci shows in her magisterial cultural biography (Mannucci 2012). Besides other factors cited above, the study of classical authors would disseminate materialist and skeptical views from the much-admired ancient world; Maréchal styled himself *"le Lucrèce français"* in an early work by that title, after the Roman materialist poet Lucretius. There was, in short, a thriving intellectual milieu—what Mortier dubs "the anti-Christian front" (*"le front antichrétien"*: Mortier 1990, 361)—of rationalistic skepticism, doubt, and (at its extreme) atheism which nurtured Sylvain's development. Much of this material, to be sure, was illegal or simply displeasing to one or another authority, hence printed outside of Paris or abroad, under false author or publishers' names, or false, even fictitious, place names (see Brunet 1866). Sometimes a book of offensively unorthodox character might be condemned by Parlement to be publicly torn and burnt, as was the fate, in 1788, of Maréchal's own *Almanach des honnêtes gens* (*Almanac of Upright People*) . Yet as Maréchal testified in the journal he edited—the well-known *Révolutions de Paris* (#212)—this only increased the prestige and price of the work, corroborating Diderot's observation that the more severe the proscription, the higher the price of the book and the more it is bought and read; the sentencing of a book causes joy among print workers and booksellers (Darnton 1991, 13).

---

4 Antonelle, Sade, and Paine are not in the *Dictionnaire*, although Paine appears in the *Calendrier des républicains* (1793) for September 27.

In a similar vein, there existed a broad current of critical biblical scholarship from the late seventeenth century onward, produced by Catholics, Protestants, and Jews, clergy and lay, in several European countries. Some of this material was generated by 'the Jewish question' regarding legal rights and enfranchisement for Jews, some by the desire and need of Christian theologians to understand their own origins and guiding texts. Again, it is Spinoza whose writing on the Bible generated much of this stream of scholarship, both pro and con; in France, Richard Simon (1638–1712) initiated rationalistic Bible scholarship. Voltaire wrote extensively on the Bible in many formats—essay, letter, pamphlet, treatise, book—with a lifelong interest that has been called "compulsive" (Schwarzbach 1971, 7) and "obsessive" (Hertzberg 1970, 285). So did Diderot, Holbach, and numerous others. In short, demystification of the sacred text was well under way by the time Maréchal took up the subject. As a well-educated Parisian—in fact a law student—and as an employee at the prestigious Mazarin Library for several years, he would have access to much of this material and to a field already well established.

But beside books, there was reality. The Revolution was never, on the whole, atheistic, despite its enemies' propagandistic efforts to portray it so; its aim was to reform, not to abolish, the extremely corrupt Catholic Church. As Vovelle observes: "If the Assembly refused on 13 April 1790 ... the demand ... that Catholicism should be declared the national religion, it did so on the grounds that 'the devotion of the National Assembly to the Catholic, Apostolic and Roman cult was never in question'" (Vovelle 1991, 13). Similarly, it did not begin as anti-royalist; the revolutionists' aim was to create a constitutional monarchy along British lines. Eventually, treasonous acts by Louis XVI and Marie Antoinette ended this possibility and led to their execution in 1793. A rich and longstanding tradition of anti-clerical writing by clergy and layfolk, some of it extending back to the Middle Ages, at last bore fruit in a series of decrees from the National Assembly—many of whose deputies, we need to remember, were clergy: this was the old 'first estate'. The new laws of 1790–93—exhaustively detailed by Latreille (1946)—included appropriation and sale of Church properties, and a requirement for clergy to swear loyalty to the new constitution rather than to the Vatican. Many did—perhaps half (Tackett 1986, 40–43); indeed, some renounced their ecclesiastical positions and went on to marry. Those who refused—the 'refractories'—went into hiding or into exile in England or North America. Anti-clericalism deepened into the short-lived 'dechristianization' campaign of 1793, during which the cult of Reason was introduced as a substitute for revealed religion, bells and other metal objects were taken to be melted down for the war effort, and Notre Dame Cathedral was transformed into the Temple of Reason, as were other churches across the country.

What a shock it must have been, then, when in May, 1794, after several years of anti-clerical legislation and anti-religious demonstrations across the country, Maximilien Robespierre, de facto leader of the revolutionary government, declared atheism an immoral aristocratic offense, punishable by imprisonment. Suddenly, admiration for the goddess Reason was replaced by reverence for a 'Supreme Being'. Motivated by political calculation—to avoid offending France's few allies, and to control a population, portions of which were demanding ever more radical reforms—Robespierre ordered massive new festivals and new holidays enshrining a new religion.

The Catholic Church, immensely wealthy and corrupt, once profoundly critiqued and punished for its sins in the early days of the French Revolution, made its comeback only a few years later. Already during the post-Robespierre Thermidorean reaction of 1794–95, churches began to reopen, and royalist priests began to return from exile in England. Working peoples' insurrections were brutally put down; the hall of government itself became, in the dramatic words of the great historian Albert Mathiez, "a place of trafficking ... an open sewer" (Mathiez 1929, 5). Laws were passed against women's activity, against popular sovereignty and political transparency. During these years, the aim of reversing the revolution was explicit among those who governed, and, as Luzzato writes, the police acted not only against the guilty but against anyone who, because of their past, their convictions or their experience, could, if need be, be guilty (Luzzato 2001, 338). In the words of a popular song of the day: "*Mais l'homme sage / dans son ménage / verse des pleurs / sur toutes tes horreurs*" (But the decent person in his household pours out tears at all your horrors: quoted in Woloch 1970, 360 n24). One can imagine Sylvain doing exactly this. And worse was coming.

Napoleon Bonaparte, commander of the French army abroad, returned from his Egyptian campaign in October 1799; the following month, he established himself as consul in a coup. Mass repatriation of *émigré* clergy and nobility continued, with restoration of their expropriated property, and works of Catholic propaganda were published and widely read. There was press censorship, government control of the arts, reversal of revolutionary laws on freedom of divorce and other family matters, preventive detention for those suspected of anti-government sentiments, police spies everywhere. The revolutionary title "Citizen" was banned (Schom 1997, 195, 291–92). There was a climate of fear for many, decadence for others. In 1801, Napoleon concluded an agreement or concordat with the once-reviled Vatican, and when he crowned himself emperor in late 1804, Pope Pius VII himself was invited to officiate.

Maréchal, who died in 1803, did not live to see this atrocity, but it culminated a process that he determined to intervene in as best he could, to remind French society of what it had accomplished only a decade before, and what remained to be done. *Pour et contre* was that intervention, recognized as such by both friends and enemies. It was not the only one, for others produced anti-religious or anti-biblical satires (see Mannucci 2012, 270ff.), while Maréchal expressed his views in other genres such as the *Dictionnaire des athées* mentioned above; in a charming but incisive epistolary novella in 1801, *La femme abbé* (*The Woman Priest*: see Chapter 8 in this collection); and in a history of Russia (1802) which enabled him to attack tyrants and their enablers. Yet here, in his Bible commentary, he expressed the depth of his bitterness and disillusion, his dismay that the new century must begin with such a defeat for liberty and equality. Nearly a decade earlier, Sade had inserted into *Philosophy in the Bedroom* a passionate exhortation to his countrymen to continue the revolution, to press rationality to its logical atheistic conclusion, to abolish capital punishment, liberate women, socialize family duties and childcare: "Yet another effort, Frenchmen, if you would be republicans" is its title (Sade 1795, 235–81). In those days, Maréchal too hoped and worked for that further effort to create what he called "that finer, grander, revolution" that would create an egalitarian society. But by 1801 he knew that this was not going to happen, for the Revolution, as Napoleon had already proclaimed, was over; its best potential leader, Maréchal's friend Babeuf, had been executed in 1797, his arrest having evoked Sylvain's most powerfully heartfelt piece of writing, "*L'Opinion d'un homme*" (*A/One Man's Opinion*, 1796) . Writing against priests and saints had not stanched the religious flood; now he must turn to the source of it all, the basis of everything wrong with the culture—its irrationality, its corruption, its authoritarianism—in a last gesture of despair and defiance.

• • •

"How odd a thing is the Bible!" observes Sylvain in his mock legendary, after a sardonic one-sentence comment on the story of Judith. How, then, does Sylvain read the Bible in his commentary on that originary text, the basis of the religion in which he and everyone he knew were raised? And what Bible did he read? His main French source, as acknowledged in the chapter on Genesis, was that of Isaac-Louis Le Maistre de Sacy (1613–1684), a priest and scholar associated with the Augustinian reform movement centered at the abbey of Port-Royal in Paris. Though not the only French translation (see Legoupil 2011), this became the standard Bible of Catholic France once its Old Testament books came out between 1672 and 1695; to this was joined a New Testament by another writer of similar doctrinal persuasion. It was often reprinted in whole or in part, with thirty-four editions in the course of the eighteenth century (Desroussilles 1986, 81); Maréchal owned a 1717 edition.[5] Yet although Sauvy observes that Sacy's translation was renowned for the clarity and beauty of its language (Sauvy 1986, 33), Maréchal is less enthusiastic than many of his compatriots, remarking that while *"fort estimable ... elle laisse beaucoup à désirer"* (quite good ... it leaves a lot to be desired:; Delany 2020,7), and throughout his commentary Maréchal doesn't spare Sacy the criticism and correction of someone who would prefer a more literal rendering. This was not an uncommon scholarly criticism of Sacy's work, even though the Port-Royal project was deliberately not literal: this the cleric-scholars viewed as "servile". Rather, their idea was to render spiritual meaning for the edification of the broad population. Indeed, one of their major points of difference with orthodox Roman Catholicism was their idea that scripture ought to be read by all. But it isn't only because of translation that Maréchal would have taken issue with Sacy's version, for the scholars of Port-Royal considered scripture to be authored by the Holy Spirit, to be read and revered *"non comme les livres des hommes"* (not like the books of human beings) but as those of God himself, *"preuves incontestables de la verité de notre Religion"* (incontestable proofs of the truth of our religion: Sacy 1701, *Avertissement*).[6] This is, of course, exactly the point of view Maréchal targets with such vigor.

Besides Sacy, many other sources were available to Maréchal, most of them acknowledged in his text or notes: other Bibles, in French or Latin (he owned a 1664 Vulgate); translations of individual books, especially Psalms, of which he owned several versions; commentaries; poems and plays about specific incidents or characters.

Some of Maréchal's reading is filtered, as might be expected, through the lens of revolutionary patriotism and the experience of a well-known writer on political affairs. Thus, he admires the Maccabees because of the early days of the Revolution, when the new French government, like the band of priestly brothers, had to defend itself against foreign invaders. In a similar vein, his

---

5 The catalogue of Maréchal's personal library sold after his death appears in several places, among them Aubert (1975, 156–74).
6 This *"Avertissement"* or preface would most likely have been added after Sacy's death. The 1701 edition in which it appears was the first printed in Paris. Modern opinion on Sacy's style seems to have swung toward Maréchal's view: Henri LeMaître writes that it is *"très étudié"* and *"cherche de dépouiller le texte sacré de ses grandeurs et de ses beautés profanes, sans reculer devant une certaine infidelité"* (very elaborate ... aims to strip the sacred text of its grandeur and its profane beauties, without worrying about some infidelity: LeMaître 2003, s.v. "Le Maistre de Saci" [sic]).

hypothetical speech for Jesus echoes fears of revolutionary France being overwhelmed by European powers, fashioning a portrait of the ideal popular leader that Jesus could have been. As with other of Maréchal's themes, this was not unique, for the Bible was used in France, as elsewhere, to prove many points on all sides. As Menozzi points out, the 1790s saw a series of biographies of Jesus, presenting him as "prototype of republican virtues ... come not only to announce liberation from the slavery of sin, but also liberation from political slavery" (Menozzi 1986, 692–93).

In a negative key, the dissolute King David is portrayed as "the Louis XIV of the Jews" and the prophet Jeremiah is denounced as a traitor to his people, preaching submission to Babylonian exile rather than resistance or flight. (Historically, of course, the many Jews who opted to stay in Persia rather than return to Israel to rebuild the temple, did very well there, founding famous academies and eventually producing the Babylonian Talmud.) The role of and respect for kings and priests, as well as those prophets who support them, is a major biblical offense for Maréchal—not surprising for a proud egalitarian and revolutionary who, during the 1790s, worked closely with one of the most radical figures in France, the proto-communist journalist François-Noël ("Gracchus") Babeuf. Maréchal's hatred of priestly authority and corruption comes through everywhere in his commentary, most explicitly in its vitriolic prefatory "Epistle" to "priests of all religions". Though it may seem bizarre that this preface urges priests to leave their posts, return to civil life and get jobs, this is just what had happened in sixteenth-century England during the Henrician Reformation, when Catholic monasteries and convents were closed and their inhabitants returned to civil life; on a much smaller scale it had also happened in the early days of the French Revolution.

Other politically grounded evaluations surface throughout. Not all of them, however, are what one might expect. Paradoxically and perhaps disappointingly, the revolutionary Maréchal does not sympathize with the Jews' grumbling and rebellion against the authoritarian Moses and Aaron (throughout Exodus and Numbers). On the contrary, he blames the populace, who become victims of brutal suppression, arguing that the Jews were not worthy of their leader but required brutalization because they are inadequate to Moses's grand vision and genius. Surely this is the tyrant's classic argument: the people require suppression for their own good—indeed, in Deuteronomy Sylvain compares Moses to Czar Peter I! Is this a latent anti-semitism, setting the worthless people against their inspired leader? Is it the consequence of Maréchal's own patriarchalist political ideal? An argument can be made for either of these interpretations, although the trope is not original: Machiavelli, for instance (who appears in the *Dictionnaire des athées*), had justified Moses's violent suppression of his rebellious followers on the grounds that innovators must use force of arms in order to prevail (Machiavelli 1513, chap. 6). Holbach, on the other hand, floated the possibility that Moses was "*un menteur impudent, un fourbe ambitieux*", even a "*fanatique*" (shameless liar, ambitious fraud ... fanatic: Holbach 1770, 20), along with many other unflattering remarks, so the option was certainly available in contemporary intellectual life.

In other places, Maréchal's literary sophistication, that of a man well read in classical and contemporary literature, evokes enthusiastic praise of some biblical books and passages, especially in the major prophets. Sublimity is a key critical term of praise in his lexicon (as it was for eighteenth-century art criticism in general), along with 'unction' (smooth flow, sweetness, feeling), energy, movement, and simplicity. Vivid imagery, intensity of imagination, and force of expression are all praised, even though these are often exemplified in sexual or scatological terms that Maréchal knows will offend the artificial 'good taste' of prudish middle-class readers. Yet in Maréchal's view, imaginative intensity must not go too far; metaphor and imagery are all very well, but must not be overly dramatic, far-fetched, or unlikely (as, for instance in Psalm 97, "the rivers applaud"). In commenting on John's gospel, he reveals a deep distrust of figurative language generally because of its abuse by religious writers, and views its excess in the Apocalypse as the effusion of a fevered brain.

Also disadvantageous is what Maréchal considers the crudity of much biblical thought and writing as compared with the Greek classics. Not all the biblical authors suffer from this comparison: Jeremiah, for example, is considered by Maréchal to be the equal of classical poets and orators, and Ezekiel XXXVII is described as more sublime than anything in Homer or Greek myth. But for the most part, scripture comes off second best. This is a venerable contrast—Athens vs. Jerusalem—going back to several Church fathers, most memorably to Augustine's *De doctrina christiana* (*On Christian Doctrine*), justifying, indeed glorifying, scriptural simplicity as against classical sophistication and elitism. Voltaire and other eighteenth-century biblical commentators made similar observations. The trope continued to flourish in the earlier twentieth century in the work of philosophers and culture critics such as Leo Strauss, Lev Shestov, and the Franco-Roumanian Benjamin Fondane; it resurfaced in Erich Auerbach's famous essay "Odysseus's Scar" (1953), and—as a Google search readily shows—in our own day at various levels of sophistication and from differing religious perspectives. It has had particular traction in Europe and among francophones because the long exclusion of Jews from citizenship created—for some, though by no means all—a sense of rivalry or conflict between Judaism and normative civil society (see Chapter 10 in this collection).[7]

Thanks to his own inclinations and an already thriving stream of critical scholarship, Maréchal gets a lot right about the Bible, much of it not generally accepted in his day by any but academic specialists or elite intellectuals, and certainly not by the average clergy or the population at large. Like most serious Bible scholars of his day, he knows that scripture is an anthology by various hands, often reflecting a priestly point of view. He knows that it is therefore not only permissible but necessary to read these documents as one reads any literary production: with a critical eye. He knows that there were many gospels, though only four of them were selected for inclusion in the Catholic canon. He knows about the Essene sect, to which some scholars thought Jesus may have belonged, and he knows that Jesus may not have existed. In his "Result" conclusion, he writes of *"l'ère commune"* (the common era), as modern scholars now do, rather than A.D. (*anno domini*, year of the lord). He uses new-fashioned terms like "ideology" (in, e.g., Psalm 6 and Job) and "civil society" (Psalm 36) as well as the newly invented *"tachigraph"* (speedometer, in Nehemiah). Many of his literary and moral judgments are irrefutable.

Nonetheless, I haven't found this text to represent Maréchal at his best or most attractive. Everyone who knew the man praises his character, noting a gentle, modest nature; erudition; delightful conversation; generosity to all and loyalty to friends; and a loving marriage with a younger woman of Catholic devotion. But in *Pour et contre* and in the handwritten marginal notes in his personal Bible (Anonymous 1712), we find a fuller picture, a more multi-faceted self-revelation than what appears in most of his other works that are not specifically religious in theme. Particularly in the handwritten marginalia, Sylvain releases a darker, more sardonic impulse: one glimpsed a decade earlier in his mock satirical legendary—*La nouvelle légende dorée* (1790), a collection of lives of women saints—that was meant to win its audience, especially women, away from Catholic devotion. In the Bible marginalia one gets a continuous, spontaneous dialogue with the text, full of sarcasm, scorn, quasi-obscene insults, scatological asides, wisecracks and cheap shots, skeptical or hostile comments about theology, demonstrations of logical or narrative flaws, cynical interpretations of behavior, and mocking interjections. There are hundreds of these, so a complete survey is impossible here; a few examples will have to suffice. A partial list of insulting words for Moses, priests, prophets, patriarchs

---

7   The conflict wasn't as developed in the United States, where Jews were not excluded to the same extent as in Europe. Partly this was due to the different constitutions of various colonies and states, several of which granted Jews the vote even before the French (see Chyet 1958).

or Jahweh includes: *charlatan, fripon, brigand, menteur, diable incarné, pillard, scelerat, execrable scelerat, imbécile, villain, fou, gaillard* (faker, fraud, bandit, liar, devil incarnate, thief, scoundrel, cursed scoundrel, imbecile, villain, crazy, big guy: perhaps with overtones of homosexuality). The Jews may be *gueux, cannibals, horrible, vilaines gens* (vagabonds, cannibals, horrible, awful people). Exodus is a *recueil de bêtises* (collection of stupidities). Crowds or the disciples are often *ânes, benets, sots, imbéciles, gueux,* or *canaille* (asses, donkeys, fools, imbeciles, beggars, low-class mob). Various statements of Jesus or other speakers are annotated as *verbiage, galimathias, fanatisme, menterie, conte d'enfans* (mere words, a confused mess, fanaticism, lies, fairy tales); much of Matthew's gospel is *mauvaise logique, mauvais raisonnement, mauvais conseil* (bad logic, bad reasoning, bad advice). Snide or sarcastic comments are everywhere. Abraham's self-circumcision and that of his son Isaac calls forth many sneers, among them: "*Et que diable cela nous fait-il?*" (What the devil has it to do with us?) and "*Puisque ce bon dieu n'aimait pas les prepuces pour quoi les avait-il faits?*" (Since this good god didn't like foreskins, why did he make them?). In Hosea 6:10, where Jahweh says that he will spread his anger like water, Sylvain ripostes: "So they'll have to take umbrellas". There are occasional vulgarities and near-obscenities: when Pharoah tells Moses *t'en va* (go away, leave), Sylvain adds "*te faire*" but omits the last word, *foutre*, from the well-known phrase *Va te faire foutre* (Go fuck yourself). When Judith claims that Holofernes didn't rape her, the note reads "*Vous mentez, putain!*" (You lie, whore!). There is also no shortage of piss and shit in various notes, especially those annotating an incident of fear. And so on.

The unfiltered response of handwritten notes in a personal Bible is not, of course, what could go into a more or less scholarly commentary for public consumption, although most of the theological objections briefly noted in the marginalia are expanded into arguments in *Pour et contre*. In the commentary, though, Maréchal expresses some of the prejudices that don't emerge in other texts or in personal relations. Jews and women, specifically female sexuality, are the two main areas where this can be seen. Both of these specially oppressed groups were much in the public eye during the Revolution (and long after), as subjects of debate in the National Assembly and other public venues. Although there were significant Jewish communities—some quite prosperous—in France at the start of the revolutionary period, and had been for centuries, Jews were not legally full citizens until autumn 1791. Their enfranchisement was hotly debated in the National Assembly and elsewhere, and enacted at that time, but this did not ensure social integration or put an end to negative stereotypes; rather, the dominant motivation was to 'reform' the Jews as a whole by making them citizens. Nonetheless, the study of Hebrew and of ancient Israel, the reception of work by famous Jewish scholars, and the social presence of intellectually gifted Jews—such as the Polish-born scholar Zalkind Hourwitz, an associate of Cloots (Mortier 1995, 127)—as well as bankers, merchants, and articulate community leaders, did create a certain respectful awareness among some intellectuals. Some took Jewish pen names, as did Richard Simon writing as Rabbin Shimeon bar Joachim. Holbach is said to have done the same, and his mansion was referred to by its frequenters as "the synagogue"—indeed by one correspondent as "the Great Synagogue of the rue Royale" (quoted in Kors 1976, 16). When the revolutionary organizer Théroigne de Méricourt addressed the radical Club des Cordeliers, she was heckled as "*la reine de Saba qui vient voir le Salomon du district*" (the Queen of Sheba come to see the local King Solomon). She pluckily responded: "*On vous l'a dit, les Français ressemblent aux Juifs, peuple porté à l'idolatrie, le plus vulgaire se prend par les sens, il lui faut des signes extérieurs auxquels s'attache son culte*" (You've heard that the French are like the Jews, a people attracted to idolatry; the most vulgar are trapped by the senses, they need external signs to anchor their religion: quoted in Bouvier 1931, 65). This last, while scarcely flattering for either party, does show an easy colloquial use of Hebrew biblical referentiality.

But Maréchal does not participate in any current of appreciation; rather, he tends to exhibit disdain for Jews as a whole, referring to them occasionally as a race or species ("*gent*"), a tribe ("*peuplade*") of brutal sensibilities, or a "*nation*": a term easily turned to the uses of anti-semitic exclusion because it implied loyalty to a foreign nation, Israel, rather than to France. In commenting Luke, he buys into the old association of Jews with money and characterizes them as nearly as despicable ("*vil*") as the Chinese (Delany 2020, 150). The same well-worn trope appears when, in manually annotating the golden calf incident, he has Aaron say, "*et moi, j'aime l'or*" (As for me, I love gold/money). In this vein, in his journalism Sylvain blamed Jews for helping to cause France's financial emergency by taking advantage of their newfound citizenship to engage in disreputable or illegal practices, thus showing ingratitude for the privilege bestowed on them (Mannucci 2012, 168–69). In the "Results" section of *Pour et contre*, Jesus's fellow Jews are referred to as "*ses compatriots dégénerés*" (his degenerate compatriots), and a disgusting anti-semitic anecdote about the Hebrews' origin in bestiality and incest, erroneously said to be by Plutarch, is uncritically recounted (Delany 2020, 188 n.19).

For Maréchal, the biblical Jews were an "oriental", Asiatic people and therefore prone to the traits of 'Orientals' that are seen in much of Jewish biblical writing: emotional excess, sensuality, lack of restraint. "Who doesn't know", he asks in Malachi, "that the oriental poets are more inflated than sublime, have more emphasis than eloquence, and are not always troubled to put justice, truth and nature into their frequent extended metaphors?" Job, Judith, and the Song of Songs are especially "oriental" despite the admiration he has for these texts; Kings II (Samuel II) shows "oriental servitude". In this way, Maréchal's Bible commentary participates in an orientalist discourse which was stimulated by, though long antedated, Napoleon's 1797 Egyptian adventure. One finds it in medieval literature (the Saracen, the Turk) and in ancient literature (attitudes toward the populations of Asia Minor or Africa) as well as in several French and English projects contemporaneous with Maréchal (Said 1978, 76–87; see also Heng 2018; Isaac 2004).

Women, like Jews, were also disfranchised. The Revolution did not rectify this exclusion despite the importance of women in rural and urban labor, the existence of women's periodicals and political clubs, the militancy of working women in the revolutionary army as well as in specific uprisings, and frequent appeals to the National Assembly by both men and women to grant them the vote and full political participation. Maréchal opposed this proposed reform, as he wrote in the well-known journal, *Révolutions de Paris*, that he edited for several years, from about 1790 to its demise in early 1794. His reasoning, like that of many of his colleagues, was the essentialist argument that 'Nature' intended women for domestic and maternal duties, not the rough-and-tumble of political life. This reasoning stands behind what is surely his most obnoxious treatise, the 1801 *Projêt* listing 138 reasons why women should not learn to read (Maréchal 1801c). Some in his day and our own have viewed this pamphlet as a (bad) joke, making a *reductio ad absurdum* out of the government's failure to educate women properly, as they needed to be in order to educate their offspring into good citizenship (Perrot 2007, 95). Others have considered it a genuine extension of his real beliefs, consistent with views expressed elsewhere.

The attitude toward female agency and sexuality that emerges in *Pour et contre* partly reflects revolutionary legislation, partly does not. Although revolutionary legislation had required proper treatment of children born outside of marriage (as many were in a period of frequent common-law unions), and had legalized divorce in 1792, female adultery (not male) remained a crime. Maréchal makes both illegitimacy and adultery special targets of disdain. Hosea memorably allegorized the Jews' attraction to other religions as an adulterous wife bearing bastards. This imagery Maréchal refuses even to translate. Later he describes it as "worthy of the bordello" (Delany 2020, 122 n.167); even as an allegory the imagery is unacceptable. The scandalous "bastardy" of Jesus, owing to the married Mary's "adultery" with the Holy Spirit, is the cornerstone of his critique of Christian theology. Elsewhere a rather narrow-minded prudery emerges, quite at odds with the hot love-poetry he addressed to his wife (see Dommanget 1950, 382). Clearly, marital sex is the only acceptable norm, and indeed always had been for Sylvain, even in his earlier pastoral poetry (Dommanget 1950, 97). Socially, of course, common-law cohabitation was quite normal among working people, especially in cities, but social reality is not always Sylvain's strong point. The explicitly erotic Song of Songs evidently caused some embarrassment: the most obviously sexual line (5:4) he declines to translate, then avoids any actual textual analysis, confining his commentary to moral and literary-historical generalities. There is a contradiction to this prudery, of course, since elsewhere Maréchal criticizes his main French source, Sacy, for bowdlerizing the Latin to accommodate eighteenth-century middle-class standards of polite discourse by eliminating sexual or defecatory imagery, yet not daring himself to comment on the "Song" beyond a few condescending remarks.[8]

Even apart from attitudes toward female sexuality, though, Maréchal sometimes disappoints. In response to the truly awful story of the incestuous rape of Tamar by her brother, engineered by a cousin and covered up by another brother, Sylvain can only muster a shallow cynical remark about Tamar's naïveté.

Elsewhere, he responds to St. Jerome's suggestion that Judith herself might have composed the book bearing her name by saying that he prefers a needle or spindle in a woman's hand rather than a pen or a sword. This despite a close friendship with two well-known women writers, one of whom, the novelist Mme. Gacon-Dufour, sat at his deathbed, wrote a memoir of his last days, and edited one of his works posthumously!

Some readers will observe, correctly, that these were normative or majority attitudes of the day regarding both Jews and women. Yet there were enough contemporaries of Sylvain—lay and cleric, men and women—who rejected them, often very publicly, in writing and in political debate, that this is not really an adequate justification. Moreover, even among earlier Catholic scholars an anti-Jewish attitude was not always necessary. For Claude Fleury (1640–1723), cleric and famous ecclesiastical historian, the Israelites offered an *"excellent modèle de la vie humaine la plus conforme à la nature"* (an excellent model of human life in conformity with nature: Fleury 1682, 1) and a simple, sensible, spiritual life far superior to the corrupt and idolatrous cultures of Egypt, Greece, or Rome. Although his view was idealized, and he did at the end of his opus have to blame the Jews for their mistreatment of Jesus, Fleury did nonetheless take a historicist perspective, inviting the reader to look at the Israelites

---

8   A similarly squeamish or evasive attitude toward sexual matters can be seen in Maréchal's commentary to the 1780 *Antiquités d'Herculanum*, where illustrations plainly depicting a homoerotic or bestial dalliance are ignored in the text (Maréchal 1781–1803).

"*dans les circonstances des temps et des lieux où ils vivoient ... et entrer ainsi dans leur esprit*" (in the circumstances of the times and places where they lived ... and thus to enter into their spirit: Fleury 1682, 5).

These retrograde attitudes of Sylvain are at odds with his professed egalitarianism. As contradictions both personal and social—common in the surrounding culture—they are not, I think, to be resolved but constitute instances, on both levels, of what today we might call combined and uneven development.

・・・

What about us?

According to polls, 20% of Americans consider themselves non-religious, though not necessarily atheists (Townsend 2012). There are specialized online groups such as Black Atheists or Black Atheist Alliance as well as groups such as Black Nonbelievers, among a minority whose majority do believe and attend church regularly (Brennan 2011). There are online networks, the Clergy Project and Recovering from Religion among others, for clergy who no longer believe in God, along with the Freedom from Religion Foundation (Worth 2012). Former conservative Republican President Reagan's son Ron publicizes a national atheist organization, the Freedom from Religion Foundation, which advertises itself on television: "Not afraid of burning in hell" is the closing line. Several military bases host a chapter of the Military Atheists and Secular Humanists, a movement that began at Fort Bragg (now Fort Liberty), North Carolina. Numerous books are published by reputable presses defending atheism, recounting its history, or attacking various religions; some of them employ rhetoric reminiscent of Maréchal's: for instance, a characterization of "the Pauline contamination" as "ravings of a hysteric" inflicted on the rest of the world (Onfray 2007, 131). Many campuses have a secular student union or an atheist or humanist club. The University of Miami in 2016 received a large endowment for a chair in "the study of atheism, humanism and secular ethics" (*New York Times*, May 22, 2016); Pitzer College in California has a Department of Secular Studies; Trinity College has an Institute for the Study of Secularism; scholars have formed an international "Nonreligion and secularity research network" with a journal, *Secularism and Nonreligion* (*New York Times*, May 22, 2016). Groups for atheists and secular humanists meet regularly worldwide. Even *Vogue* has joined the fray with a first-person contribution by a Catholic woman who has lost her faith in response to clerical abuse of children (Keane 2019, 16–18). And, in stark contrast to the Mike Pence incident with which I began, the Socialist prime minister of Spain was sworn in without a Bible, while the new Georgia county commissioner took her oath on *The Autobiography of Malcolm X* (both in June 2018).

Abroad, organized religion appears to be less popular than ever. The famous incarnation of Harry Potter, the British actor Daniel Radcliffe, declared himself an atheist, as has novelist Ian McEwen along with other writers (see Bradley and Tate 2010). In 2004, the BBC broadcast a three-part TV series called "Atheism: A Rough History of Disbelief"; it aired in the U.S. in 2007 on PBS. Atheism is the official position in Cuba, China, and North Korea (although many in these populations do believe and practice various faiths or rituals). Pew Research indicates 60 million atheist or agnostic Latino/as (with varying percentages per country, the highest in Uruguay at over one-third). Mexico has an atheist association with annual congress, as do Chile and Argentina; the Argentinians won a suit against a Jesuit university for anti-atheistic rules, and others in other countries have proceeded against school systems for discriminating against atheists. Even in Switzerland, cradle of Calvinism, the proportion of non-religious is now virtually equal to the proportion of Protestants, about 25% each (Tognina and Bechtel 2017). Also in Switzerland, in November 2018, six parliamentary women resigned from the Catholic Church to protest its "patriarchal power apparatus" and Pope Francis's denunciation of abortion (swissinfo.ch 2018).

As for France, Sarah Fainberg describes the situation in 2013 as "a steady decrease, even a crash, of Catholic faith and religious practice", observing that 35% of the general population and 64% of those between ages 18 and 24 "define themselves as completely without religion" (Fainberg 2014, 87). Admittedly, figures can't be exact: often people who define themselves as non-believers, non-observant or agnostic are reluctant to use the term 'atheist'; while some secularists oppose the Church less for theological reasons than because of its corruption, sexual abuse of children, anti-abortion or homophobic positions. Nonetheless, the trend is clear and obvious.[9]

Nor, of course, is it limited to Christians. Muslims who have left the faith are not limited to the famous names—Salman Rushdie, Ayaan Hirsi Ali—but include many internationally. The Council of Ex-Muslims, started in Britain in 2007, is now a worldwide organization; there is the group Ex-Muslims of North America, and an online movement called #ExMuslimBecause (for samples of messages sent to it, see Rizvi 2016, 72–75). As for Jews in America, over half do not believe in God, including those active in a synagogue or temple, and

---

9 For a survey of polls worldwide, with graphs and discussion, see Zuckerman 2007.

doubtless quite a few rabbis, and at least 75% rarely attend services (Putnam and Campbell 2010, 23, 138 fig. 5.1).

All this is not to claim that religion is dead (despite the claim some make that God is dead). Far from it: religion thrives in many places—often in regrettably extreme versions whether Catholic, Jewish, Muslim, or Hindu—and is likely to continue to thrive whether for psychological or political reasons. For some, it is useful: as Napoleon is said to have observed, "Religion is excellent stuff for keeping common people quiet. Religion is what keeps the poor from murdering the rich". For others, it is comforting: religion is "the expression of real distress and the protest against real distress. Religion is the sigh of the oppressed creature, the heart of a heartless world, just as it is the spirit of a spiritless situation. It is the opium of the people" (Marx 1843, 42).

Some of Maréchal's comments seem peculiarly appropriate today. For example, his remarks about David in the Psalms section seem appropriate now, as the Israeli government protests its morality and purity while committing massacres against Palestinians whom it has driven out of their homes and off their land, and practices internal government corruption that has landed more than one official before the courts or in prison. The declaration by Israel's former finance minister and government leader, Yair Lapid, that "there will be no separation of church and state here [in Israel]" (Yehoshua 2014, 173) perfectly illustrates the thinking that accounts for Maréchal's hatred of priesthood in Hebrew scripture and in any organized religion. How much more horrifying to him, as to many of us, the theocratic results of Israel's 2023 elections, or the influence of evangelical Christian politicians in shaping American foreign policy toward Israel on the basis of biblical legend! Moreover, the veracity or historicity of the Jewish Bible is once again contentious because of its use to justify political claims, despite evidence brought to light by a post-Zionist generation of historians and archaeologists showing the limits of an earlier politicized archaeology.

If the restoration of the ancient Bourbon monarchy in 1814, in the person of Louis XVIII—a brother of the deposed and executed Louis XVI—would have been Maréchal's worst nightmare, yet some developments in our own day as cited above—the existence of atheist organizations, clubs, and academic departments, the general acceptance of atheism, the widespread belief that it is possible to be virtuous without religion—might have restored some of his faith in humankind. He was, after all, always oriented toward the future. This is especially prominent in his *Fragmens d'un poème moral sur Dieu* (*Fragments of a Moral Poem on God*, 1781), published when he was only thirty-one. Fragment IX, voicing *"l'homme de bien"* (the comfortable/content man) offers this scenario:

> Un jour j'aurai pour moi tous les coeurs vertueux: ...
> Le pere à ses enfans transmettra mes écrits
> Long-tems après ma mort, utile à mon pays,
> On viendra sur ma tombe épandre quelques larmes.
> Pour moi, quel avenir peut avoir plus de charmes!
>
> One day all virtuous hearts will be mine:
> Fathers will pass on my writing to their children
> Long after my death, useful to my country;
> People will come to drop tears on my tomb.
> For me, what future could hold more charm!

And the last lines of Fragment XII read:

> Eh bien! Par nos écrits & surtout par nos moeurs,
> Dans le chemin du vrai soyons ses précurseurs.
>
> Very well! By our writing and above all by our behavior,
> In truth's road let us be its forerunners.

Some years later, Sylvain put it this way in a song he wrote for the working people of France when part of a group trying to bring about a genuinely democratic revolution:

> Je m'attends bien que la prison
> Sera la prix de ma chanson, C'est ce qui me désole:
> Le people la saura par coeur,
> Peut-être il bénira l'auteur,
> C'est ce qui me console.
>
> I expect that prison
> Will be the price of my song,
> That's what dismays me:
> The people will know it by heart,
> Perhaps they will bless the author
> That's what consoles me.
>   MARÉCHAL 1796 in Brécy, 28–29[10]

---

10 Maréchal's song, several stanzas long, was based on a popular air about a young widow alternately grieved and relieved. He wrote numerous songs which, like his leaflets on

As it turned out, prison was not to be Maréchal's fate, although it well could have been in the spy-ridden political life of his day; indeed, he had already spent several months in prison as a younger man, punishment for an iconoclastic earlier work.[11] He finished out his days in the countryside on the outskirts of Paris, in quiet retreat from political activism but continuing to read and write, see friends and family, and attract denunciation for his publications. He died of natural causes, surrounded by friends and family and had a Catholic burial in a Catholic graveyard. Although he had composed epitaphs for himself during his lifetime, it's doubtful any of them was used, and the grave itself no longer exists. Nonetheless we may end with one of them here, the same with which Maréchal ended his *Fragmens*:

> Cy repose un paisible Athée:
> Il marcha toujours droit sans regarder les Cieux. Que sa tombe soit respectée:L'ami de la vertu fut l'ennemi des Dieux.
> Here rests a peace-loving atheist:
> He walked upright without watching the skies.
> May his tomb be respected:
> The friend of virtue was the enemy of Gods.[12]

References

Alter, Robert. 2010. *Pen of Iron: American Prose and the King James Bible*. Princeton: Princeton University Press.

---

behalf of the group of revolutionaries around F.-N. ("Gracchus") Babeuf, were posted in Paris and other cities, and widely known. It would have been composed between 1795 and early 1797 (when Babeuf was tried and executed). Maréchal managed to escape identification by a police informer; as Serna observes, Maréchal *"n'existe même pas pour la police"* (doesn't even exist for the police: Serna 1997, 316 n3). The reason for this is likely, as Dommanget argues on the basis of police reports and other accounts, that the informer did not recognize Maréchal at the meeting he had infiltrated, and that documents using Maréchal's name were scarce and well hidden (Dommanget 1970, chap. 10).

11 This was his 1788 *Almanach des honnêtes gens* (*Almanach of Upright People*), a form of calendar popular at the time, but substituting political people, scientists, writers, artists and non-Christian as well as Christian religious figures from various countries for the usual saints. The book was condemned in Parlement to be publicly torn and burnt as scandalous, monstrous, blasphemous, sacrilegious, etc.; the author spent several months in prison, released through a friend's influence. It was republished a few years later and again in 1836 (Karmin 1911, 265–66).

12 This chapter is a revised version of the introduction to *For and Against the Bible. A Translation of Sylvain Maréchal's* Pour et Contre la Bible *(1801)*, translated by Sheila Delany. Leiden, Netherlands: Brill, 2020, 1–20.

Anonymous. 1712. *La sainte Bible qui contient le vieux et le Nouveau Testament: Revue sur les textes hébreux et grecs.* 4 vols. Amsterdam: Pierre Mortier et Pierre Brunet. Accessed May 23, 2023. https://search.socialhistory.org/Record/ARCH00855, items 60–63.

Aubert, Françoise. 1975. *Sylvain Maréchal: Passion et faillite d'un égalitaire.* Pisa: Goliardica; Paris: Nizet.

Auerbach, Erich. [1946] 1953. "Odysseus' Scar". In *Mimesis. The Representation of Reality in Western Literature*, translated by Willard Trask, 1–20. Princeton: Princeton University Press.

Augustine. [427] 1958. *On Christian Doctrine*, translated by D.W. Robertson. New York: Liberal Arts Press.

Barbery, Muriel. 2008. *The Elegance of the Hedgehog*, translated by Alison Anderson. New York: Europa. First published 2006, Paris: Gallimard.

Barnstone, Willis, ed. 1984. *The Other Bible: Ancient Alternative Scriptures.* New York: HarperCollins.

Belaval, Yvon, and Dominique Bourel, eds. 1986. *Le siècle des lumières et la Bible.* Paris: Beauchesne.

Benot, Yves, ed. 1958. *Le pour et le contre: Corréspondance polémique sur le respect de la posterité.* Paris: Editeurs Français Réunis.

Bouvier, Jeanne. 1931. *Les Femmes pendant la Révolution.* Paris: Editions E. Figuière.

Bradley, Arthur, and Andrew Tate. 2010. *The New Atheist Novel: Fiction, Philosophy and Polemic after 9/11.* London: Continuum Books.

Brennan, Emily. 2011. "The Unbelievers". *New York Times*, November 27, 2011.

Brunet, Gustave. [1866] 1962. *Imprimeurs imaginaires et libraires supposes: Étude bibliographique.* New York: Burt Franklin. First published in Paris.

Chyet, Stanley F. 1958. "The Political Rights of the Jews in the United States: 1776–1840". *American Jewish Archives* (April), 14–75.

Curran, Andrew S. 2019. *Diderot and the Art of Thinking Freely.* New York: Other Press.

Darnton, Robert. 1995. *The Corpus of Clandestine Literature in France, 1769–1789.* New York: Norton.

Darnton, Robert. 1991. *Édition et sedition: L'Univers de la littérature clandestine au XVIIIe siècle.* Paris: Gallimard.

Dawkins, Richard. 2006. *The God Delusion.* London: Bantam Press.

Delany, Sheila. 2020. *For and Against the Bible. A translation of Sylvain Maréchal's Pour et Contre la Bible (1801).* Leiden: Brill.

Desroussilles, François Dupigrenet. 1986. "La production Biblique Catholique en France au XVIIIe siècle". In Belaval and Bourel, 73–83.

Dommanget, Maurice. 1950. *Sylvain Maréchal, l'égalitaire ... (1750–1803).* Paris: Spartacus.

Dommanget, Maurice. 1970. *Sur Babeuf et la conjuration des égaux.* Paris: Maspero.

Eco, Umberto. 2003. *Mouse or Rat? Translation as Negotiation*. London: Weidenfeld and Nicolson.

Fainberg, Sarah. 2014. "French Laïcité: What Does It Stand For?" In *Secularism on the Edge: Rethinking Church–State Relations in the United States, France and Israel*, edited by Jacques Berlinerblau and Sarah Fainberg, 85–94. New York: Palgrave MacMillan.

Febvre, Lucien. [1942] 1982. *The Problem of Unbelief in the Sixteenth Century: The Religion of Rabelais*, translated by Beatrice Gottlieb. Cambridge: Harvard University Press.

Fleury, Claude. 1682. *Les moeurs des Israelites*. La Haye.

Heng, Geraldine. 2018. *The Invention of Race in the European Middle Ages*. Cambridge: Cambridge University Press.

Herzberg, Arthur. 1970. *The French Enlightenment and the Jews*. New York: Schocken Books.

Holbach, Paul-Henry Thiry. [1770] 2008. *Tableau des saints*, edited by J.-P. Jackson. Tangier: Coda.

Isaac, Benjamin. 2004. *The Invention of Racism in Classical Antiquity*. Princeton: Princeton University Press.

Karmin, Otto. 1911. "Essai d'une Bibliographie de Sylvain Maréchal". *Revue historique de la Révolution française* 2, 262–67 and 437–43.

Keane, Mary Beth. 2019. "A Catholic Reckoning". *Vogue* (January, 2019) 16–18.

Kors, Alan Charles. 1976. *D'Holbach's Coterie: An Enlightenment in Paris*. Princeton: Princeton University Press.

Kors, Alan Charles. 1990. *Atheism in France, 1650–1729: the Orthodox Sources of Disbelief*. Princeton: Princeton University Press.

Latreille, André. 1946. *L'Église Catholique et la Révolution française*. Vol. 1. Paris: Hachette.

Legoupil, Audrey. 2011. "Port-Royal et la Vulgate: Une entreprise de traduction novatrice". Accessed May 17, 2023. https://docplayer.fr/amp/2869800-Port-royal-et-la-vulgate.html.

LeMaître, Henri. 2003. *Dictionnaire Bordas de littérature française*. Paris: Bordas.

Luzzato, Sergio. 2001. *L'automne de la Révolution: Luttes et cultures politiques dans la France thermidorienne*. Paris: Champion.

Mannucci, Erica Joy. 2012. *Finalmente il popolo pensa: Sylvain Maréchal nell'immagine della Rivoluzione francese*. Naples: Guida.

Maréchal, Sylvain. 1781–1803. *Antiquités d'Herculanum, gravées par F.-A. David avec leurs explications par P. Sylvain M.* 12 vols. Paris: F.-A. David.

Maréchal, Sylvain. 1781. *Fragmens d'un poème moral sur Dieu*. Athéopolis [Paris].

Maréchal, Sylvain. 1788. *L'Almanach des honnêtes gens, l'an du premier regne de la raison, pour la présente année*.

Maréchal, Sylvain. 1793. *Calendrier des républicains*. Paris: Gueffier.

Maréchal, Sylvain. 1794. *La fable du Christ dévoilée, ou lettre du Muphti de Constantinople à Jean Ange Braschy, Muphti de Rome*. Paris: Franklin.
Maréchal, Sylvain. [1796] 1978. "Chanson nouvelle à l'usage des Faubourgs". In *Florilège de la chanson révolutionnaire de 1789 au front populaire*, edited by Robert Brécy. Milan: Editions hier et demain.
Maréchal, Sylvain. 1800. *Dictionnaire des athées anciens et modernes*. Paris: Grabit. 2nd edition 1833. Brussels: Chez l'editeur [Balleroy].
Maréchal, Sylvain. 1801. *Projêt: Il ne faut pas que les femmes sachent lire*. Paris: Massé.
Maréchal, Sylvain. 1801. *La femme abbé*. Paris: Ledoux.
Maréchal, Sylvain. 1801. *Pour et contre la Bible*. Jérusalem [Paris].
Maréchal, Sylvain. 1802. *Histoire de la Russie*. Paris: Chez F. Buisson.
Marx, Karl. 1843. "Introduction to a Contribution to the Critique of Hegel's *Philosophy of Right*". In *Marx & Engels on Religion*, 41–58. New York: Schocken Books.
Mathiez, Albert. [1929] 1965. *After Robespierre: the Thermidorean Reaction*. Translated by C.A. Phillips. New York: Universal Library.
Menozzi, Daniele. 1986. "La Bible des révolutionnaires". In Belaval and Bourel, 677–96.
Mortier, Roland. 1990. "La remise en question du Christianisme au XVIIIe siècle". In *Le coeur et la raison: Receuil d' etudes*, 336–63. Oxford: Voltaire Foundation.
Mortier, Roland. 1995. *Anacharsis cloots, ou l'utopie foudroyée*. Paris: Stock.
Onfray, Michel. 2007. *In Defense of Atheism: The Case Against Christianity, Judaism, and Islam*. Toronto: Viking, Arcade.
Perrot, Michelle. 2007. "Les paradoxes du berger Sylvain". In *Projet d'une loi portant défense d'apprendre à lire aux femmes* (1801), by Sylvain Maréchal, edited by Michelle Perrot, pages. Paris: Mille et une nuits.
Putnam, Robert, and David Campbell. 2010. *American Grace: How Religion Divides and Unites Us*. New York: Simon & Schuster.
Rizvi, Ali A. 2016. *The Atheist Muslim: A Journey from Religion to Reason*. New York: St. Martin's Press.
Sacy, Isaac-Louis LeMaistre. 1701. *La Sainte Bible ... trans. Monsieur Le Maistre de Saci*. 2 vols. Paris: Guillaume Desprez.
Sade, D.A.F. [1795.] 2009. "Français, encore un effort si vous voulez être républicains". In *Marquis de Sade. Écrits politiques*. Edited by Maurice Lerer, 235–81. Paris: Bartillet.
Said, Edward W. 1978. *Orientalism*. New York: Random House.
Sauvy, Anne. 1986. "Lecture et Diffusion de la Bible en France". In Belaval and Bourel, 27–46.
Schom, Alan. 1997. *Napoleon Bonaparte*. New York: HarperCollins.
Schwarzbach, Bertram E. 1971. *Voltaire's Old Testament Criticism*. Geneva: Droz.
Serna, Pierre. 1997. *Antonelle: Aristocrate révolutionnaire, 1747–1817*. Paris: Editions Du Félin.

Swissinfo. 2018. "High-profile Swiss Women Abandon Catholic Church". November 19, 2018. https://www.swissinfo.ch/eng/outrage_high-profile-swiss-women-abandon-catholic-church/44556932.

Tackett, Timothy. 1986. *Religion, Revolution and Regional Culture in Eighteenth-Century France: The Ecclesiastical Oath of 1791.* Princeton: Princeton University Press.

Tognina, Andrea and Dale Bechtel. 2017. "500 Years of the Reformation". Swissinfo. Accessed May 17, 2023. https://stories.swissinfo.ch/500-years-of-the-reformation#222986.

Townsend, Mindy. 2012. "1 in 5 Americans Admit to Choosing No Religion". July 24, 2012. http://www.care2.com/causes/i-in-5-americans-admit-to-choosing-no-religion.

Vovelle, Michel. 1991. *The Revolution against the Church: from Reason to the Supreme Being,* translated by A. José. Columbus: Ohio State University Press.

Woloch, Isser. 1970. *Jacobin Legacy: the Democratic Movement under the Directory.* Princeton: Princeton University Press.

Worth, Robert F. 2012. "From Bible-belt Pastor to Atheist Leader". *New York Times Magazine,* August 26, 2012.

Yehoshua, Avraham. 2014. "Everything is Jewish". In *Secularism on the Edge: Rethinking Church–State Relations in the United States, France and Israel,* edited by Jacques Berlinerblau and Sarah Fainberg. New York: Palgrave.

Zuckerman, Phil. 2007. "Atheism: Contemporary Numbers and Patterns". In *The Cambridge Companion to Atheism,* edited by Michael Martin, 47–66. New York: Cambridge University Press.

CHAPTER 10

Bible, Jews, Revolution

A young Parisian Jew miraculously survives war, Nazi occupation, and Franco's prisons, returning to his country in 1945. As a *kohen*, an engineer, a resistance fighter, and a commando officer, he thinks of offering his skills to Jewish settlers in Palestine, taking his chances once again but this time on a kibbutz, grenade in one hand, machine gun in the other, against English and Arabs. Or he can remain in France to become what he sees as truly French: accept baptism, marry a Catholic, baptize his children. He chooses the latter, changes his name to that on the false identity papers he'd used during the war, and lives a long, happy life during and after a brilliant career.

Much is striking about this true and poignant story (recounted to me by its protagonist), not least its rarity; indeed, it runs counter to the history of Jews in France. Few Jews who stayed in, or returned to, post-war France felt compelled to convert in order to be fully French. Earlier, during the French Revolutionary period, when 'the Jewish question' was on the public agenda and full emancipation was finally achieved (albeit incrementally), the general attitude among Jews was that no such choice was required. Not only did they generally not convert, but even those who had converted, or whose ancestors had converted (whether by compulsion or persuasion) in Spain or Portugal during the late Middle Ages and the Renaissance, reclaimed their Judaism on immigrating to France during the sixteenth and seventeenth centuries; the same was true in England and Holland (Benbassa 2001, 51–52). Even before the Revolution, Enlightenment attitudes enabled a judge to declare, in 1784, regarding a Bordeaux Jew accused of not being French, that

> in France, as elsewhere, it is not one's religion but one's origins, one's birth, that makes one French …; whether one is atheist or deist, Jew or Catholic, Protestant or Mohammedan matters little: if one is born in France of a French mother and father, if one has in no way expatriated oneself, one is a natural Frenchman and enjoys all the rights of a citizen.
> MITCHELL 2008, 185

To be sure, emancipation brought restrictions on rabbinic and communal authority and on past textual authority as well: that is, on the practical authority of the Torah, the Talmud, and centuries of scholarly commentary together comprising 'Jewish law'. Was there a way to be fully French and fully Jewish?

Despite some short-lived resistance by a very few Ashkenazi leaders, the dominant response was positive, and even those who had initially been fearful marked emancipation with joy and public celebration (Berkovitz 2004, 102–3). Ronald Schechter writes that

> Jews were capable of quickly integrating revolutionary values into their world view without abandoning or even questioning their identity ... They assimilated that culture into their own ... They recognized its values as their own without undergoing a fundamental transformation of identity. To those Jews who might have worried that they faced a choice between nations, [those who wrote about it at the time] affirmed that no such choice was necessary. The Jews could have it all: membership in a new community of equal citizens and an ancient *nation juive*.
> SCHECHTER 2003, 13, 179

The notion of a gulf between nationality and religion developed only some decades after emancipation. In the 1820s, as Jay Berkovitz writes, revived anti-Jewish attitudes and increased assimilation generated among some intellectuals an identity crisis that produced several widely publicized cases of conversion; these were, however, neither typical nor statistically significant (Berkovitz 2004, 156, 161, 237). On the centenary of the Revolution, rabbis and grand rabbis all over France acknowledged anti-semitic attitudes but unanimously celebrated *"avec une profonde ferveur"* (with deep fervor: Mossé 1890, preface) the patriotism and gratitude of Jews, who now had a country of their own: France, *"cette nouvelle Jérusalem"*[1] (this new Jerusalem: Mossé 1890, 26).[1]

Today, the effort in France to balance universality with particularity, state secularism with individual or collective observance, has re-entered civil society, partly under pressure of North African Islamic and Jewish immigration: witness the controversial 2004 ban on Islamic headscarves and other religious insignia in public schools and government buildings; or, in 2010, on the burka or *"voile intégrale"* (full coverage). As for Jews, there was the 1980 scandal of Prime Minister Raymond Barre saying that although a bomb attack on a

---

1 Mossé was grand rabbi in the Avignon area, a member of the Marseille and Madrid Academies, founder and officer of several educational organizations. His book is a collection of sermons given at special services throughout France marking the centenary of the Revolution. Its Introduction is the speech of M. Carnot, President of the Republic, at Versailles. Although this precedes the Dreyfus affair by several years, anti-semitism, especially in the military, was already sufficiently pronounced to warrant notice in this speech and in numerous of the sermons. The phrase quoted is from the sermon of Rabbi Aron of the Lunéville temple.

synagogue targeted Jews, it only hit "innocent French people"—as if Jews were neither French nor innocent. More recently, French Zionists, along with those in other western countries, have attempted to redefine Jewishness as loyalty to Israel, to the point of proposing, in a 2004 report, to criminalize criticism of Israeli policies, an effort being replicated in Canada and elsewhere as I write.[2]

The question of the Jews' civil status predated the Revolution. Already Louis XV had commissioned a report on it, and in 1787 the Academy in Metz had mandated, for its essay contest, the topic "Is there a way for Jews to be happier and more helpful in France?" The prize was shared by three contestants, among them a scholarly Jewish immigrant from Poland, Zalkind Hourwitz, who went on to become a well-known spokesman for full emancipation. After 1789, the National Assembly and the Jews themselves debated the relation of citizenship to religious practice, civic equality to religious difference, French law to Jewish law. Accordingly, the press was full of articles pro and con, political clubs held discussions, public speeches were made, tracts distributed.

The prominence of 'the Jewish question' in late eighteenth-century France lends special interest to the text I want to write about here from the perspective of that issue: the *Pour et contre la Bible* (*For and against the* Bible, 1801) of Sylvain Maréchal. Himself an atheist from a Catholic but not especially pious background, Maréchal was nonetheless happily married to a practicing Catholic; the union was childless. Maréchal served as writer and editor for the influential radical journal *Révolutions de Paris* during its relatively short publication life (late 1789–February 1794). A leading member of the so-called Babeuf conspiracy of 1796–97, he managed to escape arrest when the imminent call to revolt was betrayed by an informer. He wrote the text for many large and beautifully illustrated academic volumes; he produced numerous treatises in verse and prose, one of which cost him his job at the prestigious Mazarin Library in his native Paris, and another which brought him—along with notoriety and fortune—a short prison term just before the Revolution erupted.[3]

By 1801, when Maréchal's Bible study appeared, emancipation had already been legislated for nearly a decade, but Napoleon had not yet established the structure of consistories, Sanhedrin, and grand rabbinate that would be decreed a few years later and that remains a force in French Jewish life to this

---

2 See Debray 2010, 50 for the French report. The Canadian Parliamentary Committee to Combat Antisemitism submitted its report to an international conference in Ottawa in November 2010 and currently, in 2023, continues its campaign to criminalize criticism of Israel's policies. Further on France, see Wall 2003.

3 For detailed and sympathetic biographies of Maréchal, see Dommanget 1950 and Mannucci 2012.

day. Why would Maréchal feel the need for such a work at that moment? For several reasons, I think. One is that religion was his constant theme throughout his writing life. He had addressed the failures, corruption, and devastating social effects of religion generally ('superstition' as he and others would have it) and of Catholicism especially in many works over the years, the most sustained and explicit being probably his satirical legendary *La nouvelle légende dorée* (1790). Now he turned to the *fons et origo* behind all of it—behind the monasteries and convents, the prayers and hagiography, the crusades and confessors, the massacres and inquisitions, the cults of virginity, asceticism, self-flagellation, Mariolatry: in short, the Bible.

An even more pressing motive, I suggest, is the author's sense of an immediate social need for such a work. Napoleon's Concordat with the hated Catholic Church would not be finalized until July 1802, but preliminary approaches and formal negotiations for it had commenced as early as the summer of 1800 and proceeded thereafter in Paris, with due pomp and circumstance, hence maximum visibility. The revolutionary reorganization of church–state relations was about to be reversed; many in Paris and elsewhere were only too happy to jump onto the bandwagon in a revival of religious fervor. *Pour et contre* was launched as a propagandistic intervention against what everyone knew was coming and indeed had already begun: the rehabilitation of the Catholic Church as a social force in support of a new autocratic ruler, soon to be crowned emperor in the presence of the pope (1804). For someone who had lived through the Revolution, worked for it, publicly supported and risked his life for its most radical aims, this must have been a truly heartbreaking prospect.

The author's aim is already expressed in the title of his volume, *For and against the Bible*: a title meant to shock and to educate. It would shock the devout reader for whom scripture was a sacred document, immune from rational critique or any other "*contre*". In confronting—indeed affronting—such a prejudice, such a volume might shake something loose, cause a question to arise. The more open-minded reader would hear the title as an affirmation of biblical facticity, its manmade textuality, hence its availability to any analytical method exercised on any cultural artifact. Does this title deliberately echo the *Sic et non* (*Yes and No*) of Maréchal's radical countryman Pierre Abelard, who shocked twelfth-century theologians with critical interrogation of religious texts and dogmas? Perhaps; in any case, Abelard occupies first place in Maréchal's scandal-making *Dictionnaire des athées*, published just the previous year in 1800, and Maréchal plainly considered Abelard a kindred spirit.

"Men make books, but don't books in turn make men?" writes Maréchal ("*Les hommes font les livres. ... mais les livres, à leur tour, ne font-ils pas les hommes?*" Maréchal 1801, xxx). Given this humanist perspective, any study of the

Bible as literature would have to offer both *"pour"* and *"contre"*, for any objective evaluation of a major work of literature must take account of both positive and negative in its object of study. For this reason, no religious literature can be dismissed as simply, or simplistically, a pack of lies, for such dismissal, ignoring cultural norms, would undercut the historicist method within which Maréchal works. It would also ignore the aesthetic dimension of the work, in an essentially philistine gesture alien to Maréchal's personal sensibility as a poet and classicist. Not least, outright dismissal would violate Maréchal's propagandistic aim, i.e., to subject the Bible to the same type of literary scrutiny as exercised on any other influential text.[4]

In his preface to *Pour et contre*, framed as an epistle to ministers of all religions, Maréchal expresses his sense of urgency and dismay at developments marking the turn of the century. Here, at the opening of the nineteenth century, he exclaims, surely we can do better than to revert to the crude absurdities of the last eighteen hundred years (Maréchal 1801, VI). He acknowledges the marked *"réaction religieuse"* (religious reaction, XIX) characterizing this first year of the nineteenth century. This reaction included not only a massive return to churchgoing by once-irreligious people but also a popular taste for books such as *Génie du Christianisme (Spirit of Christianity)* by the aristocratic libertine and repatriated former exile F.R. Chateaubriand. A romanticized account of the poetry, virtues, mysteries, and 'truths' of Christianity, the work was published in 1802 and became a great bestseller; but it had been informally circulated and advertised for subscription well before official publication, and is twice mentioned in *Pour et contre* (VIII n2; IX n1).

Bible study was no novelty when Maréchal wrote: his rational-humanistic approach already had a tradition with which he was familiar, starting with the Amsterdam Jewish philosopher Benedict Spinoza (1632–1677). A guiding spirit for Maréchal and the subject of a long entry in the *Dictionnaire des athées*, Spinoza understood religion as justification and sometimes model for the state and hence Bible criticism as a way to enable a critique of governmental

---

4 This is the problem with articles by Schwarzbach 1986 and Menozzi 1986 on eighteenth-century Bible study: they dismiss Maréchal (along with other rationalist or atheist critics) as merely an anti-Bible propagandist. They ignore everything he writes about the literary–poetic value of some biblical books and the morality and wisdom in some others. They also omit to mention his forward-looking critical perspective, which was in line with an already well-established trend in French, English, and German biblical scholarship. A similarly reductive mention by Cotoni (1984, 380) fails to note that Maréchal's book is mostly about Hebrew scripture. Granted that Christian scripture is her main topic, it seems odd to omit the real character of a source and to cite from it only a few ironic phrases about Jesus, ignoring the importance of method.

structures, whether Christian or Jewish. In France there were dozens of commentaries, studies of scripture, and treatises on ancient Israelite history by Catholics and Protestants both lay and clerical, and a few by Jews. Most aimed to show the truth of their chosen doctrine, or the existence of divinity however defined; most wished a reform of religion, not—as with Maréchal—its abolition. Nonetheless their attention to linguistics, style, cultural norms, narrative, and character paved the way for later and more thoroughgoing criticism. The seventeenth century produced Richard Simon, Montesquieu, and the frequently reprinted Claude Fleury and Le Maistre de Sacy with their prolific scholarly circles. Maréchal has Sacy's Port-Royal Bible before him and frequently deplores what he sees as the Jansenist scholar's insensitivity to the subtlety and grandeur of Hebrew poetry. The eighteenth century had Duguet, Voltaire, and Diderot together with their many sources, from late-classical to contemporary, as well as the atheist Baron d'Holbach, the prince of best-selling authors (Darnton 1995, 203) and undoubtedly a major influence on Maréchal. Most of these writers' works on the Bible, religion, Jews, and related topics, as well as commentaries, critiques and biographies, were held in the Mazarin Library where Maréchal worked (see Molinier), and many were readily available commercially. Maréchal's awareness of them is displayed in other works, notably his *Dictionnaire des athées* and his *Calendrier des républicains*.

It isn't my purpose here to elucidate every sentiment or expression in Maréchal's biblical commentary; for a more detailed discussion, see Chapter 9 in this collection. I translated the work in order to introduce his interesting and, I believe, timely text to a modern audience both Anglophone and Francophone (see Delany 2020). I would hope to add it to the growing body of work on the representation of Jews and other 'marginal' or minority groups in earlier periods. It may be useful to observe how the author's politics inflects his representation of Jews, and to acknowledge the stubbornly iconoclastic voice of a writer who was not afraid to swim against the stream.

What, then, of Jews in Maréchal's Bible study? To begin with, he is an equal opportunity provocateur, addressing his prefatory tirade to *"ministres de tous les cultes"* (ministers of all religions). By accusing them of four thousand years of lies (*"Quatre milliers d'années de mensonges ne vous suffcent-ils pas?"* [Aren't four thousand years of lies enough for you?]: vi) he clearly includes Jewish as well as Christian tradition. Rabbis are not specified in the preface, nor is the Talmud, but other formulations leave no doubt as to the intended inclusiveness: he names the Bible, the Gospels, the Koran, and the Zend-Avesta as books to be burnt *"avant tous les autres"* (before all the rest: xxv) and urges the purgation from our vocabulary of all religious labels such as *"materialistes, spiritualistes, catholiques, protestans, musulmans, juifs"*(xxv). He urges all religious leaders to accept the way of reason, to get jobs, to publicly confess their sad role in deception, and to turn their work over to women, who will do a much better job of it (XXIX–XXXV). (This is not, in Maréchal's lexicon, a compliment.)

For Maréchal, Jews are an 'oriental' people, and 'oriental' is a recurrent term in his work. There were about 500 Jews in Paris during the revolutionary period, of around 35,000 in France as a whole. Approximately half lived in Alsace; another 4,000 in Lorraine; 3,500 in or near Metz; 2,300 around Bordeaux; 1,000 near Bayonne; and 2,500 in Avignon, the Comtat Venaissin, Marseille, and elsewhere in Provence (Schechter 2003, 4–7); as well as; a number of poor or transient Jews who would not have been counted. Jews whom Maréchal might have seen or met would likely have been Ashkenazi rather than Sephardi. Coming from Alsace, Germany, Poland, or elsewhere in Eastern Europe, they would not have been culturally 'oriental' (Middle Eastern). Clearly his thought is of biblical Jewry, not of Jews who addressed the National Assembly or (at the other economic pole) peddled used clothing in the streets. Although there is no hard evidence that Maréchal knew specific Jews or understood their community organization, he did share a friend—the atheist astronomer Jérôme Lalande—with the well-known Jewish writer Zalkind Hourwitz (Malino 1996, 154), who was, like Maréchal, a Parisian radical and librarian–scholar. It is intriguing to speculate whether Maréchal's patriarchal fraternity, the geriatric "*hommes sans dieu*" (men without god: Maréchal, 1797), might have been modeled on the body of elders of the local *kahal* or Jewish community council.

How are the Jews collectively to be denoted? This was an important question during the revolutionary period, both expressing and determining a position on their proper civil status. Maréchal pointedly denies them the status of 'nation' either in biblical or contemporary times, defining them rather as a "*peuplade*" (tribe: 5)—and a lazy ("*paresseuse*") one at that, requiring chastisement from Moses. 'Nation' was a term that communities of Jews used of themselves in conducting official business at the municipal or regional legislative level or at court, and the term was used of them reciprocally, so that one might speak or write of "*la nation juive d'Alsace*" (the Jewish nation of Alsace) or "*la nation allemande*" (the German nation [of Jews]) for Ashkenazim. Thus in 1760, "*la nation des juifs portugais de Bordeaux*" (the Jewish nation of Bordeaux) submitted for royal authorization a set of rules governing its taxation on behalf of its poor (Pereyre 1760).[5] This usage did not carry our modern connotation

---

5 The document offers insight into the sort of conflict that could arise in the *kahal* (community), in this case people refusing to donate the required amount to charity for support of the poor and other communal needs (as defined, of course, by the ruling syndics). Pereyre was the agent for the Bordeaux Jews in Paris (and at court in Versailles); the document is signed

of statehood or even of unity, whether ethnic or territorial. Rather it is the old medieval corporative concept of 'nation' applied to any legally recognized grouping such as the 'English nation' in a French or Polish university or, as David Feuerwerker observes, in the guild sense as the 'nation' of tin workers or lemonade sellers (*"nation' des ferblantiers, des limonadiers, etc"*.: Feuerwerker 1976, 40 n2). Indeed, there was little sense of unity among Jewish populations in France, nor any structural or organizational means of connection, so that rivalry between Ashkenazim and Sephardim on the national scale (e.g., for privileges or rights from king or National Assembly), or between wealthy governing elite and majority poor in a municipal context, could well escalate into legal or physical conflict.

The notion of Jewish nationhood was deployed by the opponents of emancipation. For them, Jewish difference was to be accepted so fully that Jews could not and should not be integrated into French society. The die-hard anti-semite Jean François Reubell, a deputy from Alsace where half the Jewish population of France lived, said: "The Jews collectively are a *corps de nation* separate from the French. They have a distinct role. Thus they can never acquire the status of an Active Citizen" (quoted in Kates 1990, 112), i.e., could not vote and hold office even if possessing the high property qualification to do so. According to another opponent of full enfranchisement, F.-B. Darracq, if Jews were to be seen as a unified or political nation, then they would be a nation within the nation, and therefore a potential fifth column with loyalties elsewhere than to France. If they are a nation, then they cannot possibly be French and Jewish any more than they could be French and English. Moreover, as a "nation" they ought to have their own laws and authorities, and ideally their own territory elsewhere than in France (Darracq 1799, 18).[6] Indeed, as Michel Winock notes, the Jacobin Society of Nancy recommended expulsion and can hardly have been the only ones to do so (Winock 2004, 24). As background to these stormy debates, it is important to remember that the nationhood of France itself as we know it today did not yet fully exist. Territories, languages, religious identity, and forms of government were violently disputed during these turbulent few

---

by him and the syndics. The document was renewed and extended three years later. Sephardi Jews were usually labeled "Portuguese" regardless of their country of origin. Szajkowski notes that some Jewish community leaders sent their poor elsewhere: to Jamaica, Surinam, or London (Szajkowski 1970, 12–14).

6 Darracq, a deputy, was addressing the Napoleonic legislative body, the Council of 500, regarding the refusal of the Bordeaux Jews to give up their cemeteries as national property. He lost and was censured; the Jews retained their cemetery (which they claimed had never been communal property but had been bought by private individuals). See also Szajkowski 1970, xx.

years; many of the territorial languages of what is now France continue to be spoken in addition to what has come to be normative French, a continuing reminder of the fierce struggle for nationhood.

For those who favored emancipation, Jews might once have been a nation— in the biblical period—but not for some 1700 years, since the Roman invasion and occupation of Jerusalem. The Abbé Gregoire, a deputy and ardent supporter of emancipation (for reasons that scholars continue to debate), wrote:

> The Jews are no longer a nation; they are only the remains and debris of a nation destroyed. One cannot give the name of nation to men who have neither territory nor sovereignty nor government ... no central gathering place, no rallying point ... He who speaks of 'nation' speaks of power, and Jewish power today is no more real than that of the Assyrians or Medeans.
> quoted in TRIGANO 1990, 177–78

Moreover, as a corporate entity under the *ancien régime*, corporate status had been dissolved when the old corporations were abolished by the new regime (Kates 1990, 113). As a non-nation, then, Jews were as deserving of French citizenship as blacks in the French colonies—who were granted citizenship just as haltingly as the Jews, in a series of acts between 1791 and 1794. For proponents of emancipation, the watchword was that pronounced in the National Assembly on December 23, 1789: *"Il faut tout refuser aux juifs comme nation, et accorder tout aux juifs comme individus"* (It's necessary to refuse everything to the Jews as a nation and grant everything to Jews as individuals: quoted in Winock 2004, 18).

Maréchal's reading of individual chapters of the Hebrew and Christian Bibles is as literary and as scholarly as he can make it. He proceeds methodically through both texts, stating his preferences and dislikes with the reasons for each, and indicating the current state of relevant scholarship. He is well aware of recently edited collections of mythological material from other cultures, of priestly redactors, and of the plurality of gospels as well as the more traditional patristic commentary and various translations. Each chapter ends with or includes a list of literary or visual artworks on that specific book or its main incident.

Genesis is *"le plus beau"* (the finest)—sublime and simple. Its universality is denied, and its cultural specificity asserted. Moses, hero of the Old Testament, makes his appearance in Exodus, which Maréchal finds less interesting than the preceding book. He suggests a naturalistic version of the burning bush: it might have been the aurora borealis, which the ingenious Moses was able to turn to his own purpose before an ignorant people Maréchal shows great admiration for Moses, who, as an extraordinary legislator and moralist, could have used his genius to its fullest extent had he ruled a more advanced people; in this, according to Maréchal, Moses was not unlike Czar Peter I (25–26).

Of course, Maréchal admits, the Pentateuch, like the rest of the Bible, is sprinkled with miracles and falsehoods; he wryly invites the French Institute in Cairo to take the trouble to verify them. This allusion is a gibe at Napoleon, whose foray into Egypt was accompanied by a large retinue of scientists and scholars: "a full-scale academy", in Edward Said's phrase (Said 1978, 83). Their job was to assist the army, pave the way for French imperialism, and open Egypt to European ideas and technologies. These *savants* founded the French Institute, and indeed the Rosetta Stone was discovered during this campaign, in 1799. Yet the project was a disastrous defeat for the French, who withdrew after three years and surrendered in the same year Maréchal published his Bible study, 1801. Not only a reminder of this humiliation and its cost to the French in lives and money, the snide remark also poses the dilemma of intellectuals. Can they really perform their function in the new religious climate, or will scholarship have to defer to the new piety and betray its principles by—as Maréchal sarcastically proposes—verifying miracles?

The Book of Ruth is declared a masterpiece of the pastoral genre. King David was "the Louis XIV of the Jews", both of them enamored of luxury and women, both weak and debased at the end of their reigns (42). This and the next Louis reappear in Maréchal's discussion of the relation of kings and priests, in connection with *Paralipomenon (Chronicles)*. Nehemiah shows simplicity, nobility, candor, and—a key critical term for Maréchal—"*onction*", a term with overtones of skilled rhetoric, emotion, and (its etymon) oil, with connotations of soothing sweet odor. The assassin Judith he sees as a patriot; surprisingly, given his critique of biblical immorality, there is no condemnation of her murderous zeal. He raises the possibility, first floated by St. Jerome, that Judith wrote her own story—a notion concretized by Harold Bloom two millennia on (Bloom 1990)—and why not, asks Maréchal, since both sexes have equal access to divine inspiration? Nonetheless, he continues, we prefer to see a needle or a bobbin in a woman's hand rather than a pen and a sword (72). This is, of course, the orthodox two-sided Catholic position on women shared by many revolutionaries, even atheists like Maréchal. Esther is magnificent, a political romance or novel, composed in honor of the Jewish nation (74). Nonetheless, despite these flashes of literary brilliance, our critic claims, the Bible is tainted by the incest, violence, concubinage, adultery, and general turpitude it portrays (79).

Job is "sublime", showing, in Maréchal's view, energy and profundity, philosophy and high poetry. The French translations, according to him, are pygmies trying to lift Hercules's knotty club. There is nothing negative to be said about this *"conte oriental"*, even though no translator, whether prose writer or *"miserable versificateur"* (lousy verse-maker: 83) comes close to the sublimity of the Latin. Each of the 150 psalms of David is briefly considered. Most are praised, some are dismissed as common, repetitive, or nothing special (*"peu de chose"*: 87, 88, 110), and some are used as indices to the character of David. No hero, David is a prideful, vengeful king, a hypocrite (*"Tartuffe"*). As elsewhere in his commentary, Maréchal deplores the violence of biblical rhetoric in favor of a poetry that teaches virtue; let the poetry perish, he proclaims, that requires butchery, let books be burnt that offer people such atrocities as are represented in some of the psalms: if tigers had a religion, it would be that of David and his imitators (98–99).

Isaiah is Maréchal's favorite among the prophets: superb, rich, sublime, exquisite, energetic, comparable to Homer and Michelangelo (160). Yet it is sad, Maréchal claims, that all this genius lacks a more useful moral purpose, a more direct use for humanity. More or less the same, pro and con, is said of Jeremiah: both prophets could have used their talent to raise the abased spirit of their nation and give it morals (182). Moreover, Jeremiah's character is too irascible, too vindictive, for a man of God (186). Ezekiel is too baroque (my word) for Maréchal's taste, with its wheels, animals, nightmares, and extreme metaphors (205), all showing an *"ivresse de cerveau"* (intoxication of the brain); yet it too is sublime, some of it more so than anything in Homer.

Maréchal's moralism comes to the fore especially in his discussion of Hosea, whose opening metaphor of adulterous fornication he denounces and refuses to translate from the Latin, indignant that enlightened nations continue to hear the echoes of *"sales chansons d'une horde demi-barbare et sans vergogne!"* (dirty songs of a semi-barbaric and shameless horde: 220–21). Only in *I Maccabees* do the Jews play a role that does them honor, according to Maréchal's revolutionary value-system: defending their homes and liberty (246). II Maccabees, though, is flat and boring and ought not to have been made canonical (251). This survey of the Hebrew Bible ends with a short excursus on its mixed style and a warning that it is not suitable for all to read.

With that we turn to the Christian Bible, which I include here because it was written by Jews and chronicles the career of the most famous biblical Jew. (This is not Maréchal's perspective: for him, Jesus is still *"Jésus-Christ"* albeit often with an ironic inflection to that title.) Maréchal's discussion opens boldly by denouncing at length the cosmic adultery that is claimed to have produced Jesus. Not that there is anything wrong with being a bastard, he hastily asserts— and indeed the Revolution had passed laws on their behalf—but why place among someone's perfections the illegitimacy of his birth (256)? Maréchal doesn't go as far as the medieval anti-Christian polemic *Toledot Yehoshua*, which hypothesizes an affair with a Roman soldier, and doesn't need to, for his point is that even within the terms of Christian myth itself, Mary committed adultery (with the Holy Spirit). He imagines the domestic disputes that must have taken place between the pregnant young wife and her aged spouse, Joseph. Recycling a passage from his bitterly satirical legendary of 1790, *La nouvelle légende dorée* (under "Mary" in the alphabetical listing of that work), Maréchal reflects that if Mary had only said "No", we would have had no pope, no masses, no inquisition or crusades, etc.; Mary would have been quite simply a carpenter's wife and mother of a little woodworker's helper (257). The adultery theme reappears in the commentary on Luke, where Maréchal appeals to honest wives and good mothers to reject this immoral scenario and its consequence, the virgin birth, that "*monstrueux dogme*" (outrageous dogma). With its magic and miracles, the story is full of absurdities worthy of the *Thousand and One Nights* (260). We are still in the realm of 'oriental' fiction, and indeed this comparison was already a trope in rationalist study of Christian texts, for Voltaire had written in 1763, "*Plus je relis les Actes des martyrs, plus je les trouve semblable aux 1001 nuits*". (The more I reread the *Acts of the Martyrs* [i.e., saints' lives], the more I find them similar to the *Thousand and One Nights*: quoted in Malino 1996, 211 n23).

The worst that can be said of Jesus is that he was willing to split families: this anti-moral and anti-social behavior shows Jesus acting like a genuine bastard (262) or sounding like a demon with "*infernal*" advice (270). Rousseau was wrong to have praised Jesus as highly as he did, for no commentary can palliate these passages. In Luke, Jesus appears as a spoilt child who deserves a whipping, and he makes the wrong choice between Mary and Martha. The best of Jesus is the Sermon on the Mount: common-sense counsel that will last forever and has no need of miracles, prophecy, or divine inspiration to be understood (265–66). John occasions an excursus on figurative language, which makes it easy for priests to say anything with impunity and deceive the people (302–3). In the commentary, other gospels are mentioned besides the four canonical ones; these four heterogeneous booklets are contrasted unfavorably with the masterpieces of classical literature (306), and a belittling rhyme of an epitaph for Jesus concludes the gospel section: "*Cy-gît un Dieu qui se fit homme, / Et qui mourut pour une pomme*" (Here lies a god who made himself man, / and who died for an apple [i.e., the apple that Eve ate, the original sin for which Jesus's death atones]).

The remainder of the Acts and Epistles are briefly commented on with respect to style and content; scholarship is duly noted. The last chapter, "*Resultat de la lecture de la Bible*" (*Result of Reading the Bible*) offers an overview of "*notre analyse impartial*" (our impartial analysis: 368), which becomes a diatribe against Christianity and its foundational text. Here, Maréchal takes the opportunity to imagine what Jesus might have become in other circumstances. Jesus could have been an authoritative revolutionary leader and freedom fighter leading the Jews against Rome; Maréchal obligingly provides sample speeches for this alternative patriotic Jesus. Nor did Jesus behave well at his trial, displaying an unattractive passivity; again, Rousseau was wrong to praise him (373–77).

The uncompromising discourse of the revolutionary martyr Gracchus Babeuf, Maréchal's friend and comrade, must have been in Maréchal's mind as a contrast to the passive, terrified Jesus of Gospel; indeed, he had written an eloquent and poignant tribute to Babeuf as the latter awaited trial and execution only four years earlier. Here was a man who did have a "*sublime théorie*" (Maréchal 1796, 1) and fought for it, a man who was both "*bon père de famille*" (good father to a family: Maréchal 1796, 3) and a champion of real equality. Yet as little as Jesus's life and death did Babeuf's death or life make the difference it could have. With enormous contempt for those who had crippled the 'real' revolution, Maréchal in effect bid farewell to political life when the Babeuf coup was nipped in the bud. He must have seen the writing on the wall and yet it would get worse: *émigré* priests would flock back to France, people would crowd reopened churches, Napoleon would become emperor, the pope would come to Paris to bless him, many of the best laws of the early days would be reversed. This is the world into which Maréchal launched his last major work, a lone atheist revolutionary voice crying in the Napoleonic wilderness with as much vitriol as it could muster:

> Blushing for the human race to which I belong, I want at least to mark the first year of the nineteenth century of the common era with a solemn protest against the cult prostituted for so long to the most absurd, useless, immoral and evildoing of all books.
> 396; DELANY 2020, 188

And the Hebrew Bible? The two testaments are equally guilty of causing bloodshed, lies, vice, and crime, and we have paid a high price for the invention of printing! Not even the Jews have benefited, for they slander other nations throughout their history book, and the slanders have been reciprocated (395). A series of bitter, insulting apostrophes concludes the chapter: the author addresses the "*livre affreux*" (awful book), Jesus, and the ordinary folk who, "*troupeau de bipeds dociles et routiniers*" (flock of docile, routinistic bipeds: 398) that they are, will now cave in to their priests. He speaks as well to the *"femmelettes du jour"* (little ladies of the moment: 399) with ebony and gold crosses on their bare breasts, and to the bought-and-sold elegant writers: no, nothing will be different from preceding centuries after all, and the friends of reason will groan for humanity yet will continue to hope even if repaid with ingratitude or persecution (399).

A short postscript attempts to mitigate this severity by recommending, instead of the Bible, Benjamin Franklin's extremely popular 1778 pamphlet *"Science du bon homme Richard"*. Not merely part of a longstanding "craze for America" (see Darnton 2003), this recommendation places before the reader one of the heroes of the radical revolution. As a working printer, scientist, political leader, and writer, Franklin fulfilled in his lifetime several roles most admired by revolutionaries. When he died in 1790, the National Assembly decreed three days of mourning, and the Parisian print workers conducted a memorial. In 1794, Robespierre invoked Franklin's invention of the lightning rod as evidence that humanity can control nature to beneficial ends by the exercise of rational thought. A second postscript to *Pour et contre* recommends the publication of morally and rationally illuminating books, concluding with the sardonic reminder that *"Eclairer les hommes vaut mieux que de les tuer pour les rendre meilleurs"* (Enlightening people is better than killing them to make them better: 404).

What emerges from this overview, with respect to Jews and Judaism, is that while part of Maréchal's representation of ancient Jews was conditioned by the revolutionary discourse about emancipation and by a devastating loss of hope for the revolution, his central concern, even when writing about the Hebrew Bible, was with Catholicism, the old revolutionary foe that had come back as strong as ever. Even during his tenure as editor of the influential radical journal *Revolutions de Paris* (1790–94), there was no in-depth coverage of 'the Jewish question' as such, despite its prominence in intellectual discourse and governmental debate. Relevant votes in the National Assembly were noted, but arguments were not described in detail. Perhaps the journal's staff took it for granted that the 1789 Declaration of the Rights of Man made full emancipation a self-evident consequence requiring no special justification. Perhaps, for one caught up in the complete social and cultural transformation that 1789 seemed to promise, the civil status of Jews was a minor footnote in the creation of a new society, and their foundational text an obstacle to that renovation. For us, at a time when religiosity tries to and all too frequently does shape public discourse and policy in the United States, Canada, Israel, France and elsewhere, a dose of eighteenthcentury French rationalism may be a healthy antidote.[7]

References

Belaval, Yvon, and Dominique Bourel, eds. 1986. *Le siècle des lumières et la Bible*. Paris: Beauchesne.

Benbassa, Esther. 2001. *The Jews of France*. Princeton: Princeton University Press.

Berkovitz, Jay R. 2004. *Rites and Passages: the Beginning of Modern Jewish Culture in France, 1650–1860*. Philadelphia: University of Pennsylvania Press.

Bloom, Harold. 1990. *The Book of J*, translated by David Rosenberg. New York: Grove Press.

Cotoni, Marie-Hélène. 1984. *L'exégèse du Nouveau Testament dans la philosophie française du dix-huitième siècle*. Oxford: Voltaire Foundation.

Darnton, Robert. 1995. *The Corpus of Clandestine Literature in France, 1769–1789*. New York: Norton.

Darnton, Robert. 2003. "The Craze for America: Condorcet and Brissot". In *George Washington's False Teeth*, 119–136. New York: Norton.

Darracq, F.-B. 1799. *Opinion de Darracq dans l'affaire des Juifs de Bordeaux*. Paris.

Debray, Regis. 2010. *À un ami Israélien*. Paris: Flammarion.

Delany, Sheila. 2012. "Bible, Jews, revolution: Sylvain Maréchal's *Pour et contre la Bible* (1801)". In *Ot Letova: Essays in Honor of Professor Tova Rosen*, edited by Eli Yassif et al., 95–109. Beersheba: Heksherim Institute.

Delany, Sheila. 2020. *For and Against the Bible. A Translation of Sylvain Maréchal's* Pour et Contre la Bible *(1801)*. Leiden, Netherlands: Brill.

Dommanget, Maurice. 1950. *Sylvain Maréchal, l'égalitaire*. Paris: Spartacus.

Feuerwerker, David. 1976. *L'émancipation des Juifs en France*. Paris: Albin Michel.

Kates, Gary. 1990. "Jews into Frenchmen: Nationality and Representation in Revolutionary France". In *The French Revolution and the Birth of Modernity*, edited by Ferenc Feher, 103–16. Berkeley: University of California Press.

Malino, Frances. 1996. *A Jew in the French Revolution: the Life of Zalkind Hourwitz*. Oxford: Blackwell.

Mannucci, Erica Joy. 2012. *Finalmente il popolo pensa: Sylvain Maréchal nell'immagine della Rivoluzione francese*. Naples: Guida.

---

7 This chapter is a revised version of "Bible, Jews, Revolution: Sylvain Maréchal's *Pour et contre la Bible* (1801)", in *Ot LETOVA: Essays in Honor of Professor Tova Rosen*, edited by Eli Yassif et al., 95–109 Beersheba, Israel: Heksherim Institute, 2012.

Maréchal, Sylvain. 1796. *L'opinion d'un homme, sur l'étrange procès intenté au tribun du peuple, et à quelques autres Écrivains Démocrates*. Paris.

Maréchal, Sylvain. 1797. *Culte et loix d'une société d'hommes sans Dieu*. n.p.

Maréchal, Sylvain. 1801. *Pour et contre la Bible*. Jerusalem [Paris].

Menozzi, Daniele. 1986. "La Bible des Révolutionnaires". In Belaval and Bourel 1986, 677–96.

Mitchell, Harvey. 2008. *Voltaire's Jews and Modern Jewish Identity: Rethinking the Enlightenment*. London: Routledge.

Molinier, Auguste. 1885– 90. *Catalogue des manuscrits de la Bibliothèque Mazarine*. 3 vols. Paris: Plon.

Mossé, Benjamin. 1890. *La Révolution française et le rabbinat français*. Avignon: Imprimerie Spéciale de la Caravane.

Pereyre, Jacob Rodriguez. 1760. *Reglement de la nation des Juifs portugais de Bordeaux, approuvé & autorisé par sa Majesté*. Versaille.

Said, Edward. 1978. *Orientalism*. New York: Random House.

Schechter, Ronald. 2003. *Obstinate Hebrews: Representations of Jews in France, 1715–1815*. Berkeley: University of California Press.

Schwarzbach, Bernard. 1986. "Les Adversaires de la Bible". In Belaval and Bourel , 139–68.

Szajkowski, Zosa. 1970. *Jews and the French Revolutions of 1789, 1830 and 1848*. New York: Ktav.

Trigano, Shmuel. 1990. "The French Revolution and the Jews". In *Modern Judaism* 10, 171–90.

Wall, Irwin. 2003. "Remaking Jewish Identity in France". In *Diasporas and Exiles: Varieties of Jewish Identity*, edited by Howard Weinstein. Berkeley: University of California Press.

Winock, Michel. 2004. *La France et les Juifs*. Paris: Seuil.

Index

Abelard, Peter   99, 105, 148, 155, 155n2, 182
abortion   87, 89, 126, 171
Acta sanctorum   98
adultery   29, 168, 188, 189, 190
Antonelle, Pierre Antoine   157, 158n4
atheism   12, 103, 106, 108, 113, 115, 121, 122, 157, 158, 160, 170, 172
Augustine, Saint   14, 164

Babeuf, François-Noël ("Gracchus")   1, 110, 111, 112, 113, 115, 137, 161, 163, 174n10, 181, 191
Balzac, Henri de   4, 9
Barthes, Roland   10, 57, 58, 70
bibliothèque bleue   119, 148
Bolsheviks   39, 44, 46, 49, 50, 51, 52, 53, 64, 73, 82, 84, 87, 88, 88n10, 89, 90
Bonaparte, Napoleon   102, 107, 112, 112n6, 137, 143, 160, 161, 168, 172, 181, 182, 188, 191
Brecht, Bertolt   1, 5, 6, 13, 37, 40, 57–70
Breton, André   20
Buonarroti, Philippe   110, 112

Canada   25n1, 28, 33, 105, 140, 141, 142, 143, 181, 193
Carlyle, Thomas   13, 26
Chaucer, Geoffrey   2, 3, 8, 14, 26, 27, 29, 32, 34
Chiang Kai-shek   62, 63, 64, 65, 66
class traitor   4, 157
Cloots, J.-B. "Anacharsis"   158, 167
contraception   87
contradiction   8, 9, 20, 21, 76, 86, 97, 102, 111, 146, 150, 169, 170
Cuba   1, 2, 74, 171

Davis, Mike   1
demystification   129, 159
Derrida, Jacques   17, 27n3
dialectic   18, 49
dialectics   3, 8, 9, 11, 12

Engels, Friedrich   4, 9, 14n2, 15, 16, 26, 29, 37, 38, 40, 115

First Nations. *See* Indigenous

Fischer, Ernst   8–9
Furnivall, F.J.   26, 27, 32

Gacon-Dufour, Madame   139, 169
Genevieve, Saint   96, 97, 121–131
Golden Legend. See Legenda aurea

Haiti   112, 112n6, 142, 143
Holbach, Baron de   157, 159, 164, 167, 184
Hourwitz, Zalkind   167, 181, 185

Indigenous   20, 134, 140, 141, 142

Jameson, Fredric   61, 146

Korsch, Karl   61, 68, 68n6
Kuomintang   62, 63

Lalande, Jérôme   109, 113, 157, 158, 185
Left Front of the Arts (LEF)   18
Legenda aurea   98, 121
Lenin, V. I.   1, 4, 9, 11, 15, 16, 17, 18, 28, 29, 37–43, 49, 50, 51, 52, 53, 61, 62, 64, 65, 76, 78n5, 81, 90, 115
Lévi-Strauss, Claude   146
Liebknecht, Karl   1, 17, 40, 43, 47, 49, 93
Lucretius   5, 158
Lukacs, Georg   50, 53, 54
Luxemburg, Rosa   1, 2, 5, 15, 18, 37–54, 83, 92

Mao Tse-tung   10, 11, 13, 15, 16, 62, 63, 65, 66
Marx, Eleanor   26, 27
Marx, Karl   1, 2, 3, 4, 11, 15, 16, 17, 25, 27, 28, 29, 37, 38, 40, 41, 48n1, 61, 172
Mayakovsky, Vladimir   13, 30n6, 73
Mazarin Library   98, 103, 121, 131, 135, 147, 155, 159, 181, 184
Morris, William   13, 26
Müller, Heiner   1, 58, 60, 69

Naigeon, Jacques-André   155n2, 157
Native American. *See* Indigenous

Paine, Thomas   13, 158, 158n4

Peng Shu-tse   63*n*3, 66
Proletkult   14, 73, 77, 78, 81

Quakers   139

Révolutions de Paris (RdeP)   96, 102, 106, 109, 110, 112, 119, 120, 135, 142, 158, 168, 181
Robbins, Rossell Hope   32
Robespierre, Maximilien   5, 107, 108, 110, 136, 137, 160, 192
Roman de la rose   129, 147, 149
Room, Avram   87
Rousseau, Jean-Jacques   97, 99, 105, 113, 148, 190, 191
Rubinstein, Annette   30, 31

Sade, Marquis de   157, 158*n*4, 161
Schlauch, Margaret   25, 28–32
Shakespeare, William   9, 17, 27, 27*n*3, 48*n*1, 61, 68, 105, 138, 147
Shklovsky, Viktor   17, 82, 101, 131

socialist feminism   84, 85
socialist realism   57, 73, 77, 78, 81, 92
Spartacus (Roman slave leader)   3, 43, 105
Spinoza, Benedict   113, 158, 159, 183
Stalin, Joseph   1, 19, 35, 37, 39, 49, 59, 61, 62, 64, 65, 66, 69, 73, 74, 75, 78*n*5, 89, 90

Tolstoy, Leo   4, 9
Tretiakov, Sergei   68, 69
Trotsky, Leon   1, 4, 6, 12, 15, 16, 18, 29, 37, 38, 39, 53, 61, 65, 66, 67, 74, 76, 78*n*5, 81, 88, 88*n*10, 92

utopia   26, 50

Voltaire   100, 105, 159, 164, 184, 190
vote   28, 30, 33, 43, 85, 102, 146, 165*n*7, 168, 186, 192

Zetkin, Clara   5, 44, 45, 46, 52, 83

www.ingramcontent.com/pod-product-compliance
Lightning Source LLC
Chambersburg PA
CBHW070624030426
42337CB00020B/3901